Frank Burch Brown
Religion and Humanit
nic Institute and State
musician and compose

RELIGIOUS AESTHETICS

God as Architect of the Universe. French miniature, mid-thirteenth century. The caption at the top reads in Latin, 'Here God creates the heavens, the earth, the sun, the moon and all the elements'.

Religious Aesthetics

A Theological Study of Making and Meaning

Frank Burch Brown

Princeton University Press
Princeton, New Jersey

Published by Princeton University Press
41 William Street, Princeton, New Jersey, 08540

Library of Congress Cataloging-in-Publication Data
Burch Brown, Frank, 1948–
    Religious aesthetics : a theological study of making and meaning /
Frank Burch Brown.
        p.   cm.
    Bibliography: p.
    Includes index.
    ISBN 0–691–07366–X :
    1. Christianity and the arts.   2. Arts and religion.   I. Title.
BR115.A8B87   1989
261.5′7 — dc20

89–33639
CIP

[Printed in Great Britain]

For Joanna

Contents

List of Illustrations

For permission to reproduce illustrations, the author wishes to thank the institutions and individuals cited below.

Preface

Even in a time when few fields of inquiry appear to have definite boundaries, it may seem odd to suggest that the field of religious studies be widened to include some kind of aesthetics. Aesthetics is not very often read by religion scholars and theologians or, for that matter, by artists, whether religious or not. Among philosophers, moreover, it seldom has been held in the highest esteem, having had the reputation of being something indulged in most often by fuzzy thinkers unable to cope with the rigors of logic, epistemology, ethics, metaphysics, and the like. It has been taken up by major theorists like Kant mainly when they have had the wish to round out their philosophy. One occasionally hears it said, in fact, that a graduate course in aesthetics is an anomaly; however difficult to read, writing in aesthetics is simply not that advanced.

One might think that theology in particular would want to keep better company. Its own reputation is already questionable enough, having been impugned in modern times by at least three kinds of critic. First there are individuals who, although religious and therefore in some sense practitioners of what theology claims to contemplate, picture theology (at least in its more scholarly forms) as too abstract, detached, and intellectual to be interesting or trustworthy. Then there are the people whom Friedrich Schleiermacher long ago termed the 'cultured despisers' of religion as a whole and of Christianity in particular. For them it is difficult to conceive that theology was ever considered the 'queen of the sciences', and easy to doubt the intellectual integrity of any sort of reflection that manages to take religion seriously. Finally there are the numerous scholars of religion itself who associate theology with an authoritarian and exclusive mentality that is inimical to the free and critical inquiry essential to the academic enterprise and thus to the academic study of religion.

So it would seem that in the eyes of many people there are problems with aesthetics, problems with theology, and – presumably – problems with any attempt to yoke the two together as part of a broader study in religious aesthetics. To such people the present undertaking is likely at first glance to appear unpromising or of only marginal interest.

There is, to be sure, one sense in which the study offered here is indeed marginal, for it definitely occupies margins where traditional divisions and distinctions tend to collapse. But for this very reason, among others, I believe it need not have only marginal import, either for those normally skeptical of theology and aesthetics or for those whose thought or work in these areas has been defined by long-standing traditions. One of my aims has been to show, in fact, that precisely the margins explored here could be of central concern to aesthetics and theology in general, and likewise to the wider humanistic study of the arts and of religion – especially at a time when more and more theorists are becoming aware of the inadequacies of standard ways of conceiving the goals and methods of these and other fields of inquiry.

With respect to aesthetics, the issues I take up and the conclusions I reach reflect a conviction shared by many, that the foci, scope, and prevalent assumptions of this field of study need to be re-examined. It is hoped that this book will provide one indication that as aesthetics begins to be reconceived, here and elsewhere, it can play a more significant role both in philosophy and in religious reflection.

Regarding the explicitly theological aspects of this study several words of clarification are in order. First, while this inquiry is theoretical and academic, the religious issues it addresses are ones I take to be of potential consequence for existing forms of religious thought and practice. There is thus a certain practical pressure exerted on this investigation that would be absent from an attempt, for instance, to determine how the ritual processes and objects of the cult of Isis might be understood in the light of Hellenistic ideas of beauty. Second, I do undertake at points to theologize. By this I mean that I attempt to take into account religious experiences, norms, and practices of one theistic tradition in particular – the Christian – and endeavor to reflect on them in such a way as to make a contribution to Christianity's own self-understanding.

Nevertheless, in this area as well, the marginal character of this particular study will be in evidence. For what I have written is not confessional or devotional; it is not church dogmatics or outright 'doxology'. Although the Christian tradition occupies the focus of much of my discussion, its claims are treated as grounds for hypothesis, conjecture, and exploration rather than as fixed and absolute norms. My overall intention, moreover, is to examine the Christian tradition in such a way as to advance the study of religion in all its forms. Thus I mean to address not only Christians and their theologians but also people more generally engaged in thinking about the humanities, culture, religion, and the arts.

In this regard my *modus operandi* is very different from that of Hans Urs von Balthasar in *The Glory of the Lord*,[1] a multi-volume work in Christian theological aesthetics, and from that of Nicholas Wolterstorff in *Art and Action: Toward a Christian Aesthetic*.[2] Likewise it differs from the tack taken by Gerardus van der Leeuw in *Sacred and Profane Beauty: The Holy in Art*.[3] I am indebted to all three authors; yet the first two write completely from within the perspective of Christianity and simply assume the truth of Christian presuppositions and affirmations. Van der Leeuw, too, while taking into account non-Christian religions and intending his work to be mainly phenomenological or descriptive, nonetheless writes from first to last almost entirely for Christians, and primarily from within the perspective of Reformed theology. These studies and my own all have sufficiently different aims that they should be regarded as basically complementary, although sometimes also corroborative or competitive with respect to their specific claims and assumptions.

All four studies differ, moreover, from a book like John Dillenberger's *A Theology of Artistic Sensibilities*,[4] which is more historical than theoretical and which deals almost entirely with the visual arts. Finally, the present inquiry and the others just mentioned are to be distinguished from books such as Thomas R. Martland's *Religion as Art*[5] and F. David Martin's *Art and the Religious Experience*,[6] which mostly circumvent issues that are explicitly theological in order to focus on particular philosophical arguments.

Any marginal, cross-disciplinary work faces daunting difficulties of communication. Even in the humanities, which have tended to employ less specialized vocabularies than the sciences, it is now virtually impossible to find a genuine *lingua franca*. To minimize inevitable frustrations and misunderstandings, I have avoided technical terms and jargon wherever possible. Anyone familiar with the fields with which I am in dialogue will recognize how restrained I have been in adopting current modes of specialized discourse. I have also relegated most of my generally brief debates with other theorists to notes at the end of the book, trying to keep them from proliferating as they are wont to do. A scholar deprived of a full arsenal of jargon and a vast array of notes must feel somewhat exposed, but I confess that setting aside some of the customary arms and armor can also be a relief. I hope readers will find it to be so.

The suggestions for further study include books whose contents and bibliographies will quickly assist readers wanting to pursue particular issues in greater depth. The publications mentioned in these suggestions and in the notes as well are a reliable indication of the kinds of source that I have most directly drawn on and reckoned with. Needless to say, however, I have not been able to cite all the writings pertinent to this whole area of inquiry and worthy of serious consideration.

From the perspective of this study it has seemed artificial and illegitimate to follow the typical academic practice of altogether excluding from consideration discourses and works that are not highly formal or somehow elite. Although value judgments and genre distinctions are both unavoidable and legitimate, they frequently are deceptive when made strictly along established lines – lines that encourage scholars to examine, for instance, Medieval and Renaissance dance music but not its counterparts in modern culture. Consequently I do from time to time make reference to ideas and artifacts found in popular and vernacular sources such as newspapers, magazines, television shows, movies, and pop music. Some of these examples will doubtless seem dated by the time this study appears in print. Popular culture is much taken by the style and person of the moment; the majority of its products have a limited 'shelf life'. Yet the points best made by way of such examples should not be affected greatly by this fact.

In treating the arts and aesthetica as a whole, this study extends some of the ideas I first developed in relation to literature and religion in my book *Transfiguration: Poetic Metaphor and the Languages of Religious Belief*.[7] By exploring basic aesthetic questions in conjunction with theology and religious reflection, I also hope to be laying the groundwork for wider-ranging essays (and not only my own) that will give more consideration to religious traditions and aesthetic issues that are glimpsed, at most, only on the horizon of this inquiry.

A book of this sort is meant chiefly to make a contribution to theoretical understanding. But where it fails to take account of ideas that emerge from praxis, it fails even in academic terms. I have tried, therefore, to pay close attention to the practical and experiential side of the arts and their religious 'uses'. In this I have been aided in part by personal and familial circumstances. Since I have occasionally published poetry and am active as a composer and musician, my own experience of secular and religious arts, and of music and literature in particular, has naturally proven to be of some value. Happily, this experience has been enriched immeasurably over the years through many hours of listening, music-making, and conversation with my brother David Brown, a pianist and composer sensitive to religious questions and quests. I appreciate his commenting on parts of this manuscript that either annoyed or excited him. My wife, Carol Burch-Brown, who is an artist and teacher, has even more consistently encouraged and challenged my perceptions and ideas regarding religion and the arts. Her specific suggestions for improving and completing this project were invaluable.

I am grateful to the National Endowment for the Humanities for a summer stipend and a fellowship that enabled me to travel widely to art collections and works of religious architecture while also freeing me from teaching duties to do the basic research for this book. A leave provided by Virginia Polytechnic Institute and State University made it possible for me to finish the writing.

The basic argument of Chapter 6 first appeared in abbreviated form in *Soundings: An Interdisciplinary Journal* and is reprinted here by kind permission of the editor. Much of Chapter 2 was presented in preliminary form at the Centre for the Study of Literature and Theology at the University of Durham, and in a somewhat more developed form at a symposium on 'The Role of the Arts in Theological Education', sponsored by the Lilly Endowment and the Yale Institute of Sacred Music, Worship, and the Arts. I am indebted to the institutions and the individuals involved for insights and criticisms which I hope are in some measure reflected in the present work.

For moral support, editorial correction, and professional prodding I am grateful indeed to David Jasper and Cathie Brett-schneider as well as to Virginia C. Fowler, Clark Gilpin, Gregor Goethals, David Kelsey, Elizabeth Struthers Malbon, Margaret Murray, Lynn Poland, Eleonore Stump, George Telford, and Maurice Wiles, all of whom read and (when I let them) improved the manuscript either in part or in its entirety at various stages of its development.

Finally I am thankful for the patience, curiosity, and kind encouragement of my seven-year-old daughter Joanna, who even now is no stranger to many of the things that have perplexed and exhilarated me as I have worked on this project. It is to her that the book is dedicated.

FRANK BURCH BROWN

1
Introduction

The Prospect of Religious Aesthetics

No one could claim that religions have no use for the arts. Even at their most ascetic, moreover, the worlds and ways of religion generally have a side that is distinctly aesthetic, if not always artistic. Pilgrimages, rituals of purification, seasonal observances, myths, prayers, holy groves and mountains, sacred dances and songs, and houses of the gods all have a 'feel' or palpable 'sense' to them – a shape or rhythm, or texture or aura. Ancient Egyptians even spoke of a special fragrance given off by deities.

It is not accurate to characterize this multi-faceted and significantly aesthetic side of religion as merely sensory or sensual; even the 'aroma' of the gods must have been, for the Egyptians, something more than just an ordinary smell. Nor do aesthetic features of religion function sheerly to enhance its emotional appeal. The 'feel' or 'rhythm' of religious phenomena acts on and with the emotions in quite particular ways, and the aesthetic form of religious acts and objects sometimes, in fact, restrains or channels emotions and sensations rather than 'watering them' (to use Plato's expression). Furthermore, aesthetic forms in religion, as in other contexts, affect ideas and volitions as well as the emotions and senses. Thus the relatively commonplace thought that the world is not entirely self-generating can become at once profound and profoundly moving when caught in the cadences and images of a Psalm or Vedic hymn. The abstract idea takes on reflective, affective, and indeed moral depth in an aesthetic milieu.

Even so, questions of aesthetics *per se* have not been widely pursued within the various religions. Although every tradition has its own explanations of why its ideals, rituals, and objects are as they are, the stated rationale is seldom concerned with factors we think of as specific to the arts or aesthetic experience.

Often the emphasis is simply on following what has been commanded or on re-enacting what supposedly was done a certain way in the time of beginnings. This way of thinking is found not

1

only in archaic contexts but also in the context of highly literate discussions. In the Protestant Reformation, for example, negative theological assessments of the arts typically were rooted in appeals to history or authority rather than in anything like a close analysis of aesthetic factors. Although the educated reformer-musician Ulrich Zwingli could muster a few psychological and practical reasons for objecting to the use of music of any sort in public worship, his main argument had nothing to do with traits intrinsic to music but with the alleged fact that music was absent from the primitive church and was not positively commanded by God. Similarly, in earlier centuries iconoclasts of all the major monotheistic religions, when arguing against the use of images, seldom pointed to any aesthetic deficiencies in the objects. Though many were offended at images simply because they are sensory and physical rather than 'spiritual', the decisive factor was that Scriptures supposedly condemn images as idolatrous. The question of how visual images could potentially be more conducive to idolatry than the mental images produced by verbal eloquence was rarely raised.

Theories in favor of aesthetic religious practice have seldom been much more fully developed. Calvin accepted some of the very music that Zwingli rejected, but he did not elaborate on his justification, which relied heavily on the classical idea – transmitted partly through Augustine – that music can move the heart and will. Again, Gregory the Great promoted the use of images on the grounds that they provide a 'Bible' that can be read by the poor. Yet precisely how imagery is 'read', and exactly how it reinterprets what is told in Scripture and celebrated in liturgy, was something he left largely unexplored. Thomas Aquinas, while affirming the veneration of images on the grounds that the movement of the soul toward the image is at the same time its movement toward the thing imaged, never paused for long to ponder how the aesthetic qualities of the image might affect one's response to what is thereby imagined.

Meanwhile, in the Eastern Church sophisticated defenses of icons had indeed been put forward, often on the basis of incarnational theology. Even here, however, the main matter of concern was the ontological relation between material image and spiritual archetype, not the distinctive aesthetic features of the image itself. The genuine icon (as opposed to an idol) would need to be painted with a modicum of skill and in the right way; but mainly it would need to represent something or someone deemed to be real and truly venerable.

Undoubtedly the widespread theological neglect of aesthetic factors in religion is related to the fact that over much of Christian history the prevalent theological and moral climate has been such as to generate considerable ambivalence and suspicion regarding things sensory and bodily. Augustine, for example, expressed mixed feelings about the beauty of Ambrosian chant. What troubled him was the fear that, to the extent to which either the melody of the hymn or the voice singing it was beautiful, it was likely to lure one's attention away from the very truth it was meant to convey. Such artistry moved him to tears, but it also perplexed and grieved him. For him and countless others the association of aesthetic experience with sensory perceptions and bodily delights tainted its powers with an unwelcome worldliness.

Yet even in our time, when the ascetic strain within Christianity is by no means prominent, such prolific Christian theologians as Hans Küng, Karl Rahner, and Karl Barth – all of whom have at moments acknowledged and reflected on the religious import of the arts – have devoted but a minute portion of their enormous output to considerations that are in any overt way aesthetic as well as religious. Theologians such as Tillich and Berdyaev or, earlier, Schleiermacher and Newman have been exceptions; and even these thinkers, for all their aesthetic sensitivities, have not been nearly so well read in aesthetics *per se* as in other areas of philosophy and theology.

As for scholars of religion who are part of the secular academy, the bulk of their work has focused on such things as religious beliefs and history, institutional structures and changes, the formation and meaning of myths and sacred texts, and the effects of modernism on religion. It has been precisely the aesthetic dimension that has been neglected. Moreover, when this dimension has in fact been scrutinized, as in studies of religiously significant music, literature, dance, or visual art, aesthetic theory as such has rarely figured prominently in the discussion.

Naturally, however, the relative neglect of aesthetics on the part of theologians and religion scholars has not been entirely without reason. First of all, during the late eighteenth and early nineteenth centuries – when thinkers began to become intensely interested in interrelations between religion and the imagination and when, almost simultaneously, the techniques of modern secular scho-

larship were first being applied consistently to the study of
religious texts and practices – aesthetics *per se* was just in its
infancy as a self-conscious philosophical discipline. Second, at the
time when later religion scholars of the nineteenth and twentieth
centuries began to take up topics that one would think of as most
pertinent to aesthetics – topics such as the nature of religious
language and ritual – aesthetics was in actuality largely governed
by formalist or other purist principles that obscured its possible
relevance. Indeed, by the middle decades of this century, the most
relevant point that might have been drawn from aesthetics was
often being overstated there as the claim that, as far as aesthetics is
concerned, the form simply *is* the content; or, in terms of communication theory, the medium *is* the message. Since this formulation offers little to someone searching for the deeper meaning of
myth or trying to figure out whether the symbolic language of the
Bible (or the *Tao Te Ching*) is in any way true, or even how it
functions precisely as symbolic, the promise of dialogue between
aesthetics and religious reflection did not really begin to be
fulfilled.

At least in English-speaking countries a similar neglect of
aesthetics could be found within philosophy, where the influence
of a narrow empiricism and positivism caused questions of meaning and truth to be severed completely from questions of aesthetic
form and content. Certainly the formalism and purism dominant in
aesthetics itself gave philosophers little reason to question their
assumption that aesthetics was properly treated as a quaint and
useless ornament to the profession. In the idealist tradition,
meanwhile, Hegel had long before declared that Truth and the
Spirit had progressed beyond the phase of major artistic expression, which suggested that aesthetics was left with nothing urgent
to do.

It is therefore a signal development that in recent years scholars
in the field of religion have increasingly turned to theories of art,
narrative, and poetic metaphor to help interpret religious modes of
thought and expression. Likewise, religion scholars have begun to
examine closely particular arts such as literature and painting, and
to study the artistic qualities of the central sacred text of Western
culture – the Bible. Yet it has become clear that the study of specific
forms of religious art and language must be connected with a
broader understanding of the artistic and aesthetic dimensions of
religion and culture.

One consequence of this realization is that students of religion have begun to pay more attention to aesthetics (broadly conceived), and a smaller number of Christian thinkers in particular have begun to reconsider the place and possibility of what has been termed specifically 'theological aesthetics'. At the same time aesthetics itself has been undergoing a veritable revolution that has begun to make it an important testing ground for theories of mind, culture, language, knowledge, imagination, and the like.

The Present Study: Its Aims and Premises

Promising as these developments may be, religion scholars and theologians have just begun to consider how they might be furthered and what they mean for the overall study of religion or, more narrowly, of Christian faith. Accordingly, the purpose of the present study is twofold. First, it is meant to draw on, and indeed actively to engage in, aesthetics at the points at which it now holds the most promise for religious reflection. This aspect of the study addresses questions potentially of interest to anyone concerned with aesthetics as such or with the academic study of religion. Second, this inquiry stresses how Christian theology in particular could be informed by aesthetics and explores ways in which it would necessarily change, were it to incorporate aesthetics into itself in much the same way that it has incorporated ethics.

To do any of this, however, it is necessary to reconsider not only the shape of theology but also the very basis of aesthetics, and so to understand how aesthetics might begin to have something more substantial to offer theology and the study of religion. Our critique in the area of aesthetics has two major prongs. It questions the widespread reduction of aesthetics to the philosophy of art; for this practice can make aesthetics seem pertinent only to a rather restricted and often elite sector of human making and meaning. And it questions any tendency to interpret aesthetic phenomena in purist terms. In doing so, it at once criticizes persistant purist inclinations within modernist aesthetics and distances itself from the advocates of 'anti-aesthetics', who in reacting against such purism and the ideologies affiliated with it proceed to reject aesthetics in general as irremediably purist and hence as ultimately bankrupt.

Of course many things can be meant by the term 'purist'. Within the present context, however, those theories are termed 'purist' that in various ways see anything that can be considered aesthetic as something essentially self-contained rather than as interactive. At their most extreme, they assume or claim that whatever is aesthetic is by definition or by nature autonomous and unalloyed: neither religious, cognitive, moral, practical, nor political. Or if, as often happens, the purist does see aesthetic phenomena as having some hidden or perhaps incipient moral, religious, or cognitive dimension, this is understood to be essentially intuitive, contemplative, and preconceptual in nature – uninvolved with ideas or with such things as religious life as a whole or with moral choices.

Now if this is what purism entails, it may seem that an analysis and critique of 'high modern' purist aesthetics would largely be superfluous, whether launched from the platform of anti-aesthetics or from a mediating position that maintains ties with aesthetics *per se*. Few people outside professional philosophy and literary theory have ever completely believed in the main purist dogmas anyway. They never have conceived of art as absolutely autonomous, sheerly self-referential, or ineffable in meaning. One might assume that any criticism of these notions would just reinforce what common sense already tells them.

And doubtless it would, in some degree. Yet our commonsense resistance to purism is neither thoroughgoing nor entirely trustworthy. The less extreme form of purism, which pictures anything aesthetic as purely affective and preconceptual, manifests itself in many of our everyday notions of art and beauty, as when we say that through art we simply express how we feel. Besides, common sense today certainly includes at least some idea of what one means by 'aesthetic', and this very idea often carries with it covert assumptions allied with purism of the purest kind.

To glimpse how even the more extreme form of purism finds its way into our ordinary thought processes, we might think about the fairly obvious fact that, for aesthetics of any sort to be an intelligent enterprise, there must be things that we can legitimately regard as aesthetic: aesthetic objects (aesthetica), aesthetic experience (aesthesis), and aesthetic making (poiesis). For specifically religious or theological aesthetics to make any sense, moreover, aesthetic phenomena – or aesthetica in the broad sense – obviously must in some cases be religious themselves or have religious import.

Most of us are inclined to assume that these two conditions are easily met. For example, works such as Giotto's *Madonna Enthroned* (Uffizi Gallery) and Guillaume de Machaut's fourteenth-century

Messe de Notre Dame constitute objects that are plainly aesthetic and undeniably religious. From the standpoint of this study, however, the question is whether this commonsense intuition about the religious capacity of art can be squared with our equally commonsense ideas about aesthetic traits or 'properties'. If it cannot, we have rather shaky grounding either for aesthetics as a whole or for religious and theological aesthetics in particular.

Let us see, therefore, how well our everyday notions of the things we think of as aesthetic help us sort out the relation between the aesthetic and religious aspects of the works mentioned above. Most of us, it seems safe to presume, would not hesitate to admit that aesthetic appreciation of a Giotto tempera painting or a polyphonic Mass by Machaut has sometimes been keenest among connoisseurs little interested in the possible religious meanings and functions of these works. Most of us also would be quick to acknowledge that in a liturgical setting the question of the aesthetic merit of such works does not inevitably arise and that, indeed, inferior pieces of liturgical art often can serve religious purposes equally well, if not better. We may be conscious, too, of theological admonitions to focus on God in the act of worship instead of focusing on the beauty of the singing, the loveliness of the stained glass, and so forth. In the context of the liturgy (we may have been told) none of these things is to be valued for its own sake. And yet valuing beauty for its own sake is precisely what is supposed to be involved in adopting an aesthetic attitude.

This train of thought quickly leads to the deduction that there can be no strict correlation between the realm of the aesthetic and the realm of the religious; whereupon it may further occur to us that, despite exhibiting a certain mutual compatibility, these two realms should perhaps be thought of as quite different. For if aesthetic and religious values or perceptions were not in the end distinct, we reason, then religious devotees would all be aesthetes, and aesthetes would all be saints. One would need to have a cultivated religious sensibility in order to appreciate the aesthetic qualities of a Giotto, and the liturgy would always require nothing but the best in art and aesthetic design. It is good when art and religion can meet in a work of painting or music, we conclude, but they are hardly in the same business and should not be confused.

Such observations readily coalesce into the idea that for something to be aesthetic it must be simply autonomous and hence *not* religious or moral or anything of the kind. The more philosophically inclined among us may put it this way: What is recognized as genuinely aesthetic in a religious context is precisely what cannot be converted even in part to religion proper without losing its identity as aesthetic. Anything aesthetic placed in the service of religion becomes something else, because it no longer has a properly aesthetic function; to the extent that the function of religious art remains aesthetic, it is to that very extent not religious.

Although we may balk at this point, sensing that something has gone awry, this philosophical deduction does seem to be consistent with the line of commonsense thinking we have just now traced. From the perspective of this study, however, the purist thesis thus deduced will not do. By excluding any intrinsic or intimate connection between aesthetica and religion, it effectively eliminates the very rationale for theological aesthetics that we said seemed so intuitive and, again, commonsensical. It also leaves unexplained many of the most conspicuous facts about religion and art. It allows us no vantage point from which to see very clearly why religion bothers at all with works of art or why it ever entertains considerations of aesthetic quality. It gives us no understanding of why aesthetic objects and processes in some circumstances actually *are* forms of religion. And it fails to shed light on why art that is not religious might be of religious significance or why, once a work of art is put to religious use, even its aesthetic qualities can seem rather different from those it exhibits in a gallery or concert hall.

Finally, such purist aesthetics, in both its sophisticated and commonsense forms, tends to render us morally naive. That is, aesthetic purism can make us oblivious of how the practice of aesthetic making and the exercise of aesthetic taste could be either constructive or destructive at a moral level, being involved with power, personality, gender, ideology, and class as well as with the expression and appreciation of something 'for its own sake'.

Purist ideas, while meant to rescue the aesthetic object from moralistic marauders, thus can end up domesticating it. Something labelled 'aesthetic' may be expected to be provocative or beautiful, interesting or touching, but it is not supposed to have overly serious designs on us – no serious affiliation with intellectual or moral suasion, with blindness or insight. If it did, we fear, everything aesthetic would surely be susceptible to the carpings of philistines and to the censure of ideologues, religious and secular alike. Yet we also sense that at the very moment that aesthetica are hermetically sealed off from the rest of our human world, they lose some of their interest and power, just as a 'primitive' cultic object typically does when placed behind museum glass, accompanied merely by a map and a label: Dogon mask.

Given our difficulty in finding a commonsense antidote to the aestheticism that willy-nilly creeps into our casual and formal theorizing, it is no wonder that a number of theorists today have begun to suspect that the very idea of the aesthetic – largely a legacy from the Enlightenment – has been somewhat 'aestheticized' from the start. The question then becomes: Is it better to reform the idea or to jettison it?

As we have noted, many in the current theoretical avant-garde would relegate the concept of the aesthetic to the large heap of historically interesting notions whose time has passed. These thinkers often put forward views that are avowedly anti-aesthetic in that, as one such theorist points out, they challenge the whole network of ideas that they believe is inherently associated with the concept of the aesthetic. In one way or another they dispense with 'the idea that aesthetic experience exists apart, without "purpose", all but beyond history, or that art can now effect a world at once (inter)subjective, concrete and universal – a symbolic totality'. The advocates of the anti-aesthetic likewise question the notion that taste is capable in principle of asserting universally valid claims. Furthermore, in their practical criticism they aim to be sensitive 'to cultural forms engaged in a politic (e.g. feminist art) or rooted in a vernacular – that is, to forms that deny the idea of a privileged aesthetic realm'. In sum, the anti-aestheticians regard the 'adventures of the aesthetic' as one of the 'great narratives of modernity' that has come to an end.[1]

Some of these same thinkers, and others as well, have been described as practising 'paraesthetics' as opposed to anti-aesthetics. But in the end this amounts to much the same thing. In the view of one interpreter of the 'paraesthetic' practice of Foucault, Lyotard, Derrida, and others, what one finds in their work is 'something like an aesthetics turned against itself or pushed beyond or beside itself, a faulty, irregular, disordered, improper aesthetics'. It is more a 'parasitical, transgressive, critical aesthetics than a "true" aesthetics', since it is preoccupied with 'the mutual contamination of the aesthetic and the non-aesthetic'.[2]

As will soon be evident, the present study voices and echoes such anti-aesthetic and paraesthetic critiques of modernist ideas of the aesthetic. It may seem strange, then, that we do not adopt the anti-aesthetic stance *per se* or employ all the tactics of the para-estheticians. The reason, quite simply, is this: The strategy of anti-aesthetics and paraesthetics is either to reject aesthetics outright or to render aesthetic discourse acutely problematical. Neither anti-aesthetics nor paraesthetics is designed to renew the enterprise of aesthetics itself by clarifying what is distinctive about aesthetica even in their 'impure' relations with politics, morality, or religion ('religion' being, in much of this rhetoric, emblematic of all that is rigid and authoritarian). Because the discourse acceptable to most of these alternative approaches to art and related phenomena is predominantly semiotic, political, psychoanalytical, or socio-logical, one notices much that traditional aesthetics ignores; yet one also is left with no means of accounting satisfactorily for the *distinctive* ways in which artistic and related phenomena function within cultural systems. One misses what is peculiar to artistic mediums of relation and exchange, for which the term 'aesthetic' is as good as any.

What one recent writer says in response to strictly sociological, materialist, and specifically Marxian approaches could be said, *mutatis mutandi*, in response to strictly semiological or psychologic-al approaches as well:

> The sociology of art [still] needs a theory of the aesthetic. . . . [Sociology] must recognize and guarantee the specificity of art. The experience of it, and hence its evaluation, cannot be reduced to the totally extra-aesthetic aspects of ideology and politics, although . . . an aesthetics which ignores the social and political features of aesthetic judgement is unacceptable and distorted.[3]

To take an anti-aesthetic approach, perhaps by treating artworks merely as 'texts' like any other texts or as ideological constructs like any others, would be necessary only if the idea of the aesthetic were all wrong – which is doubtful. To take a totally paraesthetic approach, as in Derrida's astute yet persistently deconstructive reading of Kant's *Critique of Judgment*,[4] would be imperative only if one could not, for instance, read Kant critically while simul-taneously using his illuminating inconsistencies to formulate a constructive theory of the aesthetic/non-aesthetic relation.

Likewise, we will decline to follow Hans-Georg Gadamer in his wish for aesthetics to be absorbed into hermeneutics.[5] Gadamer and his mentor Martin Heidegger both describe how one 'listens to' and 'lets happen' the non-objectifiable meaning and truth of art. In this fashion both thinkers provide a corrective to the relative superficiality of modern aestheticism.[6] Nevertheless, Gadamer can propose the absorption of aesthetics into hermeneutics only because he joins Heidegger in manifesting a strong inclination to homogenize the worlds and purposes of art. For these thinkers art is something inherently lofty or deeply traditional (as in the ritual art Gadamer alludes to). It always is the veiling/revealing and 'setting-into-a-work' of ineffable truth.

One cannot complain that interpretation theory, or hermeneutics, ignores issues of meaning and truth as they arise in connection with art. Yet aesthetica are enormously varied in form, purpose, and effect; not everything aesthetic is at all artistic, and not everything artistic or aesthetic has directly to do with anything we think of as true or even meaningful. Part of the realm of the aesthetic (albeit a smaller part than traditional aesthetics has supposed) is the sheerly delightful within perception, or the noticeable-for-its-own-sake, which can freely exist beyond even truth-as-event or meaning-as-meaningfulness. If one insists on always approaching this side of aesthetic phenomena through the questions of hermeneutics, one misses an aspect of aesthetica and aesthesis that deeply affects whatever is aesthetic and artistic – even its peculiar ways of being meaningful or true.

All of which is to argue that for religious (or, more narrowly, theological) aesthetics to be viable, it needs to be based on a reconstruction of aesthetics that, on the one hand, draws on the anti-aesthetic and hermeneutical criticism of purist aesthetics and, on the other hand, utilizes insights that emerge from conversation with aesthetics as commonly conceived. Consequently, the approach taken here represents neither anti-aesthetics nor conventional aesthetics but what might be termed, instead, 'neo-aesthetics'.

For our neo-aesthetic project to be carried out, we must revise prevalent ideas of what is involved in the meaningful making and make-up of aesthetic objects, processes, and experiences. As already indicated, it will be especially important to analyze carefully major differences among things we consider aesthetic. This means, of course, that we should acknowledge from the start that the term 'aesthetic' is conceptually rather elastic – as one would expect, given that it applies to phenomena that elude perfectly clear conceptualization. While we still may find it convenient to speak abstractly of 'the aesthetic' (and of 'the religious', too), we must guard against any assumption that we are thereby referring to some ideal, uniform, and completely autonomous realm or entity. In point of fact, as we will see in our critique of Kant's dichotomy between free and dependent beauty, our claim will be that the very distinction between aesthetic and non-aesthetic is relative; it marks a continuum. At or near one pole of the continuum are qualities of form, process, sense, and imagination that we can notice or appreciate almost entirely in and for themselves, apart from any logical, cognitive, semantic, practical, ethical, or religious considerations. Such qualities and experiences can be regarded as aesthetic 'pure and simple'. At their purest (which still is a purity tainted by associations the mind always brings in some degree to any experience), they are exemplified by the beauty of a snowflake's geometry, by what Roland Barthes calls the rustle of language or the grain in a singer's voice, or by what Julia Kristeva speaks of as the element of heterogeneity in discourse, resistant to what we think of as meaning and signification.[7] Near the opposite pole are expressions and objects that are valued almost exclusively for logical, utilitarian, moral, religious, or cognitive reasons and that therefore are minimally aesthetic.

In between are most of the things we think of as being meaningful or moving artistically and aesthetically. The complexity of such aesthetica is not always evident just from the expressions we use to describe them. Terms such as 'graceful', 'elegant', 'sublime', or 'beautiful' do not necessarily call to mind anything beyond purely aesthetic interests. Frequently, however, such aesthetic terms do reflect judgments encompassing factors that are not immediately aesthetic, although they have aesthetic consequences. We speak of the *Oresteia* as having aesthetic power and grandeur. Yet, were this trilogy somehow deprived of all moral, political, psychological, or religious seriousness, it would retain little of the aesthetic grandeur and power we now ascribe to it. This means that the work's more purely aesthetic traits (such as the dramatic form and the 'flavor' of Aeschylus's poetic language) are but subordinate elements within a complex aesthetic whole, the qualities of which affect and reflect non-aesthetic perceptions. We know that the *Oresteia* is significantly aesthetic, because any attempt to translate it into sheerly moral, political, or religious discourse diminishes its import significantly.

Yet we know that the work is not aesthetically pure, because even its aesthetic effects depend in part on dramatic engagement with concerns of the sort just now mentioned.

Again, the well-known thirteenth-century Bible illustration showing God as architect of the universe (see frontispiece) has formal integrity and pleasing lines and colors that give aesthetic delight when considered strictly in themselves. But the delight becomes richer and more complex, even at an aesthetic level, when one takes into account factors that are not immediately or necessarily aesthetic. One can be struck by the historical fact that the iconography of this miniature is rather unusual. One's intellectual curiosity can be aroused when one notices that, as God holds in his left hand the spherical world which is being created, this world is made visible to us in a fascinating cross-section. It is of theological interest, moreover, that God actually is imaged here, and imaged as an alert and intent architect. In our view, all of these 'non-aesthetic' sources of satisfaction can condition and enhance our aesthetic appreciation of the work experienced and valued as a whole. By the same token, aesthetic appreciation also can be diminished by factors not immediately aesthetic. This picture might seem to us a less wonderful or delightful work of art inasmuch as we object to its reinforcing the stereotype of God as male or inasmuch as we would prefer to envision the world not as a product of divine architectural skill but as an extension of God's own being: as God's body.[8] Neo-aesthetics is distinguished by the attempt to take seriously such complex aesthetic responses and judgments and to recognize the extent to which they are ingredient in all of culture, and not least in religion.

Indeed, we will see that nothing religious is completely free of the impact of aesthetica and their varied yet distinctive traits. By the same token, every aesthetic perception and realization undergoes critical evaluation and experiential reinterpretation, often within religious contexts. To trace, acknowledge, evaluate, and articulate such meanings-in-process can best be thought of as a kind of artful practice requiring of us new discipline and new disciplines if it is to be pursued.[9]

The Strategy in Brief

In helping to lay the groundwork for such a pursuit we will not simply be looking for a clearer understanding of how the words 'aesthetic', 'artistic', and 'religious' are ordinarily used. Too often they are used carelessly and inconsistently. Nor are we necessarily hoping to stipulate meanings that will win out over all others in the linguistic marketplace. The marketplace is too large and populous for that. Our aim, instead, is to locate important aesthetic and religious phenomena variously pointed to by these terms and others of the kind, and then to employ such terms with sufficient care that we can attain new insights into what is religiously meaningful within aesthetica. Thus the method used here is an unorthodox combination of the analytical, the phenomenological, and the hermeneutical, each modified and rid of its more technical trappings.

In keeping with common practice, our treatment of aesthetica deals more with art than with other aesthetic phenomena. This is because the different levels of the aesthetic, and the different uses and transformations of the aesthetic in religion, can best be observed through a study of the meaningful making – the poiesis – that occurs in art, and through examining what we ourselves make of art in aesthetic experience (aesthesis). Yet the artistic and the aesthetic are not coextensive or entirely correlative; consequently one cannot proceed as though the nature of artistic making and meaning can fully be understood without considering a wider range of aesthetica. Hence we try to take into account certain aesthetica that no one regards as art or that no one thinks of *only* as art.

The stages of this study can be described succinctly. After we have examined in the next chapter the fundamental reasons for rethinking aesthetics and have outlined the potentially extensive and vital role of aesthetics within theology, we take a closer look at the question of the identity and nature of aesthetica themselves, which we subsequently relate to the means and ends of artistic making and to its capacity for religious meaning. We then examine several of the most important varieties of religious aesthetic experience evident to, or manifest within, Christianity. With these in mind, we turn to explore the question of the extent to which religious experience understood within a Christian framework is ever sufficiently aesthetic to require aesthetic judgment and sensitivity – or taste – of the devotee or saint. Naturally the question of taste brings up the whole issue of standards, which we deal with by way of a discussion of classic and non-classic norms in the arts and in the Christian tradition.

The final chapter reflects further on how the particular assumptions and practices of a religion necessarily shape its aesthetic ideals in a distinctive manner and influence its aesthetic experiences. Thus we observe that theology and religious reflection can contribute actively to aesthetics itself, even if some religious aesthetic theories are likely to make most sense to those who actually embrace the various ideas, practices, and commitments that together comprise a given religion's unique 'way' and supply its own inner dynamic.

2

Can Aesthetics be Christian?

Aesthetics, Theology, and the Example of Ethics

Within the context of the present inquiry, to ask whether aesthetics can be Christian is also partly to ask whether aesthetics can or should play a major role in the thought of any specific religious tradition, whether Christian, Muslim, Jewish, or some other. Our answer therefore will be framed in such a way as to emphasize features of Christian theology that to some extent may be representative of religious reflection undertaken within many different traditions. Furthermore, given the aims of our inquiry as a whole, our answer obviously will need to constitute some kind of 'yes'.

Nevertheless, it probably would be good news for Christian theologians if we were able to demonstrate in this study that aesthetics could not conceivably be Christian – that, in fact, it should continue by and large to be accorded a religiously neutral status similar to that of mathematics or physics. Since aesthetics is primarily theoretical, Christian aesthetics would necessarily be a task for Christian theorizing, which at its most distinctive and systematic level is undertaken by theology proper. Theologians, however, have enough to do as it is. Many of them already feel some obligation to take account of theories from such diverse fields as economics, history, politics, sociology, psychology, linguistics, semiotics, hermeneutics, epistemology and, certainly, ethics. One hesitates to propose that the theologian also acquire sophistication in the field of aesthetics. Yet, as we shall see, this is the least that is called for. In fact, it is altogether possible that theological aesthetics should now constitute a branch of Christian theology in some ways comparable to theological ethics and likewise should inform the practice of theology as a whole.

The suggestion that aesthetics may have as much theological relevance as ethics could easily sound naive. It is worth recalling, therefore, that Christians have not always been certain where

16

ethics itself fits into Christian theology. Among those many Protestants who have been preoccupied with grace and salvation almost to the exclusion of sanctification, concern for ethical theory and practice has been secondary. And while moral theology has a venerable place in the Catholic tradition, those numerous Catholics whose ethical reflections have been based on theories of natural law have assumed that there is nothing peculiarly Christian about most ethical principles, because (it is supposed) all truly reasonable human beings have at least the potential of apprehending the greater part of what is ethically right or wrong without the aid of Christian revelation and ecclesiastical teaching. Thus, historically speaking, it turns out that neither Protestant nor Catholic theology has consistently highlighted Christian ethics as such. In fact, ethics has become a separate theological discipline only in modern times.[1] Furthermore, the status of the theory and practice of Christian ethics has remained problematical enough that as recently as a decade and a half ago a prominent theologian found it worthwhile to devote a whole book to the question *Can Ethics Be Christian?*[2]

Yet it must be said that the idea of Christian ethics was by then commonplace. It came as no great surprise that the question the book posed was answered in the affirmative. As for the present, it can safely be said that relatively few theologians have serious doubts about the legitimacy of Christian ethics within theological reflection. Graduate degrees are offered in the subject and authors write about such specialized topics as 'evangelical' ethics.[3]

The fact that ethics has moved from a peripheral to a focal position within Christian theology does not prove that aesthetics should do likewise; it only indicates that perhaps it *could*. But if aesthetics is to become a central theological concern, the process will be more complicated and arduous than it has been for ethics. It is true that, as Hans Urs von Balthasar has impressively shown, Christian theologians throughout history often have employed aesthetic categories in their descriptions of the nature of God, the cosmos, the Christian life, and the Kingdom. Von Balthasar's own writing demonstrates, moreover, that theology can order its own language and reflection in such a way as to exhibit aesthetic integrity, proportion, and a certain *claritas* befitting its objects and aims.[4] Nevertheless, with regard to a number of issues that one clearly can identify as basic to aesthetics, the Christian tradition has largely been silent, cryptic, or at any rate inconclusive. This is

as true of those traditions of Christian thought that include beauty
among the names of God or among the transcendental attributes of
Being as it is of those for which the word 'beauty' itself smacks of
the world, the flesh, and the devil. And it has rarely been more
obvious than at present, just when ethical theory (by contrast) is in
some way on the mind of almost every theologian.

There simply is no denying that, with a few notable exceptions –
Augustine and Pseudo-Dionysius, or von Balthasar and Tillich in
our own era – the theologian has exhibited slight interest in
aesthetic theory *per se*. Von Balthasar himself, it should be
observed, employs a quite minimal theoretical apparatus, albeit
one applied with great theological insight. Theologians of art such
as Gerardus van der Leeuw, Nathan Scott, John Dixon, Roger
Hazelton, David Harned, John Dillenberger, Hans Küng, Karl
Rahner, and Tillich too, rely rather little on aesthetics proper. Even
Nicholas Wolterstorff, himself a philosopher (and Calvinist) who
draws extensively on contemporary aesthetic theories in his
attempt to point the way toward a Christian aesthetic, passes over
or rejects a great deal of what has been said by aestheticians,
whether Christian or not. And though seminaries and graduate
programs in religion offer a modest number of courses on particular forms of art and particular artists, offerings in theological or
religious aesthetics are so unusual as to seem exotic.[5]

Thus, by and large, it seems that if there are solid grounds for
Christian theological aesthetics, they are not ones that can be
established in a satisfactory fashion – as perhaps those for ethics
can be – merely by appealing to what is already implicit or tacitly
acknowledged within Christian doctrines, institutions, traditions,
or Scriptures and by showing that, after all, Christianity has a
distinctive and unwavering commitment to this kind of inquiry.
The truth is that, unlike ethics, aesthetics is not *prima facie* the sort
of thing in which Christianity would take a keen interest. One has
some difficulty imagining a book on the aesthetics of Jesus or an
article on new trends in evangelical aesthetics. The very idea of
Christian theological aesthetics constitutes a challenge to prevalent
ways of thinking about theology and implicitly challenges certain
presuppositions about the nature of aesthetics as well.

Precisely because theology and aesthetics have such a tenuous
relationship, the options for finding a basis for theological aesthetics come to this: One can either interpret theology anew and in
such a way that theology's actual and possible connections with

aesthetics become evident, or interpret aesthetics anew and in such a way that its theological relevance cannot be missed. In point of fact, both approaches are valid and necessary. But they cannot be taken simultaneously. Our strategy here will be first to move toward the reformation of aesthetics, showing why it has been less than inviting to both humanistic and theological inquiry and then indicating how aesthetics might be transformed, for its own sake as well as for that of theology. Then we will venture to suggest how theology itself can be reoriented so as to provide a context for aesthetic reflection. This alone will not result in a Christian aesthetic but, rather, in the nucleus of a theory of why Christian aesthetics is possible, plausible, and to some extent unavoidable.

Rethinking Aesthetics

In an essay written almost half a century ago, Dorothy Sayers laments what she takes to be the fact that, although there are writers on aesthetics who happen to be Christians, there is 'no Christian aesthetic – no Christian philosophy of the Arts'. That this is the case seems to her nearly incredible because, in her view, 'if we commit ourselves to saying that the Christian revelation discovers to us the nature of *all* truth, then it must discover to us the nature of the truth about Art among other things'.[6] It plainly follows from Sayers's argument that any rethinking of aesthetics that could be of value to theology or to Christians in general would necessarily be done from the standpoint of theology itself and of what Christianity regards as revelation.

A similar view of the proper source for theological aesthetics is expressed by von Balthasar. In his multi-volume work *Herrlichkeit*, or *The Glory of the Lord*, von Balthasar warns against the dangers of an aesthetic theology – a theology that is reduced to a preoccupation with the beautiful in a limited sense – and accordingly stresses the need for a legitimate theological aesthetics. Von Balthasar appears to believe, however, that only an aesthetics directly derived from revelation will be useful to theology. For, as he explains, he means by 'theological aesthetics' a theology 'which does not primarily work with the extra-theological categories of a worldly philosophical aesthetics . . . but which develops its theory of beauty from the data of revelation itself with genuinely theological methods'.[7]

Although the arguments of Sayers and von Balthasar are laudable in their intention to motivate work in theological aesthetics, they unfortunately are specious. The major premise employed in each case is that, in the words of Sayers, 'Christian revelation discovers to us the nature of all truth'. From this it naturally follows that revelation must show us whatever is true about art and beauty. The major premise, however, is patently false. Christian theology may indeed want to say that no truth can be inconsistent with fundamental Christian understandings of self, others, world, and ultimate reality – truth having its source in the very God that is made known in Christ. It should be obvious, however, that Christian revelation is not what has discovered to us the nature of the truths of logic or quantum mechanics, of language or the interpretation of dreams. Nor is it, consequently, the sufficient means by which we can discover all other basic truths, such as those pertaining to art and aesthetics. Thus there is little reason to believe that whatever insight and theoretical understanding the aesthetician requires is immediately available in the form of revealed theology. Nor does it stand to reason that, just because theology can indeed make its own contribution to aesthetics, only aesthetics that begins with revelation can be pertinent to theology itself.

That said, however, we must stress how unlikely it is that philosophical aesthetics would have been so generally ignored by theologians if it already were replete with ideas tailored to theological interests or even to the interests of humanistic inquiry at large. As it happens, post-Enlightenment aesthetics often has slighted or suppressed the very aspects of aesthetic theory that might attract and enhance such interests, or indeed those of philosophy itself as a whole. This fact, together with confusions seemingly endemic to thinking about matters so far removed from the world of clear-cut concepts, is in no small degree responsible for the familiar complaint about the 'dreariness' of aesthetics[8] and for the sense among many theorists that the subject of aesthetics, if not so 'entirely misunderstood' as Ludwig Wittgenstein claimed,[9] is at least very much in need of being rethought.

Exactly what sort of rethinking is called for? And how might it be carried out in such a way as to discover the latent theological promise within aesthetics itself? To begin to answer these questions – and in this chapter we can only just begin – we need to review several major features of aesthetic theory in the modern period, taking care to notice the conceptual difficulties inherent in each of these aspects of the modern tradition. Of particular relevance are modern conceptions of the very nature of aesthetics, of aesthetic experience, and of art; for these are conceptions that, if let stand, inevitably must constitute major obstacles to the whole enterprise of theological (or religious) aesthetics. Looking first at ideas about aesthetics as an area of inquiry, we will examine in the next section ideas of aesthetic experience and art.

Aesthetics proper started out by being something it would never be again. When Alexander Baumgarten coined the term 'aesthetics' in 1735, he was thinking of the Greek adjective *aisthetikos*, which means 'perceptible, or concerned with perception'. (Thus the noun *aisthetika*, transliterated into English as 'aesthetics', literally means 'perceptibles'.) As this etymology suggests, Baumgarten originally meant aesthetics to be the science of sensory perception in general – including the science of poetics, which was to be concerned with the sensible forms we call works of art. By 1750, however, Baumgarten had come to equate aesthetics with what he formerly had called poetics, declaring its proper object to be beauty and the 'perfection of sensitive cognition'.[10] This new meaning of the term 'aesthetics' was not far from the meaning that would be established within the lifetime of Kant and would remain current until now – namely, philosophical reflection on the nature of art and beauty and of response to both.

At this point in history, however, it is far from evident that art and beauty necessarily go together, that beauty is all that solicits or warrants aesthetic attention even outside of art, and hence that aesthetics as it has usually been conceived forms a coherent field of study. Mindful of modern music like Penderecki's searing and frightening *Threnody to the Victims of Hiroshima* and of post-modern plays like those of Tom Stoppard, the theorist is now keenly aware that not all art is easily or even sensibly thought of as beautiful. Nor, of course, can one call all beauty artistic unless one insists on thinking of sunsets, oak trees, and trout as quite literally artworks of God. And it seems evident that, heard from a distance, the chants and roars of a crowd at a sports stadium can be aesthetically interesting and exciting without being judged beautiful, ugly, or indeed artful. Add to this the claim of certain theorists that some contemporary art is so dependent on imperceptible intellectual and social factors as not to be especially sensory or aesthetic at all, and one begins to realize why traditional aesthetics appears to lack a subject matter of sufficient coherence to give the field unity.

It has been proposed more than once that, in order to remedy this incoherence, philosophy of art should be divorced from aesthetics, leaving aesthetics to inquire not into the nature of art as such but simply into the beautiful, the grotesque, the sublime, and so forth. The trouble with such a suggestion is that aesthetics without art would be like astronomy without stars – not impossible, but altogether less interesting. Extensive theoretical study of art apart from aesthetic considerations would be even sillier and more futile; for, however important it may be to distinguish between the artistic and the aesthetic, artistry almost invariably works with, or plays off from, aesthetic means and ends.

It seems, then, that aesthetics might better be made broader in scope than narrower. In point of fact, aesthetics should perhaps be nothing less than basic theoretical reflection regarding all aesthetic phenomena, including their modes of significant interrelation with, and mediation of, what is not inherently aesthetic: abstract ideas, useful objects, moral convictions, class conflicts, religious doctrines, and so forth. The coherence of the field of aesthetics so conceived would derive from its central interest in aesthetica – a term we can use technically to denote not perceptibles (as in Greek) or beautiful objects alone, but all those things employing a medium in such a way that its perceptible form and 'felt' qualities become essential to what is appreciable and meaningful.

From the standpoint of religious studies and theology, this broad notion of aesthetics potentially has great advantages. Conceived of in this way, aesthetics obviously can reflect on religious arts, including liturgical music and church architecture, for example, and perhaps can illuminate how aesthetic and religious perceptions coalesce or compete in various forms of secular art. It also can look beyond art and, in so doing, can reflect on ritual or prayer, or on the role of the aesthetically mysterious in religious expression and the importance of the aesthetically monotonous in pilgrimage or acts of penitence. Aware of the mutual influence between medium and message, it can ponder whatever differences there may be between theologies or traditions in which the word is dominant and those that give more attention to visual media, dance, or music. And instead of confining itself to an analysis of how something can be enjoyed strictly for its own sake, aesthetics can enjoin significant semantic and epistemological issues regarding modes of meaning and truth and the degree to which each is *sui generis.*

Furthermore, specifically theological aesthetics, once it has freed itself from the tyranny of the beautiful, need not foreclose on the question of whether fragmentation, mystery, darkness, and imbalance affect the very being of God and qualify the very form of the Reign that Christians believe has no end. It can acknowledge, therefore, that human notions of harmony, light, and proportion may not always be reliable guides to any ultimate state or process of aesthesis. In any event, an aesthetics that searches beyond the beautiful allows for the possibility that beauty itself, besides being just one among many names of God, may also be just one of God's many *aesthetic* names.

No one would suggest that this broad conception of aesthetics has emerged as the dominant one today. For one thing, there still is a tendency for aesthetics to collapse into philosophy of art instead of contemplating aesthetica of all kinds. Besides this, we have seen that there is an inclination on the part of the more radical recent thinkers to doubt that the very distinction between the aesthetic and the non-aesthetic is useful – a doubt that we must here be content to allay little by little.

Where the 'neo-aesthetic' approach advocated here does join with contemporary theory at large is in regarding the traditional ways of drawing the distinction between aesthetic and non-aesthetic phenomena as inadequate. The view of aesthetics presented here likewise accords with the growing pluralism within recent aesthetic theory; for aesthetics of the sort envisioned here could incorporate approaches ranging from the phenomenological or analytic to the hermeneutical, semiotic, or deconstructive. This means that we assume, with many other theorists today, that there is a high degree of flexibility and permeability in the boundaries separating aesthetics from such fields as linguistics, critical theory, and cultural criticism. But we also assume that, once we have opened aesthetics to currently fashionable considerations of politics, semiotics, and 'erotics', we have no grounds for ruling out the less fashionable considerations of theology and religious practice.

These, however, are just the sorts of consideration that modernist theory has systematically excluded and that, especially as regards theology, the more radical post-modern theorists see mostly in a negative light. We need to remind ourselves, therefore, why modernist aesthetics took the route it did, and how. As we do so it will soon be plain that the modernist legacy in thinking about art and aesthesis, even more than the constricted modern understanding of the enterprise of aesthetics as a whole, naturally tends to militate against the very conception of genuinely theological or religious aesthetics.

The Aesthetic and the Religious: Theory at an Impasse

We have suggested that aesthetics is best constituted as the study of the nature of aesthetica of all kinds and that, in view of the heterogeneity of aesthetica themselves, it will utilize ideas and methods adapted from other fields of study, thereby crossing traditional boundaries between disciplines. In this way we have depicted aesthetics as a field naturally opening out onto such areas as theology, hermeneutics, and the history and phenomenology of religions.

It nonetheless remains to be seen whether in fact aesthetic phenomena can and do bear religious freight and, if so, under what circumstances. That is – to borrow traditional terminology – we must determine whether beautiful and artistic things, when truly considered aesthetically and in themselves, have much at all to do with religion. Modernist aesthetics has been strongly inclined to doubt that they do. And while the basis for such thinking has lately been challenged in important respects, problems inherent in modernist ideas of art and aesthetic experience persist in many post-modern permutations. Consequently our immediate task is to indicate how these particular ideas developed and why they are questionable.

For many Romantics and their heirs, the notions of art, beauty, and religion were closely intertwined and sometimes thoroughly confused. It appears to have come naturally to Chateaubriand in 1802 to give to his large volume called *The Genius of Christianity* the subtitle *The Beauty of the Christian Religion*. Blake, Coleridge, the Schlegels, Schelling, Ruskin, even Pater – these and other Romantics and Victorians found it easy to utter the words 'art', 'beauty', and 'religion' together in one breath. 'The Whole Business of Man is the Arts', wrote Blake; 'Jesus & his Apostles & Disciples were all Artists'; 'A Poet, a Painter, a Musician, an Architect: the Man or Woman who is not one of these is not a Christian'.[11] These

aphorisms, albeit eccentric and heterodox, lay claim to the central-
ity of artistic imagination for the life of morality and religion. In this
respect they are typical of much aesthetic theory that originated in
Romanticism.

Many later thinkers were to conclude, however, that the Romantics and their followers neglected to draw crucial distinctions
between the aesthetic and the religious and thereby failed to justify
the connections they saw. Hence, the main currents of modern
aesthetics flowed on into a different channel, rapidly becoming
more secular: more interested in the autonomy of the aesthetic
realm and in the legitimacy of art for its own sake. By the latter part
of the nineteenth century, formalism and aestheticism of various
kinds were not to be held back. Philosophers, critics, and artists
now emphasized the uniqueness and purity of aesthetic experience and its objects.

As one might expect, it was Immanuel Kant who earlier had set
the tone for this genuinely modern development when he said that
our discernment of the beautiful is disinterested, non-cognitive,
and amoral. Subsequent theorists (who eventually ignored Kant's
further claim that the beautiful, as an end in itself, is a symbol of
the morally good) invented notions like 'aesthetic distance' and
'aesthetic attitude' to extend and reinforce Kant's thesis that the
beautiful is inherently isolated from moral, theoretical, and practical interests. Accordingly they forgot that, for Kant himself, beauty
is often 'dependent' – that is, allied with purpose and meaningful
content, and so subject in some degree to conceptual interpretation
and to the influence of larger human interests, some of which are
social and religious. In the process of being made and seen through
formalist and aestheticist eyes, both art and beauty were removed
from direct commerce with ideas, religion, society, and morality.

This line of thought, having become conspicuous in the late
nineteenth century, continued to be prominent in theory and
practice until the last quarter of the twentieth. Its impact was
evident even on theorists like Benedetto Croce and his admirer
R. G. Collingwood, neither of whom could be considered formalists. Early in the twentieth century these philosophers put forward
ideas that, in effect, reduced genuine art to nothing more than the
imaginative expression of feeling or, in other words, to the
expression of what Croce called 'lyrical intuition'. Although Croce
and Collingwood both had a high regard for feeling of this sort,
claiming that intuitions expressed in art serve abstract thought by

providing the imaginative link between sensation and intellection, they nonetheless regarded aesthetic intuitions in themselves as wonderfully useless, devoid of *actual* emotion or of entertainment value, and admirably inert at the conceptual level. In their view, for instance, the person truly interested in the artistic and aesthetic value of the prehistoric cave paintings at Lascaux would simply ignore their probable ritual and magical connections.[12]

In our own day, if not in the most recent hour, one comes across countless similar examples of the diminution of the aesthetic and the further diminution of art. The late Monroe Beardsley, for example, argues in his prolific and widely esteemed publications that moral, historical, cognitive, technical, and intentional factors are extrinsic to anything aesthetic; and since, in his view, art is pre-eminently aesthetic, he maintains that such factors are extrinsic to the consideration of art *qua* art.[13] In a related vein, the British philosopher Harold Osborne, long-time editor of the *British Journal of Aesthetics*, writes (without apparent fear of contradiction) that 'neither linguistic nor visual art, even when it is representational, is appraised aesthetically, i.e., *as* art, by reference to the amount, completeness, accuracy, or specificity of the semantic information it conveys'.[14] That is to say, aesthetic appraisal is carried out without referring to any of those things that ordinarily would make communication meaningful. Jerome Stolnitz, author of widely esteemed historical and theoretical studies in the so-called aesthetic attitude, takes the same tack when he boldly argues that to read a novel as art is to read it 'aesthetically', in consequence of which moral considerations are simply excluded.[15] Needless to say, self-consciously formalist art critics such as Clive Bell and Clement Greenberg embrace closely related ideas, as do the New Critics in literary theory of the mid-twentieth century. Presumably none of the above would take exception to the memorable but now rather worn dictum of Archibald MacLeish that 'A poem should not mean / But be', which in their view doubtless would sum up the *raison d'être* of any work of art.

This whole tendency to equate the artistic with the aesthetic and then to treat the aesthetic as inherently isolated from everything else is most revealingly exemplified in the account of aesthetic perception given by Virgil Aldrich in his textbook *Philosophy of Art*. There Aldrich likens our perception of the aesthetic aspects of an object to our perceiving the familiar duck-rabbit figure in one way rather than another.[16] His point is not that the duck-rabbit itself affords much aesthetic pleasure; no, this ambiguous figure is relevant, Aldrich says, because it shows how one can perceive something in two very different and mutually exclusive ways. In fact Aldrich's interpretation inadvertently makes it plain that the so-called duck-rabbit is really a duck/rabbit. One can see the figure either as a rabbit or as a duck but not as both at the same time. The image either has big ears or it has a bill, but it does not have big ears and bill simultaneously. Similarly, Aldrich suggests, one can see an artwork like the Parthenon in terms of non-aesthetic properties such as the physical weight of the marble, the growing imperialism and collective pride of Periclean Athens, the function of the building as a temple, and so forth; or one can see it as a work of art, attending to aesthetic features such as its unity-in-diversity, formal balance, proportion, expressive strength, and gracefulness. What Aldrich makes absolutely clear is that he thinks these two modes of 'seeing-as' must be mutually exclusive.

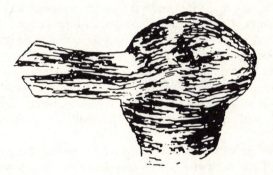

Such either/or thinking about aesthetic experience deserves careful scrutiny, for it entails an aesthetic purism that is oddly pervasive, extending well beyond the strict versions articulated by rigid formalists. Philosophers such as Ernst Cassirer and Nelson Goodman, for example, depart from Kant far enough to regard art as a mode of constructing the worlds we humans inhabit; but Kant's presence is felt nonetheless when they insist that the worlds of art are quite separate from worlds constructed by other means.[17] In a parallel vein Martin Heidegger suggests that the worlds made or revealed through the work of art are not at all the worlds uncovered or fabricated in other, more 'objective' and 'objectifying' ways.[18] And while neo-Thomist philosophers such as Jacques Maritain and Etienne Gilson attribute to art a capacity for bringing about the sensible or intuitive cognition of things that are known at another level through abstract reasoning, they nonetheless fail to see how theoretical understanding and poetic intuition could both be altered substantially in a process of reciprocal exchange and mutual transformation. Identified with a long tradition according to which the beautiful – along with the good and the true – is an irreducible, transcendental attribute of being, the latter philosophers nonetheless have little conception of how the order of beautiful making and meaning not only overlaps but also interacts with the orders of moral reason and critical inquiry, and hence with the apprehension of the good and the true.[19]

Similarly, for Susanne Langer and Mikel Dufrenne, what art expresses through its non-discursive forms is the life of feeling – its anticipations, tensions, and resolutions. And for Dufrenne at least, feeling is one kind of knowing. Yet, having thus connected art with life, these thinkers make it clear that the virtual, aesthetic expression of the forms of feeling differs altogether from other modes of expression and never substantially engages that side of the mind concerned with practical or rational reflection.[20] Sometimes even the American pragmatist John Dewey ties the aesthetic so closely to the dynamic rhythm and organic 'feel' of expressive forms and satisfactions that he cannot deal adequately with the content of the satisfactions and thoughts formally shaped and aesthetically expressed.[21]

While there are very significant differences among these various theories of art and aesthetic experience, they all at some point yield (perhaps, as in the case of Dewey, quite against their basic intentions) to one or more purist temptations in their thinking about art and aesthetica. These temptations present themselves most vividly in the guise of three related but separable assumptions: first, that the value of art *qua* art derives from nothing other than its capacity to maximize purely aesthetic qualities and pleasures; second, that all aesthetic qualities are ones apprehended in the act of 'free' contemplation and thus never appeal to genuinely conceptual thinking or practical impulse, or therefore to any aspect of morality or religion that is not already essentially aesthetic and thus sheerly 'felt'; and, third, that as a consequence the exercise of taste is unalloyed and exclusive, entirely concerned with form or with a unique sort of feeling expressed by the 'object itself', which one values for 'its own sake'.

In view of the prevalence of such assumptions about art and aesthetic experience, it is not surprising that it has so seldom occurred to modern theologians and religious thinkers to try to formulate a religious aesthetic, or a theology of art and beauty, that could have the weight of a theological ethic. Too much has been excluded from the aesthetic and artistic at the very start.

It would take at least a book – the rest of this one, in fact – to construct an adequate alternative to the views of art and aesthetics sketched above. In due course we will want to turn directly, if only intermittently, to recent or recently resurrected aesthetics for assistance. Yet often such theorizing has been better at criticism than at construction, and even its more constructive ideas must be dealt with judiciously and selectively when we come to explore in greater depth the relation between aesthetica and religion. It is not sufficient to point out that leading analytic philosophers such as Arthur Danto, Joseph Margolis, and George Dickie have rejected one or more of the modernist premises referred to above, and perhaps represent the majority of current Anglo-American aestheticians in doing so. Nor is it enough to cite the radically different hermeneutical approach that Hans-Georg Gadamer elaborates partly on the basis of Heidegger's phenomenological ontology. For that matter, we cannot be content just to rely on the post-structuralist semiotics of art proferred by Umberto Eco and, in a psychoanalytical version, by Julia Kristeva, or merely to trot out the critiques of formalism by Suzie Gablik and Norman Bryson in the field of visual art, the neo-Marxist analyses of the politics of art, or, indeed, the ideas of some thinker unduly neglected or oddly used by aesthetics in the modern past – a Wilhelm Dilthey, for example. All of these thinkers have in some fashion informed the theorizing in which we will be engaged. Yet they do not constitute a united front that simply can be mobilized to take over the terrain of any possible and future aesthetic. And none of them adequately analyzes the crucial relation between aesthetic and religious phenomena.

In any case, our approach at this particular stage can be relatively independent. What we now must do is indicate elementary theoretical grounds for questioning what we have found to be the most troublesome modernist assumptions about aesthetics and art, and then establish a reasonably secure basis for an alternative approach. This will enable us to suggest how such an approach could become an important part of theology itself, should theology be able to rethink its own tasks and methods in the way aesthetics has begun to do.

Religious Aesthetics: Or, Farewell to the Duck/Rabbit

In his *Religio Medici* of 1643 Sir Thomas Browne remarks that music – even 'Taverne Musicke' – has a profound effect on him. 'There is something in it of Divinity more than the eare discovers', he says. 'It is an Hieroglyphicall and Shadowed lesson of the whole world, and Creatures of God; such a melody to the eare, as the whole world, well understood, would afford the understanding. In briefe, it is a sensible fit of that Harmony, which intellectually sounds in the eares of God.'[22]

Even apart from Browne's dubious though venerable assumption that God is all intellect, this is a statement that would confound many moderns. But it is not so very different from the thinking of the thoroughly modern Igor Stravinsky, who, for all his association with formalism, maintains that 'music comes to reveal itself as a form of communion with our fellow man – and with the Supreme Being'.[23] We might place both of these views alongside the belief of Karl Barth that the Kingdom of God can be likened to a composition by Mozart, which is at once 'beautiful play' and virtually the equivalent of a parable.[24] It is important to note, moreover, that we can find related ideas in the writing of that arch-formalist Clive Bell. Having declared 'significant form' to be the defining characteristic of genuine art of all ages, Bell claims, on the one hand, that such form is something to which representational content and human interests as a whole are irrelevant. On the other hand, however, he theorizes that when we consider the formal significance of an artwork, and thus see it as an end in itself, 'we become aware of its essential reality, of the God in everything, of the universal in the particular, of the all-pervading rhythm. . . . It is that which gives to all things their individual significance'.[25]

The kind of self-contradiction that we have observed most clearly in the case of Bell actually is not uncommon. Similar contradictory ideas can be found in statements made by Kandinsky or Mondrian, Schoenberg or Stravinsky, or by a number of New

Critics.[26] The modernist, prone to exhibit what we can now term the 'duck/rabbit' mentality, tends to think of an experience or object as either aesthetic or non-aesthetic. Since the work of art is regarded as an aesthetic object *par excellence,* the modernist takes great pains to establish the extraordinary autonomy and self-referential 'meaning' of the art object. Thus we are told that the artwork's function is merely to shine forth in its fullness of being – a plentitude to which all cognitive, social, moral, or religious meanings are supposedly irrelevant. But because, even after all this, something like a halo of meaning remains to grace the work, and because a work that signifies nothing might appear truly insignificant, the modernist lapses into contradictions in an effort to account for the work's genuine significance and for what can now only appear to be some sort of meaning-beyond-meaning. Taking what seems like a leap of faith, our modern theorist will suddenly sound strangely like Sir Thomas Browne, making trans-cendent cognitive and metaphysical claims for the work of art, treating it as a unique mode of knowing, a particular embodiment of the universal, a veritable icon simultaneously aesthetic and religious (or moral or infinitely wise). The doctrine of eucharistic transubstantiation, which repeatedly has been alluded to in mod-ernist poetics, sounds scarcely more mysterious than does mod-ernist talk about the ineffable presence and ontological depth of a poem or a painting that has already been declared to be self-contained and devoid of reference or meaning.[27] In view of the contradictions entailed in the modernist approach, one could be forgiven for preferring the language of Browne himself, which at least acknowledges the mystery at the very start.

Understandably, however, the most common *post*-modern re-sponse to what are sometimes seen as essentially Romantic contra-dictions within modernist theory is not to call for a return to the neo-Platonism of Browne. Rather, the post-modernist typically is inclined to argue that any residual halo of meaning surrounding the putative aesthetic object is itself but another sign within a universe of opaque and finally unilluminating signs, all of our own making. In this case, one has making without meaning, or making in which all meaning is merely made up.

What is left for the theologian informed by such post-modern aesthetics is perhaps a deconstructive atheism of the sort proposed by Mark C. Taylor in *Erring: A Postmodern A/theology.* Yet such an a/theology is also caught in contradictions (however willed and conscious) – not so much because it rejects the affirmations intrinsic to Christian theology as because its very premises tend to undercut those alternative affirmations implicit in its own ever penultimately joyful dance of words, which seems after all to depend on at least a ghost of positive presence and meaningful signification. Taylor, for example, declares that there is an affirmative as well as a negative a/theology. Accordingly he asserts that, with the necessary end of meaning and logos, of God and self, and of purpose and history, there comes 'mazing grace', carnivalesque play, and a delightfully endless, errant, and useless wandering that supposedly becomes the only available way of 'totally loving the world'.[28] But the affirmation made here is undermined by the fact that, in effect, we have just been denied any real world and any source or means by which to love it meaningfully, since the universe allegedly is nothing more than insignificant signs and since self and meaning – not to mention God – have been deconstructed. Why the paradoxes of this position are preferable to the traditional ones at which Taylor balks (often for understandable reasons) is finally unclear.

It seems possible, at any rate, that some of the moves made by Taylor and certain other post-modernists are unnecessary. This is not, of course, to say that modernism and its antecedents can be left in place. Rather, it is to observe that perhaps modernism should be faulted more for its concepts of making, meaning, and experiencing than for its persistence in somehow supposing that there actually are meanings – even profound meanings – for us to make out. To see how this could be so in the sphere of aesthetics, we need to return briefly to the duck/rabbit and the mode of perception it represents.

Intriguing as the duck/rabbit figure may be to thinkers as diverse as Ludwig Wittgenstein, E. H. Gombrich, and Virgil Aldrich, it is not a good model for understanding aesthetic perception and its relation to aesthetic objects. All that the duck/rabbit demonstrates is that perception can sometimes be an either/or affair. It does not demonstrate that this is always the case or that it is even usually the case when one attends to artistic and other aesthetic objects. What makes the duck/rabbit tempting is that, on this model, if one claims that a given experience is aesthetic, one automatically seals it off from the intrusion of extrinsic criteria appropriate to abstract ideas, political and utilitarian interests, and conventional moral and religious claims. The problem is that what has been separated so radically cannot then be joined again without contradiction; and, as we have seen, the impulse to re-join the aesthetic with something more or higher or deeper has proven to be virtually irresistible, which seems to indicate that the impulse is in some way elicited by aesthetica themselves.

Clearly a better model for thinking about aesthetic experience would be one that allowed for the integrity and uniqueness of works of art or aesthetic objects without completely severing their connection with what is not already inherently artistic or aesthetic. This would allow us to justify in theory our common perception that, for example, the beauty and sublimity of Chartres Cathedral – its grace, dizzying height, and powerful integrity – are at once aesthetic and religious, with its religious import modifying its aesthetic impact, and vice versa.

We can take a step toward explaining this phenomenon by modifying the model of perception Aldrich and others rely on in explaining aesthetic experience. It is in fact commonly the case that perceptions, instead of neatly alternating, co-inhere in multiple layers and are subject to mutual influence in a given milieu. This phenomenon is to some extent present in virtually every act of perception. Something cannot be perceived at all except *as* whatever one takes it to be, however tentatively; and with this relatively primitive act of perceiving-as, other modes of perception are combined, so that what is perceived *as* something is often also perceived on, in, or through another perception. Thus the white disc suspended in the evening sky is perceived *as* the moon; yet, perceived *in the context* of proximity to the horizon, it is perceived to be larger by far than when seen directly overhead. The act of seeing-as is here conditioned by seeing-in-relation.

Some of the processes by which such perceptual transfigurations are achieved would appear to be analogous to the various mental and linguistic processes by which metaphor and metonymy transform and combine meanings from different semantic fields, thereby achieving a surplus of meaning. Tranquility, for example, can be perceived *in* what one sees *as* the face of a saffron-robed Buddhist monk who is seated in a rock garden before a sculpture that he in turn sees *as* an image of Bodhisattva *in* whom tranquility is manifest and (metaphorically) exemplified. At such a moment and in such a context one can 'see' a sort of tranquility that might not be seen at all if one saw the 'same' expression on the monk's face as he walked about Hong Kong in ordinary attire. On another occasion merriment is heard *in* a tune that becomes both metaphor and exemplification; for one hears it *as* an Irish jig *through* which one can perceive something of the spirit of the Irish people. Indeed, this aspect of Irish spirit is perceived as such and in this way nowhere else, because the music is not literally a transcription of Irish life, although it participates in and expresses that life. Again, Sir Thomas Browne hears something *as* divine *in* the sensuous, microcosmic order *on* which he perceives audible music to depend. And this is an order *through* which he glimpses a further, strictly intellectual order that he associates *with* the non-sensuous harmony perfectly understood only by the being he regards *as* God.

Obviously one may question the philosophical and theological biases of a Thomas Browne, or argue over which of the various perceptions described above is literal or metaphorical, or deeper or more penetration. One also can debate whether a given perception should be described in terms of perceiving-as, perceiving-in, et cetera. What is important here is that various of these perceptual modes, some aspects of which we can legitimately term aesthetic, are multi-layered, interdependent, and largely simultaneous. This emergence of multi-dimensionality and complexity within aesthetic experience warrants further comment and explication.

Within the experience of music described by Sir Thomas Browne, for example, one can detect several levels of aesthetic perception. There is his perception that the sounds are organized enough to be called music, which is an almost spontaneous realization of sense and intellect requiring only minimal aesthetic awareness. His perception of the music as melodious and pleasingly harmonious is different, although probably simultaneous, and it is simply and strictly aesthetic – a delight in sense and form that is not in any evident way practical or moral or intellectual. Yet it is fair to surmise that the particular aesthetic enjoyment Browne takes in this music is colored by his hearing *in* it something more. For Browne this additionally pleasing component of the music he hears is partly a function of his tacit awareness of theology and of his evident love of God, whom he terms the 'first Composer'. This largely non-aesthetic, tacit dimension of awareness makes for a further resonance in the sounds he hears, since he now hears them as the incarnation of inaudible cosmic harmony and as truly – albeit mysteriously and metaphorically – divine. To suppose that at this more complex level his perception is in no way aesthetic simply because it is in some way intellectual and religious would be to fall prey to the duck/rabbit mentality and thereby to miss the obvious: that the music really *sounds* different to Browne because he brings to the sound a mentality and sensibility that allows him to hear the graceful and harmonious features of the music as the adumbration of Grace and Harmony writ large.

To make matters even more complicated, it likewise stands to reason that, almost inevitably, Browne's ideas and feelings regarding what is true of God and the cosmos surely would in turn be shaped and colored by the very music they help interpret. That is to say, Browne's experience of music takes on a meaning that would affect his experience of God, because for him music is meaningful as the audible manifestation of harmony that really is divine.

What these partly religious examples show about aesthetica is that, while some are relatively simple and pure, others become exceedingly complex as they relate to ideas, convictions, and feelings beyond anything merely sensory or formal. So much, then, for the duck/rabbit and the prevalent modern assumptions that all aesthetic experience is inherently pure, self-contained, and affective, with art existing to provide an utterly unique sort of pleasurable feeling or intuitive knowledge that is sealed off from other modes of thought and experience. We also can bid farewell to the correlated assumption that aesthetic taste and attention is essentially exclusive of all intellectual, moral, practical, or religious factors. Certainly this leaves us in a better position to account for the religious meanings that Stravinsky, Barth, Bell, and Browne all profess to find in aesthetic works and objects; because, on this account, we can see that religious attitudes, thoughts, and convictions can shape and be shaped by what is aesthetic.

In arriving at this point, we have criticized and begun to modify prevalent modern notions of aesthetics, art, and aesthetic experience. Although we have not yet attempted to offer a definition of art or anything like a thoroughgoing phenomenology of aesthetic experience, we have lent support to the intuition that, whatever their nature, art and aesthetic experience often are important to religion in a variety of ways and therefore invite theological reflection. Indeed, we have suggested that what is aesthetic can itself sometimes be religious. At such junctures aesthetics and religious reflection must converge; for each can fully understand itself only through the transformations wrought through contact with the other. Accordingly, our last step in this portion of our study is to try to indicate what in general it would mean for Christian theology to engage in aesthetics.

Aesthetics in Theology

Even though Christian theology's dealings with aesthetics have been minimal, various theologians who clearly identify themselves as Christian have maintained that theology has no *a priori* reason for neglecting the aesthetic dimensions of religion and life. Von Balthasar, for instance, argues that it is 'not necessary that, as generally occurs in our century, theology renounce aesthetics, whether unconsciously or consciously, whether out of weakness or forgetfulness or even a false scientific attitude. For if it were, theology would have to give up a good part – if not the best part – of itself'. For von Balthasar, it seems, what makes theological aesthetics possible at all is the belief, first, that what is holy and divine somehow takes perceptible and imaginative form and, second, that beauty in form is not simply a distillate separated from truth and morality. In von Balthasar's view, the beautiful form 'as it appears to us is beautiful only because the delight that it arouses in us is founded upon the fact that, in it, the truth and goodness of the depths of reality itself are manifested and bestowed'.[29]

These are judgments that John Henry Newman surely would have supported. Writing a century before von Balthasar, he declared: 'Revealed Religion should be especially poetical – and it is so in fact. While its disclosures have an originality in them to engage the intellect, they have a beauty to satisfy the moral nature. It presents us with those ideal forms of excellence in which a poetical mind delights, and with which all grace and harmony are associated'.[30]

For anyone attuned to such positive theological assessments of things aesthetic, Søren Kierkegaard's withering sarcasm regarding religious aesthetics comes as something of a shock: 'They talk in lofty tones of the cleverness and profundity of St Paul, of his beautiful similes, etc. – sheer aesthetics. . . . Only to clerical ignorance would it occur to praise Paul aesthetically'. To praise Paul for aesthetic reasons is to act in ignorance, Kierkegaard thinks, because Paul is thereby admired for being 'what in an apostle is a matter of indifference' and what essentially he is not: a creative genius, a stylist – 'whereas in fact he has no affinity either with Plato or Shakespeare'.[31] The Kierkegaardian tone is echoed by the poet W. H. Auden when he opines that, to a Christian, 'both art and science are secular activities, that is to say, small beer'.[32]

Such differences in theological aesthetics can easily be over-stated. Kierkegaard and Auden by no means despise art, and von Balthasar and Newman by no means advocate aestheticism. Nevertheless, the theological contrast in their stances toward aesthetics is significant, potentially reappearing in other guises as differences concerning liturgics, ideas and images of God and world, modes of proclamation and moral action, approaches to Scripture, and so forth. Given such differences, it makes no sense to speak of a single, uniform relation between aesthetics and theology, as if every theology would need or want to engage in aesthetics in the same manner. Any such uniform approach is further ruled out by the simple fact that theology takes many forms. Aesthetics may be one thing when done in the context of an academic ecumenical liberal North American systematic theology and quite another thing when done in the context of a Catholic liberation neo-orthodox Central American practical theology.

Yet, despite this fact, one can think of several important respects in which Christian theology of every kind most likely would be affected by acknowledging and in some measure incorporating aesthetics. Likewise there are several ways in which Christian theology of nearly every variety might inform aesthetics and impress upon it configurations of Christian value, experience, and thought.

Before we examine any of these, however, one basic point needs to be made – namely, that there is a sense in which doing aesthetics is not so much a theological option as a theological necessity. The question is only whether it will be done consciously and well. When Cardinal Ugo Poletti recently decided to ban all so-called profane music from the churches of Rome, he may have thought of his criteria as strictly theological rather than as aesthetic. For the ban extended to all classical music that could not be designated 'religious' and suitable for performance 'in the presence of the Most Blessed Sacrament', as a consequence of which most of the music of Mozart and Beethoven, for example, was immediately prohibited.[33] Yet in the ears of many trained musicians and aesthetically astute listeners, a great deal of what ordinarily is identified as church music, even when written expressly for use during communion, is conducive to a sentimental response that tends to violate the very spirit of the Mass; whereas the Adagio movement of Beethoven's String Quartet opus 59, no. 1, for instance, can convey a deep sense of reverence. Although the judgment of such listeners need not be made normative for all people and settings, neither should it be ignored.

The whole question of what makes a given work of art in any sense religious calls for aesthetic acumen as well as theological reason; indeed, it requires theological reflection that is also aesthetic. This suggests that even the theological failure to recognize and address aesthetic issues already entails (erroneous) aesthetic judgments and commitments. For theology inevitably deals in matters of aesthetic pertinence, even when it does so blindly. How, then, can it proceed with open eyes?

If we answer, 'by including aesthetics within theological discussion and curricula', this can only sound glib and premature unless we articulate more clearly why and how aesthetics has a distinctively theological vocation. But to do this depends, of course, on some understanding of the vocation of theology itself.

In general we can say that Christian theology is the attempt to understand and reflect methodically on the identity, meaning, and truth of what the Christian tradition confesses, celebrates, and practises. To reflect on these things within a Christian framework is to engage in theo-logia (thinking and talking about God), because God is considered the ultimate reference point for all Christian life and practice.

For the most part, to be sure, theology does not talk directly to or about God, but talks about other discourse that does just that. Thus it normally constitutes a second-order discourse, with the primary discourse being actual prayer, praise, and so forth. Even so, theology as carried out within the Christian community is never completely detached and speculative. As one scholar recently has emphasized, Christian theology in the most inclusive sense is both a deliberate undertaking whose end is knowledge (of God and the Kingdom of God) and a cognitive habit of the soul, manifest as an existential and sapiential component within faith itself.[34] That aesthetics has a theological calling thus will be evident if it can be demonstrated that faith characteristically or frequently has a component that we can identify as aesthetic and that variously enters into the more highly reflective tasks of theology. It turns out, in fact, that it is possible to relate aesthetics to theology with respect to at least four aspects of theological reflection arising out of Christian faith and tradition. These we can identify as theology's concern for *truth* and for *meaning*, and as its choice of *subject matter* and of *method*. In relating aesthetics to these theological concerns and choices, we will be relating it to issues toward which neither a von Balthasar nor a Kierkegaard could be indifferent, however much they might differ in response. Although our treatment of these matters must at this point remain rather sketchy and abstract, in later phases of our study we will see that their concrete implications are far from negligible.

Because truth has been such a dominant concern of theology and faith, we will treat it first and at greatest length. A theology or faith totally unconcerned with truth may be conceivable, but it is hard to conceive that it could be Christian. What theologians (and other thinkers) mean by 'truth' is, of course, subject to variation. Some think of truth primarily as correctness or as the correspondence between what is said or thought and something 'out there' that is real and definite. Others think of truth primarily as coherence, or as disclosure and event, or as that which genuinely empowers and liberates. But, however it is conceived, truth is almost always regarded as warranting assent and trust. Accordingly, there has never been any doubt on the part of Christians that the God of Christian faith is not the God of lies but of truth and that any theology worthy of assent would need to take truth seriously.

Now, it must be admitted at once that the objects and practices we today associate with art have been suspected, at least from the time of Plato, of having a less than total commitment to truth. Furthermore, the truths that beautiful objects and arts manage to embody in sensible form often have been deemed lower in kind than those that are purely intellectual and spiritual. Traditionally, theology still might value sensible beauty and artistic products, because these move the heart and will and perhaps point toward invisible beauty that is eternal and divine. Besides, the theologian can say, God condescended to take on flesh, thereby showing that pure spirit is not all that even God requires in dealing with a world of material things and of creatures endowed with bodies, emotions, and imaginations. Scripture itself uses figures and poetry to communicate with such creatures as we. Nonetheless, religious truth that is expressed beautifully, figuratively, and artistically has long had the reputation of being (at the very most) a vivid but less precise expression of what can be said more properly in systematic, conceptual discourse. Normally, therefore, the plain and literal sense of Scripture is what has been sought out when the truth of its claims has been at issue. Similarly, for the Church's ongoing interpretation of the truth *as* truth, the inquirer has looked not to its poetry and art or even to its liturgy (though these are acknowledged to have their own unique value) but rather to doctrinal statements and theological texts.

Yet the understanding of aesthetic and artistic making and meaning that we are pursuing suggests a quite different understanding of this matter. Let us consider more carefully the fact, for instance, that any theology worthy of the name cannot avoid reflecting on whatever truth may be disclosed through media rich in aesthetic qualities. In the first place, we should not underestimate the extent of this theological reliance on aesthetic mediations. Even supposing that some of the truths in which Christianity has a stake can be arrived at directly by means of logic and metaphysics, it remains the case that, if any conceptualization is to be theologically convincing, it somehow must resonate with more primary religious or quasi-religious language and experience. And this frequently bears conspicuous aesthetic marks, as is evident in parable, apocalypse, liturgy, sacred song, spiritual exercises, the rhythms of ecclesial life, and even in the tensions and resolutions of moral and humane relationships. Without establishing a profound connection with these things, no idea or system can be either intelligible or true for religious faith; for it will not be true to what in language and experience is religiously meaningful, whether as part of culture at large or of one religious tradition in particular.

The religious and theological importance of significantly aesthetic phenomena may, of course, be ignored or denied. Thus some Protestants attempt to do nothing other than proclaim the 'plain and simple truth' received from the Bible. Yet aesthetic factors are involved even here where they are seldom recognized as such. The relatively unceremonious style of worship and pulpit rhetoric often associated with Free Church Protestantism has an aesthetic rhythm and impact of its own. Furthermore, however artless the Scriptures often may be, their aesthetic dimension is by no means negligible. While scholars and preachers (past and present) frequently have overlooked literary approaches to the Bible in favor of historical, textual, and doctrinal analyses, the majority of biblical scholars today recognize that biblical writings have at all times engaged readers to a significant degree by means of story, image, and symbol. Accordingly, the theologian may need to treat them in some measure as meaningful and truthful in the manner of art.

Even the theologian in pursuit of historical truth cannot escape data relevant to aesthetics, although again the aesthetic dimension may go unnoticed. Certainly there is an aesthetic aspect to any overall depiction of the evolving shape and emerging meaning of history, such as one encounters in theological accounts of salvation history or in the radically transformed versions of those accounts given by Karl Marx, for example, or Teilhard de Chardin. Moreover, particular historical events pondered by theologians, from the fall of Rome to the Holocaust of the present century, become significant enough to be 'historic' only as they are given imaginative form that expresses the dramatic import of life lived out before God and under the duress of time. Likewise the lives and deaths of saints, martyrs, and contemporary Christians become real for the faithful only insofar as they can be told and depicted effectively, and hence artfully, even if with sometimes modest or unrefined means. It is no wonder, then, that the most notable recent history of the changing image of Jesus through the centuries repeatedly links that image with aesthetic perceptions.[35]

On an older hermeneutic the theologian alerted to the aesthetic form of many of Christianity's most faithful expressions might directly proceed to search out the kernels of truth carried by the husks of aesthetic form. Now, however, it is widely agreed by critics and philosophers of art that the *meaning* of a symbol, poem, or other aesthetic expression cannot fully be expressed in any other form. And since such *truth* as is disclosed through an appreciably aesthetic form cannot entirely be separated from the totality of the meaning, it follows that the truth disclosed aesthetically is not entirely separable from the aesthetic form itself.

From this it follows that, without aesthetic sensitivity, theology is in danger of misunderstanding the very character of its primary data and of the central truths it ponders – a danger descried by Coleridge and other Romantics and later by various Victorians, as when Matthew Arnold lamented that religion had come to insist (in vain) on being factually true.[36] Thus, ironically, it may be a theology sensitive to aesthetics that can best reply to Kierkegaard's attack on religious aestheticism. For such a theology might be able to show how scriptural style – even the sometimes inelegant style of Paul – may after all be relevant or even crucial to its utterance of truths that transcend 'sheer aesthetics', forsaking overtly beautiful phraseology for rugged diction and audacious paradox.

Yet theology cannot satisfactorily appropriate aesthetic truth simply by becoming aesthetic itself or by failing to exercise its own rational capacities. The theologian therefore should be wary of following those who would obliterate every distinction between the aesthetic (or figurative) and the rigorously reflective (or conceptual). This is a danger present in Arnold's own defense of poetry as that which, in contrast to dogmatic religion, will more and more 'interpret life for us' and 'console us',[37] and it lurks also in those later writings of Martin Heidegger that seem to grant not just primacy but also absolute supremacy to poetic and artistic modes.

A more adequate understanding of the relation of the aesthetic realm and its truth(s) to that of theological concepts is that they exist in mutually transformative, dialogical relationship. Aesthetic perceptions give rise to thought (to paraphrase a familiar slogan), and thought modifies aesthetic perceptions in such a way as to give rise to further aesthetic creation and insight.[38] Whatever theology receives from its more aesthetic sources – whether in Tillich's interpretations of ontological depth disclosed through expressionist painting or in Augustine's autobiographical probings – it transforms through a large measure of critical reflection, conceptual clarity, and rational order, reconstituting both meaning and insight at a different level. Whatever an aesthetic medium receives from theology – whether in Van Eyck's Ghent altarpiece or in T. S. Eliot's *Four Quartets* – it reinterprets through imaginative particularity and depth; through sensory immediacy and affective form. It thereby changes what it makes its own. In this ongoing, dialectical process, it seems probable that whatever the believer or theologian can call truth is always known impurely and in part, and known differently through the different modes of thought and expression that endlessly give and receive in relation to one another.

None of this discussion of theological truth would make sense, however, if it were not also the case that theology and aesthetics are linked with respect to matters of meaning, since only what is meaningful can be true. In fact, as we already have implied, aesthetics – having a keen ear for the subtlest sorts of meaning – appears to have special potential for joining with hermeneutics to tune theological instruments of interpretation. Together they can emphasize that the meanings we find most meaningful, especially when shaped aesthetically, are by no means static or always intellectually manageable; nor are they ever simply given, even by grace, totally apart from the context and constitution of the receiver. And aesthetics in a neo-aesthetic mode would be bound in particular to stress that the creation and transformation of meaning through aesthetic media, while not confined within conceptual categories, is not restricted to preconceptual activity. Thus when Dante responds to Aquinas, or when Bach responds to Lutheran and Pietistic theology, the result is a religious expression that is in some sense *post*-conceptual as well as pre-conceptual, and *post*-reflective as well as pre-reflective, because the art is significantly changed by the concepts and reflections it responds to and reinterprets. In turn art may yield new religious meanings that could not otherwise belong so vividly to the logic and language of faith.

In highlighting the gifts that aesthetics brings to the theological analysis of meaning, we should not suppose that theology's own role in reflecting on questions of distinctly aesthetic meaning is totally passive. On the contrary, specifically theological aesthetics can shape aesthetic analysis by providing an interpretive framework within which Christians can understand and appreciate the larger meaning of aesthetically significant media, acts, responses, and works. From a properly theological point of view, for instance, the doctrines of creation, incarnation, redemption, and eschatology can serve such a purpose, alerting aesthetics to dimensions of creativity, expression, beauty, and the like that foreshadow or participate in what Christians mean by salvation or sanctification, by prophetic pronouncement or beatific vision, or – perhaps most of all – by sacrament or sign. At a number of points in history, in fact, Christian theologians have invoked the doctrine of the Incarnation and the principles of sacramental theology to legitimize a qualified yet positive valuation of the material, sensory order with which the arts have so much to do.[39]

For any of this to be done effectively, however, the focal subject matter of theology must itself be modified and extended in several ways. Most obviously it must be expanded to include more thorough study of the arts themselves, including their historical role within (and in reaction to) the Christian tradition. Any attempt to interpret Christian faith and what George Lindbeck calls the 'grammar' of Christianity, or 'the framework and the medium within which Christians know and experience',[40] cannot hope to be adequate if it excludes such study of the arts. Yet basic questions of how the arts can possibly attain religious significance, how they differ in function and impact, and how they relate to theology *per se* cannot be addressed adequately apart from aesthetic sophistication, which is what theological aesthetics as a distinct subject is equipped to provide.

At the same time that aesthetics illuminates the theological import of the arts and makes their history and analysis topics for theological study, it can contribute to the recovery of nature as a major subject of theological reflection – something that has rarely been the case since the latter part of the nineteenth century. Whether nature be glimpsed in the terror of Pascal's vision of the silent, infinite spaces or in the gracious bounty of earth that is celebrated in the Psalms, it mediates aesthetically and physically the beyond-ourselves that Christian theological aesthetics cannot well escape and that from the standpoint of Christian faith still calls forth awe and dread, and praise and thanksgiving.

We have seen, then, that theology can neither adequately understand the meanings nor satisfactorily interpret the truths of its primary sources without engaging to some extent in aesthetics. And we have noted that the aesthetic qualities of art and nature, together with the analysis of aesthetic theory itself, demand to be focal subjects within theologies taking aesthetics seriously. What we will confirm in conclusion is that, although in these and other ways the very consideration of aesthetic issues raises new questions for theology, they are questions that are intrinsic to every major method of theologizing.

To understand the validity of this last claim should by now require no major step. It is commonly agreed, for example, that both historical and dogmatic (or doctrinal) theology attempt at the very least to understand what Christianity has meant and affirmed in the past and that theologies of a systematic, apologetic, or philosophical sort perennially seek ways to interpret or criticize the tradition in the light of new ideas and experiences. We already have established, however, that such theological pursuits cannot well neglect aesthetic expressions of religious sensibility. Such expressions (and not only those that constitute what David Tracy and others would call Christian classics) are a vital part of the living body of Christian faith.[41] Thus they also call for the theoretical understanding that aesthetics is potentially and uniquely equipped to provide.

Further examples of the relevance of aesthetics to the various methods of theologizing are not hard to come by. It seems plain, for instance, that because nothing strikes us as more relative and changeable than aesthetic judgment, an important part of theology would be inquiry into how religious judgments that are made using substantially aesthetic criteria can be in any way reliable and valid. This, one might say, is a task for theological hermeneutics, which in turn is relevant to almost every field of theology. And if it is the case, as we have suggested, that many instances of what Christianity terms 'revelation' take aesthetically significant form, then more careful and exhaustive inquiry must also be made into how aesthetic form becomes ingredient in that which is disclosed, and whether such a form can be religiously decisive. This inquiry would be crucial to theology that is apologetic or fundamental (or, as we might prefer to say, philosophical).

As for the large question of just how religious truth and meaning is apprehended and appropriated when presented in a significantly aesthetic form, what seems called for is a theological critique and rehabilitation of the concept of taste, which leads into practical theological issues concerning the role of aesthetic proclivities and sensitivities in the formation of religious communities – surely something for ecumenical theology to contemplate. This would also prompt further consideration of the ways in which aesthetic values and perceptions affect moral habits, standards, and choices.

In view of these various representative paths and methods of aesthetic theological inquiry, it seems no exaggeration to say that theological aesthetics can contribute to, if also complicate, virtually all methods and branches of theology: moral, practical, fundamental, biblical, historical, and even systematic. In the process it is bound to take on a distinctively Christian shape because of the nature of the evidence it takes seriously, the religious understandings it brings to the task, and the character of the primary communities for whom and to whom it speaks.

To engage in theological aesthetics obviously is to cross traditional boundaries between theological fields. In doing this, one recognizes that these boundaries are constructs the somewhat arbitrary nature of which seldom is acknowledged institutionally – by faculty appointments, administrative priorities, curriculum designs, or indeed by church programs and the budgeting of clergy time. For this reason theological aesthetics occasionally might be irritating and unpopular in practice and positively disconcerting in theory. Yet, as this phase of our study has argued, a relatively adequate theory could support the view that such an enterprise is theologically significant.

Accordingly, we must move now from a general survey of the basic grounds for theological aesthetics to a more careful consideration of issues that any religious or specifically theological aesthetic must undertake to address. At the same time, we must try to refine further the aesthetic theories themselves, so that they can be put to more effective use in theology and in the broader study of religion. Our next goal in this regard is to develop a clearer and more complete picture of the nature of aesthetica, particularly as they take on qualities that we think of as religious. For it is of course with aesthetica that even religious and theological aesthetics begins.

3

Art, Religion, and the Aesthetic Milieu

Aesthetics, Anti-Aesthetics, Neo-Aesthetics

We have seen quite clearly that, when using standard concepts of the nature of the aesthetic, it is difficult to conceive how theological aesthetics could be a sensible, let alone significant, enterprise. For it has commonly been assumed since the time of Kant that part of the point in calling something aesthetic at all is to say or imply that, in this respect at least, it is not to be evaluated in terms of religion or morality (or indeed in the light of scientific or pragmatic considerations). Insofar as something is appreciated for aesthetic reasons, it is to be appreciated for its own sake, not for the good it can do or the understanding or devotion it can enhance. Or so the usual thinking goes.

This line of thought, which is purist in its assumptions about the nature of aesthetic phenomena, has been challenged of late by members of the anti-aesthetic or 'paraesthetic' camp. These thinkers claim that the idea of the aesthetic basically is a fiction fabricated by the Enlightenment – a fiction none too benign in its association with systems of privilege and power, with hierarchy and authority, and with 'logocentric' metaphysics and monopolistic theology.[1] Yet, as we have pointed out, it is not clear that aesthetics can simply be supplanted by anti-aesthetics, with its almost exclusive reliance on political, semiotic, sociological, and psychological models of thought. There are liabilities associated with the anti-aesthetic habit of regarding aesthetic objects as 'texts' like any other texts; for in identifying them merely as forms of 'inscription',[2] one finds it difficult to conceive of any truly distinctive role they might in principle play in either religion or culture. Besides, not all objects and satisfactions are signs or symbols, or projections or ploys. They are not all political or practical, moral or religious, or even nostalgic or sentimental. Thomas Aquinas is saying nothing implausible when he speaks of an untrammelled delight that is taken in the very perception of something beautiful; similarly, it is with reason that Kantians speak of a somehow 'disinterested' interest taken in things that are aesthetically admirable.[3] However inadequate as an overall account of the aesthetic, these ideas seem applicable to the pleasure we might derive from watching rippling waves on a lake or from listening at dusk to doves calling at the edge of a wood.

There remains the possibility, of course, that some of the standard versions of aesthetics are not so attached to purism as the discussion so far would suggest and that, consequently, both anti-aesthetics and the 'neo-aesthetics' we ourselves propose are superfluous. Anyone familiar with a wide range of expressive, mimetic, semantic, or cognitive theories in aesthetics must realize that certain ones, far from being purist in intent or by logical necessity, exhibit tendencies that, if followed out consistently, would lead somewhere other than to purist conclusions.[4]

In reaction against older didactic or ornamental theories of art and beauty, even moderate 'purists' have, to be sure, usually ended up restricting the aesthetic to the realm of the pre-conceptual and/or the sheerly affective. Yet it is not obvious why this should hinder the attempt to locate a meaningful nexus between the aesthetic and the religious. After all, various theorists in the Romantic and neo- or post-Kantian lines have identified religion itself with ineffable meaning and with a certain kind of feeling – a feeling of the All, the Whole, or perhaps the feeling of absolute dependence on the Holy and Wholly Other. Thus there is nothing to prevent someone's saying that the arts and other aesthetica can be deemed religious inasmuch as they produce this very feeling or its symbolic analogue.[5]

Now, this notion of aesthetic experience and its relation to religious feeling surely is not all wrong; but neither is it all right, or right enough. For one thing, it ignores the variety and particularity within both religious and aesthetic experience. For another, it does not help us to tell what is aesthetic about certain religious feelings, or vice versa. Given that one can feel anger or surprise or disappointment without aesthetic effect, why should one consider the religious feeling of absolute dependence or of awe before the Holy to be intrinsically aesthetic? And if we said merely that religious feeling could *become* aesthetic, why would this not simply be an admission that religion can be distorted or diluted? To say that art and religion are both a matter of feeling provides no sure escape from reductive notions of either art or religion. Even supposing we identified aesthetic feeling with a primordial and intuitive form of knowledge, this would give us no reason to associate such feeling with anything other than a germinal moment in the religious life.

In point of fact, however important feelings or primitive intuitions may be to religion, faith and religious life evidently involve much more: personal commitments, intellectual concepts, moral acts, social alliances, ritual enactments, and so forth. The claim that religious feelings or intuitions could exist at all if isolated from some of these other elements is dubious in the extreme.[6] Consequently the notion that a purely aesthetic feeling could generate or constitute a deeply religious experience is equally dubious.

Hence, like the anti-aesthetic alternative, even the modified purism that confines art to feeling and sheerly intuitive knowledge leaves much to be desired. We therefore come back to the thesis that what seems to be required for religious and theological aesthetics to be viable is a form of aesthetics that would pursue a course between the purism that in various ways is entailed in traditional aesthetics and the anti-aestheticism or paraestheticism that rejects aesthetics as being by definition purist. Cognizant of more or less pure aesthetica, such reformed aesthetics – which we are terming neo-aesthetics – also would venture to analyze complex aesthetic milieux constituted by the dynamic interaction between aesthetic forms or qualities and non-aesthetic ideas or perceptions. It is such a theory that we now are ready to pursue in greater detail.

If we are to make good on our claim that some kind of neo-aesthetics is both possible and necessary from the standpoint of religious reflection, we must inquire further into the makings of aesthetica. After surveying in general the sorts of thing that qualify as aesthetic and noticing along the way what it is that is *not* notably aesthetic within our experience, we next will need to look more closely at the distinguishing marks of aesthetica. To do this we will examine two exemplary aesthetica, observing how complex some of their aesthetic qualities are and how elusive of purist theorizing. Then we will see how one classic expression of purist aesthetics – Kant's theory of free and dependent beauty – can be modified so as to help us to characterize the varied traits of aesthetica and to understand the religious relevance of milieux that we are calling aesthetic. This in turn will prepare us to explore, in the chapter to follow, the nature and religious significance of specifically artistic making and meaning.

In Search of Aesthetica

As we noted early on, 'aesthetica' is a coinage from Greek that is used here as a technical term to denote significantly aesthetic objects of all sorts (and by extension to denote aesthetic phenomena in general). Being descriptive rather than honorific, the term does not, even in the narrower of our definitions, serve to designate only things that are regarded as admirable and beautiful, or indeed ugly and distasteful. There are some objects or events productive of memorable aesthetic effects that seldom occasion any value judgments at all. One thinks, for instance, of the rhythmic, raspy cry of the diminutive chickadee, which seems neither beautiful nor artistic but clearly possesses formal and 'felt' qualities that can capture one's attention.

The word aesthetica, then, does not denote only things that normally elicit judgments as to their beauty or value. Neither does it denote all or only physical sensations, or things as they are apprehended strictly by the senses (literally *aisthetika*, or perceptibles). In late antiquity there was the philosophical distinction between *aisthetos*, the world of sensible matter, and *noetos*, the world of mind. But a burning sensation, while indeed having a material cause and physical effect, is not something notably aesthetic in our sense of the word, and neither are things like sticks of chalk or pieces of gravel when perceived in a normal fashion; whereas a poem read silently, and without much attention to the residual sounds of the words or the visual appearance of the text, does nonetheless achieve aesthetic effects.

It could be objected that, in lacking a distinctly sensuous surface, literary works are atypical among aesthetic objects. Yet even in one's apprehension of the highly sensuous Impressionist art of Monet, what one appreciates aesthetically always has to do with more than sheer sensation. It typically involves (among other things) attention to abstract compositional relations, awareness of a distinctive style, and consciousness of how in this style the flecks of paint, the highly saturated colors, and the blurred outlines all are used to approximate the act of seeing and the moment of vision. Such features of artistic intention and craft are never matters of sense-data or sensation alone; yet one's awareness of them affects one's response to the immediately perceptible elements of the art. They therefore are aesthetically relevant. That is to say, they are *mediately* aesthetic.[7]

If the term aesthetica does not refer merely to things usually considered beautiful or to sensations or sheerly sensory impressions, still less does it refer to something that is noticed or evaluated strictly in terms of its physical properties, whether sensed or intellectually apprehended. In point of fact, the object normally regarded as the source of aesthetic experience may have minimal physicality. If I toss in the fire a piece of paper on which is printed William Ernest Henley's 'Invictus', I (perhaps unfortunately) have done nothing to destroy the poem, although my destruction of the printed object may have hindered someone's access to the aesthetic object. Of course many aesthetic objects really were lost when classical Greek bronzes were melted down over the centuries in order to produce weapons, coins, and the like. This does not prove, however, that the properties of the aesthetic objects were ever completely physical. Although the aesthetic qualities of extant bronzes from classical Greece are due partly to physical features of the medium, the strictly physical fact that many large bronze sculptures are hollow, as a result of the 'lost wax' method of casting, plays no part in their aesthetic effect. Aesthetically they are no less weighty or imposing for being empty at core.

From the fact that the aesthetic object cannot be reduced entirely to sensory or physical properties we should not leap to the conclusion that the object of aesthetic experience is actually just an abstraction like 'the beautiful', 'the grotesque', or 'the sublime'. The aesthetic traits of some objects can be classified using such abstract aesthetic concepts, but no concepts as such capture aesthetic interest.

It also must be said that at times an object of aesthetic attention and source of aesthetic response can be an event or process as much as a product or stable entity. A ritual like the Muslim Hajj, which with its circumambulations of the Ka'bah shrine and other dramatic acts manifests vivid aesthetic qualities, is less a thing witnessed than a process undergone. Likewise the experience of reading a story such as Tolstoy's *The Death of Ivan Ilych* is less like gazing at the well-wrought urn celebrated in the poetics of the New Critics than it is like going through an ordeal – wrestling with some angel who in at last departing leaves us changed.

These observations put us in something of a quandary. We keep referring to aesthetica as objects, but the more we think about them the less object-like they seem. Despite ourselves we may sound as though we are saying that something that is deemed an aesthetic object – an aestheticon – is only an ephemeral 'object' of our imaginative attention, and nothing solid or lasting at all. In fact, however, sensory and physical traits are not aesthetically negligible. Whether actual or imagined, they are, as it were, the body of the aesthetic. Still, they never completely constitute the aestheticon, which is (in current jargon) 'supervenient' in relation to them.[8]

Yet even if it is now plain that we are not eradicating the physical, sensory, and perduring side of things considered to be aesthetic, we nevertheless may sound as though we would agree with Roman Ingarden when he claims that what we call an aesthetic object proper is just the (perhaps cumulative) imaginative 'concretion' or 'plenishment' of an artwork that in itself exists in an intrinsically schematic and somewhat incomplete and indeterminate state. In that case we might also be embracing Ingarden's idea that, because we and others never respond in exactly the same way to the same work of art, no work of art *qua* work is – strictly speaking – an aesthetic object; rather, it is but the ideal basis or 'foundation' of multiple aesthetic objects.[9]

While we need not embroil ourselves in all the controversies surrounding this issue, the issue itself is germane to the larger discussion of which things we should think of as aesthetic and how we are to picture their relation to other things. It is important to acknowledge, for instance, that works of art are indeed – as Ingarden says – 'realized' as aesthetic objects by the respondent, and realized differently by different individuals at different times. This means that not all aesthetic traits are predetermined by the work of art (or other object of appreciation).

Contrary to what Ingarden supposes, however, our aesthetic experience is founded on the belief that we are responding to the work of art or natural object itself, if only in one possible way among many. Emile Zola writes of having seen and admired Manet's painting *Olympia*, which had offended numerous viewers with its unprettified nude and her black cat.[10] Debussy reports of hearing Wagner's *Parsifal*, which he pronounces to be, despite the silliness of some of the poetry, 'incomparable and bewildering, splendid and strong', and in fact 'one of the loveliest monuments of sound ever raised to the serene glory of music'.[11] No doubt these illustrious artist-critics would have been amazed to be told that in neither case did they respond to the work of art itself – that is, to anything the artist actually made – but only to the object they imaginatively constituted on the basis of the work. Surely it would be reasonable for them to retort that, on the contrary, what they were doing was responding to the work of art itself *as* aesthetic object. At any rate, this is what the present theory would claim.

Nevertheless, we need to reckon with the fact that (to take another example) one person may find Philip Glass's opera *Satyagraha* to be tedious and its ending anticlimactic while an ardent companion finds it mesmerizing and its conclusion serene and uplifting. Given the difference between these responses it seems that either the artwork or the aestheticon, or both, must differ too. How so?

This difference could be caused in one of two ways. On the one hand it may be that our listeners, despite their contrasting responses, are attending to basically the same aesthetically relevant features of the opera: the proportions of the parts, for example, or the fit between the music and the words, or the extent to which the libretto, drawn as it is from the *Bhagavad Gita*, illuminates the moral and spiritual values of the pivotal figure, Gandhi. Perhaps the listeners agree that the music is repetitious. For one of them, however, the repetition sounds ostentatious and abrasive in a peculiarly minimalist way; for the other it evokes and projects a state of meditative concentration, the interweaving textures and barely perceptible rhythmic permutations suggesting the possibility of mystical release from attachment to mere temporality and to the consequence of action.

Insofar as the two listeners are listening to and for the same things, it makes sense to say that they do in actuality hear the same work of art and consciously 'intend' the same aesthetic object. This is analogous to saying that two alert readers of this very sentence have indeed read the same thing. But the aesthetic object (the artwork experienced aesthetically) is *in effect* rather different for each of the two listeners. For one of them it is boring and unimaginative; for the other it is subtle and inspired. Correspondingly, readers of the same sentence frequently react differently to what they have read in the same way.

On the other hand it may be that the opera listeners are attending to very different aesthetically relevant features of the work of music – the one to melody and harmony, the other to text and rhythmic flow – even though they hear the same pitches, tempos, and textures. This is not unlike the situation in which one reader pays attention to the historical accuracy of a sentence in Gibbon while another notices only its diction and sonority. With respect to the work of music, the greater the divergence in what is attended to and listened for, the greater the *virtual* difference in the work that each listener hears. Even here, however, we would say that the opera's publicly recognized identity, both as work and as aestheticon, is singular. It is best thought of not as two operas but as one; for its identifying features are at least potentially accessible to any listener. And it is to the one opera that conscientious listeners intend to devote their inevitably varied and shifting attentions.

From our discussion so far we can conclude that what we consider to be the aesthetic object is precisely and only that to which we respond aesthetically, and that it exhibits formal, felt, and 'intentional' qualities that emerge from physical and sensory traits without being identical to either. It appears, moreover, that our aesthetic response always entails at least peripheral awareness of what the object may be beyond our particular experience, and even beyond anything immediately aesthetic. Our response to a work of art depends on understandings of genre, style, and meaning that are never immediately given in perception itself. Similarly our response to a natural phenomenon depends on our tacit awareness of non-aesthetic features that color the aesthetic effect. A sunset is not just a lovely hue in the distance but also the 'dying of the day' and so looks different from a sunrise with identical colors.

This indicates that, contrary to what a host of theorists suppose, aesthesis proper is not restricted to some rarified 'aesthetic attitude' in which one necessarily contemplates nothing but a narrow range of purely aesthetic features.[12] What is experienced, even in aesthetic immediacy, is not experienced as only immediate and aesthetic. This point helps explain why it is possible and necessary to speak not so much of an isolated aesthetic object and purely schematic artwork as of an aesthetic *milieu* – a milieu of immediately and mediately aesthetic factors – essential to the very constitution of the work as a complex aesthetic entity. As we shall see, this also is paramount to any reflection on how aesthetic and religious perceptions could ever coalesce or mutually interact.

Because almost anything has qualities that can be experienced as aesthetic under certain conditions, we now need to be clearer about which things are most appropriately called aesthetic objects, and when. It seems that the label 'aesthetic object' (or 'aestheticon') applies to two kinds of entities. First, there are objects that are made, displayed, or presented with the primary purpose of evoking aesthetic response. Second, there are those objects that one at least temporarily considers specifically with respect to their capacity to evoke such a response, even though such a capacity is unintentional, incidental, or of secondary interest.

Of the objects that are unintentionally or secondarily aesthetic, many are natural processes and products, inanimate as well as animate: a storm at sea, a weathered stone on the shore, a sailor's 'expressive' face. Others are artifacts, such as a sail or a ship. By contrast, objects that are primarily aesthetic are generally either *objets d'art* that no longer serve any practical purpose or else things (or parts of things) that are made or presented as fine art.

An object that in one context is seen primarily as aesthetic may in another context be responded to as aesthetic only in a secondary or unconscious way, if at all. Leaning on Michael Polanyi and gestalt psychology, we can say that in one context the perceptual gestalt is such that the purely aesthetic features of an object serve as the focus of one's awareness, although one has a subsidiary or tacit awareness of its other features;[13] in another context the reverse may be true. This is not a case of duck/rabbit alternation but of a shift in the focus of one's attention. Displayed in a museum of art, the bejewelled sardonyx and gold chalice that Abbot Suger consecrated for use in the Abbey Church of St Denis makes a different impression from the one it usually would make in a liturgical setting; it has a different effect when seen primarily as aestheticon than when regarded primarily as a eucharistic vessel. Yet the gestalt in either case exhibits appreciably aesthetic qualities; the whole perceptual milieu remains significantly aesthetic.

The aesthetic milieu thus comprises everything in focal or subsidiary awareness that, within a particular context, is either immediately or mediately aesthetic in effect. While in every moment of aesthetic perception the borders of an aesthetic milieu are indefinite, certain things at a given moment lie beyond them. If, in an isolated instance, some jewel in Suger's chalice happened to have been donated in exchange for political favors, for example, this can now largely be forgotten in beholding the object. It is incidental to the object's purpose and appearance. That the chalice could have been made at all only by virtue of ecclesiastical wealth and political power in the midst of rather widespread poverty is less easily ignored, being relevant to its emblematic meaning and ambiguous function within a system of sharing grace without equally sharing goods. Such considerations possibly diffract the object's radiance, its *claritas*.

As we have begun to see, differences among aesthetica have consequences for the ways in which the term 'aesthetic object' can be applied. With respect to an object that is unintentionally, incidentally, or secondarily aesthetic, the label 'aesthetic object' can be attached only temporarily or in a qualified way. For navigators and fishers the sea becomes an aesthetic object *per se* only under certain conditions and for a limited time, somewhat in the way Judge Jones temporarily becomes umpire on a Saturday afternoon when he is asked to organize a baseball game for the neighborhood children. This is true in spite of the fact that, even when an object ceases to be thought of as aesthetic, it may continue tacitly to have aesthetic effect – as when the stormy 'mood' of the sea affects even a sailor in no mood to contemplate it. By contrast the intentionally and primarily aesthetic artifact such as the ballet *Swan Lake* or Debussy's *La Mer* is something we continue to identify as an aesthetic object despite its other identities, somewhat in the way that Izaak Walton is thought to have remained a devoted trout fisherman while being an author and many other things as well.

Yet we may wonder how something that is institutionally and publicly certified as a work of art can have traits as an artwork that are not relevant to its identity as aesthetic object. Actually it is not hard to show that some of the properties of a work of art are irrelevant to its normal realization as aesthetic object.[14] It is plain, for instance, that the rejected early drafts of Beethoven's Fifth Symphony are part of the evolution of the work of art but have no impact on the way we normally hear the music. Likewise, the fact that portions of this symphony were written laboriously plays no part in our aesthetic experience of it, which would have been the same had Beethoven managed to work more quickly.

Having considered the question of which things belong to the class 'aesthetica', and under what circumstances, and how they differ in general among themselves and from other objects, we are in a position to make a number of observations about the connection between aesthetic objects and religious objects. First, the fact that a religious object or event may not be thought of as aesthetic does not necessarily prevent it from being tacitly so. The rhetorical power of a Puritan sermon may owe little to ornament and depend instead on a certain severity or plainness of style and earnestness of delivery; but the tone, rhythm, and diction carry and underscore the meaning, and do so aesthetically, in a manner that a sheerly matter-of-fact presentation could not.

Second, as we have seen, there is no inherent contradiction in saying that a given aesthetic object is simultaneously a religious object. Aesthetica usually have multiple identities. Thus, while a religious object such as a chalice may only occasionally be thought of primarily as an aesthetic object, this does not keep it from being considered on those occasions as *both* aesthetic and religious. Nor does the object cease functioning aesthetically when this function is only subsidiary; otherwise there would be no need for a chalice that is used in worship to be beautiful or elegant or, in some settings, relatively crude and simple.

Third, there is no way of telling *a priori* which elements of religion will at some point have aesthetic relevance or which aesthetica will accrue religious significance. Although the aesthetic milieu in any given context of perception excludes much that is religiously relevant, nothing religious is in principle excluded from mediately aesthetic relevance.

Fourth, the fact that an art object such as a Salvador Dali *Last Supper* has a public identity as religious does not guarantee that its aesthetic effect or its virtual identity as a work will always – or even ever – be religious. The public identity of the work directs but does not dictate how it will be received and realized. Conversely, an object productive of aesthetic effects that often have religious import may not have a religious public identity. This seems to be true of many of the world's higher mountains, for instance, or of the austere and craggy heights of the late Beethoven string quartets.

Fifth, given that the aestheticon is constituted not by anything so simple and definite as physical makeup or sense data, but rather by a process through which the work manages to *work with* the mind and self in a variety of ways, the role of the respondent and of the social and cultural context in the constitution of the object cannot be minimized. What one *makes of* an aestheticon, religiously, surely will depend partly on concerns, values, and expectations that one brings to the experience, and not only on factors immediately associated with the work itself.

Finally, because of the complexity in human making and in our response even to things not humanly made, no aestheticon, be it secular or religious, is likely to be constituted as a perfectly pure aesthetic essence. Absolute aesthetic purity – Kant's perfectly 'free' beauty – exists only as a hypothetical limiting case.

By this juncture, then, we have begun to find considerable complexity and diversity hidden under the convenient label 'aesthetic'. But we have not examined particular aesthetica with sufficient care to allow us to characterize with any precision the distinctively aesthetic traits of the aesthetic objects constituted in experience. It is to this task that we need to turn, since it will have a direct bearing on how we understand the means by which aesthetica become religiously meaningful. As we consider two rather different objects whose status as aesthetica could hardly be in doubt, we will see more clearly than ever that, while these objects exhibit markedly aesthetic traits, not all these traits are ones that traditional aesthetics can account for. This will prompt us, in the last two sections, to try to describe more adequately the distinguishing features of both 'pure' and 'impure' aesthetica.

Exemplary Aesthetica and Deficient Aesthetics

In the first century BCE the Roman engineer and architect Pollio Vitruvius singled out three characteristics of good architecture: *utilitas*, *firmitas*, and *venustas* – or, in the standard neo-classical rendering of Sir Henry Wotton, 'commodity, firmness, and delight'. A commodious building is suited to its function; a firm building is sturdy; a delightful building is pleasing to look at, walk through, or occupy. Good architecture is all these things.

When deciding which of these features should be called aesthetic, the theorist inevitably chooses the last, and with good reason. Nevertheless, there is considerable ambiguity in the word 'delight' and uncertainty about the relation of aesthetic delight to other aspects of architecture. Thus there are good grounds for doubting that this traditional way of distinguishing the aesthetic from the non-aesthetic truthfully reflects the nature of many aesthetica or even of architecture itself.

That things actually are more complicated becomes apparent

when one tries to think about the aesthetic features exhibited by particular objects and actual works, because often these features turn out to be qualified by apparently non-aesthetic factors, including both 'firmness' and 'commodity'. For our purposes two examples of the convergence and intersection of the aesthetic and the non-aesthetic will suffice – one taken from architecture, the other from contemporary art.

If there is anything which stands as a paradigm of Christian art, it is the architecture of Gothic cathedrals. No one approaching or entering Chartres Cathedral, for example, could doubt that this is an aesthetically rich work imbued with distinctively Christian – and specifically Medieval Christian – ideas and values (Plate 1). The Christian influence is observable in everything from the iconography of the stained glass, the sculptural program on the exterior, and the cruciform shape of the building to the rationale behind the inlaid labyrinth of the nave and the symbolism of the mathematical formulas used in working out the proportions and dimensions of the overall structure.

In fact what is still today at least as obvious as the cathedral's capacity to 'delight' is its usefulness as a religious edifice, and a 'firm' one at that. The building not only houses but also abidingly enhances, and symbolically enacts, worship. As theologians of the High Medieval period would have said, in keeping with ideas expressed by Augustine long before, the edifice of the church can be regarded as the earthly image of the eternal, Celestial City, the Heavenly Jerusalem. And the process by which it is brought to completion is, to borrow Otto von Simson's apt paraphrase of medieval thought, not only the physical labor but also 'the gradual "edification" of those who take part in the building, the illumination of their souls by the vision of the divine harmony that is then reflected in the material work of art'.[15]

The fit between Gothic style and meanings such as these was envisioned from its very inception by Abbot Suger, who in the twelfth century supervised the construction of the first Gothic church architecture: the new choir of the Abbey Church of St Denis. In words that bring to mind the much later musical and theological observations we have cited from Sir Thomas Browne, Suger reports that 'delight in the beauty of the house of God' gave rise, in his contemplation, to the sense that he had arrived at some 'region of the universe which neither exists entirely in the slime of the earth nor entirely in the purity of Heaven'.[16]

Now, once a building is seen as 'commodious' to religious acts and attitudes, and once its 'firmness' is seen as symbolically derived from what believers avow to be metaphysically the firmest of foundations, what remains of purely artistic and aesthetic 'delight'? In what does one's delight consist, even aesthetically? How does this differ from other kinds of aesthetic response? And in what way does the aesthetic object evoking such a different 'delight' correspondingly differ from others?

As we ponder these and related questions it will be helpful also to reflect on a kind of artwork that is in no obvious way useful or 'commodious' but on which there is nonetheless a similar convergence of aesthetic and non-aesthetic concerns and perceptions. In 1987 the directors of the Eiffel Tower Company proposed to celebrate the 1989 centennial of the tower by launching a circular 'light ring' into orbit around the earth.[17] This inflatable ring, designed to remain in orbit for as long as three years at an altitude of 480 miles, would consist of one hundred luminous Mylar spheres connected by thin tubing. Nearly fifteen miles in diameter, it would be a work of art visible to 'Earthlings' in almost every country, to whom it would appear to be as large and bright as the moon.

In some ways more audacious than the *Tour Eiffel* itself, though certainly not relatively so ambitious as the building of Chartres Cathedral, the project even as it was proposed created a stir – not so much among artists as among scientists, who feared that its brightness would seriously interfere with astronomical observations and could damage priceless image photon counters connected to a number of telescopes on earth. An even worse threat was posed, at least potentially, by a more easily launched back-up project called *Arsat*, which would consist in a curved, reflective 'sail' that supposedly would focus sunlight into an intensely bright cross in the sky.

In addition to being thought objectionable for practical and scientific reasons, both of the 'space art' projects seemed to be legally and morally questionable. Apparently either work of art would violate at least the spirit of a resolution passed in 1985 by the International Astronomical Union, which stated that 'no group has the right to change the Earth's environment in any significant way without full international study and agreement'.

Such mundane considerations evidently did not occur to Pierre Comte, who first conceived the idea of *Arsat*. He wrote, 'I simply tried to create an object that was beautiful, with pure lines and a dreamlike vocation: a star in the sky, but one born of human hands, a mad dream'. One would not be surprised to learn that the light ring itself was meant to fulfil aims similar to the ones Comte poetically expressed, which we can safely term aesthetic.

There is no question that, unlike any cathedral, these artifacts were envisioned first of all as art, and indeed as art that would be pragmatically and cognitively useless and thus purely aesthetic. Yet, like a cathedral, they were bound to evoke other responses as well. In point of fact it is possible that the light ring, if ever placed in orbit, might even come to have religious meaning for some person or group. One can speculate, for instance, that for the few remaining neolithic-style societies isolated in what we call remote regions of the world, the sudden and inexplicable appearance of an object rivaling the moon in radiant splendor could be astonishing and possibly disturbing; among these groups, some of which presumably would cherish traditional beliefs in the sacrality of astral objects, religious doubts or radically new divinations might ensue.

As is also the case with every major cathedral, the works of space art would be sure to have political overtones as well. To launch a commemorative object that would temporarily constitute a new moon might to some people seem sheer lunacy; but it could be the sort of 'mad dream' – in the words of Comte – that would lift France's slightly sagging reputation among the avant-garde, setting in the heavens a sign of the untrammelled French spirit.

Confronted by the mingling of so many apparently non-aesthetic concerns in the experience of aesthetic objects, one realizes how rarified and hypothetical is the idea of a strictly aesthetic experience in the realm of art. But that is not the central point of dispute or inquiry here. A theorist like J. O. Urmson, for instance, would readily admit that normally our satisfaction in, or dissatisfaction with, architectural and artistic objects is 'multiply-grounded'. He thus would acknowledge that the three traits of good architecture distinguished by Vitruvius can be appreciated to some extent simultaneously. What he would deny is that the properly aesthetic component of that response is in any way conditioned by the non-aesthetic factors we have mentioned.[18]

What we are interested in affirming is exactly what Urmson denies. That is, we are asking whether it is not in some cases true that, contrary to what Urmson claims, our aesthetic response *per se* is 'multiply-grounded' rather than pure, and interactive rather than inert. Even more to the point, we are asking whether the distinctively *religious* factors in Gothic architecture, for instance, affect its specifically *aesthetic* qualities, in which case the aesthetic traits of Chartres must be delightfully complex.

To these crucial questions we obviously are prepared to answer 'yes'. We have in one way or another asserted this very thing from the start. But before we can incorporate this affirmation into a fuller analysis of the characteristics of aesthetica, we must listen to one other voice of stark opposition, since it is that of a religious philosopher of the first rank. On this matter Etienne Gilson takes a position that Urmson doubtless would admire. While insisting that religion can and must place certain constraints on art dedicated to its service, Gilson maintains that the object so constrained ceases to be genuinely artistic and aesthetic. In his view the religious and the artistic (or aesthetic) belong to completely different orders. Although one can imagine a work that somehow manages to meet the requirements of each order, the criteria for success in the two areas are altogether different, for the ends are quite distinct.

To emphasize this last point Gilson reminds us that 'one and the same material object [such as a work of architecture] can serve two different ends and, inasmuch as it does, it is two distinct objects of apprehension'.[19] In Gilson's eyes, therefore, the building we call Chartres Cathedral must be two things: a religious object and an object of aesthetic delight. As the former it is a means of worship concerned with the glorification of God and the salvation of humanity; as the latter it is a beautiful object enjoyed for its own sake. Consequently what is aesthetically good about the building can have nothing directly to do with what is good religiously, or vice versa.

Gilson's theory stands as a classic example of what we have discussed as the kind of duck-rabbit (really duck/rabbit) thinking that eventuates in purist aesthetics. What makes it of special interest here is that, as Gilson elaborates on his ideas, it becomes exceptionally plain that when purist aesthetics is incorporated into religious reflection, it results in purist theology as well. Gilson, to be sure, joins other neo-Thomists in acknowledging that, along with the true and the good, the beautiful is a transcendental attribute of being and therefore brings one to 'the threshold of the sacred'. Yet he stresses that beauty is the most 'modest' of the transcendentals because it is 'merely the good of sensible apperception of being'. In short, beauty has its own area of specialization, which in the ultimate scheme of things is inferior to both the true and the morally good; for beauty is needed by religion strictly 'in order to win access to the hearts of men'.[20] It would seem that from Gilson's point of view a theology that stooped to engage in aesthetics would be doing so simply out of the need to condescend to the human frailty exhibited in our inability to seek or take the truth straight. Such theology would hardly expect to be informed by the aesthetic forms of Gothic architecture and still less by the literal and imaginative flight of a 'light ring' launched into space. Whether it could be adequate even as theology is another question.

In pursuing now a different course we will want to show clearly that this dispute with Gilson (and others) is not merely a quibble over words, with Gilson happening to take the word 'aesthetic' in a narrower, stricter sense than is advocated here. About this there should be no doubt if in the final two sections we can proceed to describe diverse and distinctively aesthetic traits which in part are ones that purism either misinterprets or fails to discern. Our two prime examples of aesthetica will prove useful in this regard, as will ideas from an unexpected source – Immanuel Kant – who rightly or wrongly has functioned as the fountainhead of modern purist aesthetics.

The Aesthetic Continuum

In René Wellek's foreword to a recent selection of the writings of Kant, he boldly asserts: 'Kant's aesthetics and reflections on the theory of criticism seem today as true and relevant as in 1790'.[21] In supporting this assertion Wellek is careful to point out that while Kant upholds the autonomy of the aesthetic realm he is no wooden formalist; for in the end Kant wants to see art as bridging the gulf between the world of nature and the world of moral action, between intuition and thought, and imagination and reason, and thus as ultimately pointing to the 'supersensuous' and noumenal reality underlying all appearances. Yet, as Wellek himself comes near to admitting, it seems clear that Kant's own strategy of constructing clear-cut dichotomies necessarily frustrates his attempt at bridge-building.

Our own aim is to show that Kant's distinction between beauty that is free (or self-subsistent) and beauty that is dependent (or conditioned) can in fact be modified so as to overcome the formalism and purism latent within his emphasis on the 'free' end of this polarity. Later theorists seldom have paid much attention to dependent beauty, on the presumption that what Kant finds important to say about beauty proper can be said without any reference to its dependent, conditioned form.[22] There even has been some doubt that, to Kant's way of thinking, beauty that is conditioned could really be beauty at all. Yet we will see that in this distinction and Kant's treatment of it – albeit interpreted in a way not foreseen by Kant himself – one can find important clues regarding the marks and traits of what actually appears to be an aesthetic continuum between the 'freely' aesthetic and the totally 'dependent'.

As Kant explains in *The Critique of Judgment* (1790) beauty that is free, pure, and unconditioned cannot be made or evaluated according to rules alone, described or interpreted through concepts, or put in the service of ulterior purposes.[23] The delight that it gives is directed toward the object rather than the subject; and the object in this respect is autonomous, even though beauty strictly speaking is (for Kant) not a property of the object itself but of what the subject makes of the object in 'reflective judgment'. What is beautiful, therefore, is valued for its own sake. And it is discerned only by means of taste, the judgments of which have universal, intersubjective validity.

Although Kant's list of the perfect exemplars of free, unconditioned beauty includes things like flowers, sea shells, music without words, and ornamental designs on wallpaper, he appears to allow for the possibility that something like a representational picture also could be free in its beauty as long as it is the beauty of the representation that gives delight and not anything extrinsic, such as its historical or economic value, its fidelity to that which it depicts, or the artistic skill displayed in the depiction. In all the latter instances the beauty of the object is judged at least partly in terms of one's concept of some purpose it is to fulfil, with the result that it is not free of the influence of nonaesthetic concerns.

It seems clear that the works of space art that we have discussed would be aesthetica of the sort Kant thinks of as 'free' and 'pure', since they are conceived of as both enjoyable in themselves and useless – 'beautiful, with pure lines', as the designer of *Arsat* says. It seems equally clear that Chartres Cathedral would not normally be such an aestheticon. In fact Kant explicitly excludes churches from the class of objects exhibiting free beauty. Thus he claims that the beauty of an object having a built-in purpose such as the enhancement of worship can be 'pure' in one's perception of it only if one either has no idea of the object's purpose or else abstracts a 'free' form of beauty from the form ordinarily understood to be conditioned by a purpose.[24] Phenomenologists in the twentieth century would describe this special mental act as 'bracketing' the actual purpose of the purposive form.

Applying Kant's theory to objects other than beauties, and thus to things and events Kant himself did not intend to describe, we can say that the (relatively) pure and unconditioned form of the aesthetic includes objects of perception or imagination that are noticed or appreciated in their own right and, in this sense, for their own sake. Contrary to what Kant would have supposed, however, these could be such things as oddly shaped clouds on the horizon, which may strike us as neither beautiful nor ugly. In addition aesthetica that sometimes are rather freely noted or appreciated might include the tactile qualities of rosary beads or the strangely affecting smell of incense, or perhaps even the evocative taste of Proust's *petite Madeleine* cake dipped in tea – things of the sort that philosophers generally have tended to regard as marginally aesthetic (in the sense relevant here) because insufficiently detached from ourselves, unlike the objects perceived through the principal cognitive organs of eye and ear. Kant himself would have said that these things, although in some way aesthetic, provide sheerly sensual gratification rather than the disinterested delight afforded by beauty. At points he seems to say the same thing about colors and tones (as distinct from paintings and compositions). What he thereby ignores is the contemplative and object-oriented ingredient within certain ways we have of attending to such things, which distinguishes this attention from sheer consumption and indulgence.

Assuming that with Kant's help we now have isolated several distinctive marks of at least one level of the aesthetic, we need to determine – again partly with Kant's help – what it is that one actually notices or appreciates about objects bearing these marks. With respect to such aesthetica, what are the qualities that capture our attention or cause our delight? One does not, after all, attend to or take delight in something merely because it is *not* cognitive, moral, useful, satiating, or holy.

Neither Kant nor anyone else has come up with a completely satisfactory answer to this question. Yet Kant surely is right in thinking that what evokes aesthetic response of the purest sort has much to do with form, as this is apprehended in the free play of our 'cognitive faculties' (specifically imagination and understanding) without any genuinely cognitive or practical result. But we would add that sensual qualities make their own contribution, and we would heed later 'expressive' theorists when they argue that the qualities of form and sense that strike us as aesthetic are those that are 'felt', and often felt to be 'expressive'. With respect to the 'felt' qualities of beautiful form in particular, scholastic and classical thinkers reasonably contend that we are delighted by what we perceive to be the integrity and wholeness of the object, by the harmony of its parts, by a just proportion in the relation of parts to the whole, and often by a certain radiance or *claritas* emanating from the object. Other thinkers have recognized that imbalances and incoherencies likewise create aesthetic effects.

Taking a cue from theorists like John Dewey, moreover, we would emphasize that what captures our attention and appreciation may involve qualities that emerge from a dynamic process. In such 'integral' aesthetic experience it is often the case that anticipations and expectations are aroused, are then somehow complicated, intensified, and perhaps frustrated through temporary conflict, and in the end are resolved in such a way that equilibrium is restored, though in a state of transformation. At other times, in contrast to Dewey's rather explicitly orgasmic and implicitly 'masculine' version of aesthetic experience, aesthetic qualities may emerge from an expansive filling out, from an improvisatory and multi-directional filling in, or from some other nonlinear development or envelopment. This is evident in much non-Western art and in many Western works currently celebrated by feminists.

As for *why* we might enjoy such things and processes, the reasons once more are less than perfectly plain. It is not highly informative just to say, as Kant does, that the free play of our cognitive faculties happens to give pleasure, beautiful form being in accord with the indeterminate standards of our own reflective judgment. In any case, whatever the merit of this explanation and others we can offer, such speculations are better postponed until we take up the question of aesthetic and artistic meaning in the chapter that follows.

Just now we need to pursue the second and commonly neglected half of Kant's distinction between two kinds of beauty. Whereas the first kind of beauty is free, pure, and unconditioned, Kant speaks of the second as dependent, impure, and conditioned. Although we shall see that Kant vacillates in what he thinks this means, he makes it clear that the latter beauty is perceived and evaluated at least partly in terms of concepts and purposes that are not aesthetic. These establish rules, or at any rate constraints, regarding how beauty is to be shaped and employed. In this way beauty is made to serve the practical ends of politics or religion or morality.

The dependency of beauty has its advantages, according to Kant. For instance, it allows one to establish certain objective norms for how a church is to be made beautiful. Thus (to use an example of our own) theology determined that the apse of Chartres Cathedral should be the focal point of the architectural design, because that was where the high altar was located and where the Mass was most visibly celebrated.

At the very least the use of reason allows one to set limits to the kinds of beauty acceptable for a given purpose. During the Counter Reformation, as is well known, the Catholic Church placed restraints on the use of highly elaborate polyphony in musical settings of the Ordinary of the Mass. This was not because the settings were insufficiently beautiful but because the many-layered, overlapping vocal lines obscured the text, which to begin with had provided the liturgical *raison d'être* for the music. This kind of constraint is, to Kant's way of thinking, all to the good, as long as the good one seeks in this context is not beauty in and of itself.

Finally, Kant says, dependent beauty has the benefit that when we reconcile aesthetic with conceptual norms, we experience a total harmony of mind. And this marks an increase in 'our *whole faculty*' of 'representative power'.[25]

With this last, somewhat enigmatic statement we are given a foretaste of Kant's famous and often debated assertions concerning what he calls 'aesthetic ideas', his exposition of which warrants our scrutiny. We are further prepared by Kant's reflections on the sublime and on other departures from the beautiful *per se*, all of which precede his discussion of aesthetic ideas produced by means of the beautiful arts.

Although Kant's treatment of the sublime sheds light on the whole distinction between free and conditioned aesthetica and leads up to the interesting discourse on aesthetic ideas, the topic actually is taken up separately from that of the beautiful. This is largely because, in Kant's view, the sublime (whether 'mathematical' or 'dynamic') has no clearly imaginable and limited form, however overawing or moving may be the objects we loosely call by that name. What makes for the sublime is not some perceived harmony between form and our faculty of understanding but rather the sheer ability of our reason to transcend the frustration of our strictly cognitive powers as they try to reckon with what is beyond their reckoning. Reason accomplishes this by supplying an abstract idea essential to the sublime – the idea of the boundless or infinite – that transcends anything we can sense and literally imagine. This so impresses us that what we judge to be sublime is not so much the object 'as our own state of mind in the estimation of it'.[26]

This point is made in a different way when Kant claims that in the case of the 'dynamic sublime' we recognize the enormous and potentially threatening power of phenomena encountered in nature – lightnings or cataracts or towering cliffs – and yet sense that in our very humanity and personhood we are morally superior to these and, as such, ultimately are impervious to any merely natural disaster. To make such a deduction, however, requires feeling and mental 'movement' as opposed to taste and the restful contemplation always entailed in the judgment of the beautiful. In this way, too, the sublime is different from the beautiful. Yet it still is aesthetic, since it is not determined or encompassed by precise concepts, rules, and purposes. And one's estimate of it is still something that one can expect others with proper preparation to share.[27]

There are good reasons to doubt Kant's conclusion that our response to the sublime is not oriented toward the object (natural or artistic). But the main point of relevance here is that the sublime is aesthetic and that, as aesthetic, it often appears on analysis to be more dependent and conditioned than free and unconditioned.

To be sure, this last point can be supported only by drawing out implications from a number of observations Kant makes along the way. What he explicitly says is quite different. He insists, for example, that if a purely aesthetical judgment is to be made regarding those virtually boundless objects of nature that we (metaphorically) term sublime, we must look on them without our usual intellectual concepts and ideas of purpose. To judge the starry heavens to be purely sublime we must forget about cosmic order or the work of the Creator and respond strictly to what our eyes see: 'a distant, all-embracing, vault'. Similarly, we cannot let our knowledge about the ocean and its creatures and depths influence our aesthetic response to it; the sea must remain for us a flat, watery, and bounded surface.[28]

Ironically, however, the sheerly visual appearance that Kant urges us to judge seems far less sublime once it is deprived of all those associations that he wants us to purge. And Kant's recommended way of looking, which supposedly permits the sublime to be apprehended in aesthetic purity, finally rests – according to Kant himself – on much more than what the eyes can give, for it entails mental maneuvers and moral reflections that require much 'greater culture' than does the judgment of the beautiful. Indeed, Kant states, 'without development of moral ideas, that which we, prepared by culture, call sublime presents itself to the uneducated man merely as terrible' and frightening.[29]

Since even these moral ideas do not absolutely determine or encompass one's judgment of the sublime, Kant seems to think that the sublimity they make possible can remain utterly free. But this seems inconsistent. One could argue on similar grounds that there is no reason why concepts of the cosmos and notions of the creatures and mysterious depths within the sea would strictly determine one's response to the starry heavens or the ocean. If they nevertheless condition this response, the same surely can be said of moral ideas deemed essential to the very existence of the sublime. Thus, if 'conditioned' means modified or influenced rather than strictly determined, we can safely say, with or without Kant's blessing, that there is no estimate of the sublime in nature that is not conditioned by philosophical, moral, or religious considerations.

Finally, one's impression that much (if not all) sublimity is conditioned is reinforced when Kant mentions artifacts that he himself actually thinks of as sublime (in a manner of speaking). These artifacts include such edifices as the pyramids of Egypt and St Peter's Basilica in Rome. Presumably Chartres Cathedral might be in this class as well, if one judges that its scale, mysteriously lighted interior, and soaring height are such as to prevent its being beautiful *per se*. Such sublimity seems undeniably genuine, and yet Kant openly admits that it would *not be pure* because it is partially determined by non-aesthetic purposes.[30] In this respect it seems to be strictly analogous to dependent beauty. We can conclude, therefore, that if we are to speak of sublimity in either art or nature, it is likely to be of a kind that is to some extent dependent and conditioned.

One begins to notice, in point of fact, that almost any form of the aesthetic that Kant envisions as deeply significant at a human level is something he has difficulty containing within the class of perfectly free and unconditioned aesthetica. So it is that he observes that, when one is already inclined to judge something to be beautiful, it can or will happen that one takes an interest in the communicability of one's pleasure in it, which then 'increases its worth in an almost infinite degree'.[31] Kant goes on to point out, moreover, that simultaneous with one's act of judging something in nature to be beautiful, one can take an interest in its very existence and actual presence. This interest, in Kant's view, is not the same thing as taking pleasure in beautiful form pure and simple. Yet, again, he asserts that it adds immeasurably to one's pleasure – so much so that if a lover of natural beauty were to discover that an exquisite birdsong or a lovely garden was not real but merely a product of human ingenuity and artifice, that person would no longer take anything like the same delight in it. Kant then goes so far as to declare that every beauty of nature is appreciated *only* when accompanied by the thought that it is actually nature that has produced it. The mind, he remarks, 'cannot ponder upon the beauty of nature without finding itself at the same time interested therein' – that is, interested in the fact that natural phenomena actually exist and really are encountered in experience. Such interest, which to Kant's way of thinking pervades our estimate of nature's beauty, cannot characterize aesthetic judgment at its purest. Nor can our accompanying moral intuition (incapable of proof) that the supersensible ground of nature ultimately is no more heedless of us than of nature itself. This intuition, however, partly explains why our interest in natural beauty is something 'akin to moral' and why 'nature speaks to us figuratively in her beautiful forms', as a kind of cipher.[32]

We are now a long way from the totally pure and unconditioned beauty with which Kant and we began. It seems, in fact, that the appreciation of the aesthetic qualities of nature, whether sublime or beautiful, is something that rarely if ever occurs in the purest imaginable form. The same holds for one's apprehension of the sublime in art. What, then, of the remaining branch of the aesthetic: artistic beauty? At its most significant, is it utterly free or is it partly conditioned? To answer this we must move on to Kant's discussion of aesthetic ideas.

Kant leads into this discussion by way of an analysis of genius, since genius (properly trained) is as essential to the production of artistic beauty as taste is to its apprehension. Although Kant believes that beauty, whether artificial or natural, is what pleases in the mere act of judging it, he states that art – as the product of genius – is judged in the light of one's understanding of what it ought to be.[33] This already qualifies in some measure the purity of most art, which at its best is animated by *Geist* – soul, spirit – that elevates it above the level of mere neatness and elegance and minimal beauty. Such spirit-animated beauty, while in some sense free, evidently is not so pure as the beauty of wallpaper, which may account for why Kant assures us that taste (in the narrow sense he intends) cannot fault any work that lacks it. Nonetheless it is more significant; for it 'puts the mental powers purposively into swing, i.e., into such a play as maintains itself and strengthens the mental powers in their exercise'.[34] This assertion reminds us of Kant's earlier claim that the dependency of beauty can result in an increase in our whole faculty of 'representative power'.

That which by virtue of genius animates the material of art and invigorates our mental powers is specifically the presentation of 'aesthetical ideas'. An aesthetic idea is nothing other than 'that representation of the imagination which occasions much thought, without however any definite thought, i.e. any *concept*, being capable of being adequate to it; it consequently cannot be completely compassed and made intelligible by language'. The aesthetic representation, be it symbol or metaphor, is justifiably called an idea in that it strives to express something, even if what it strives after lies beyond the bounds of concrete experience and precise conceptualization. Thus 'the poet ventures to realize to sense, rational ideas of invisible beings, the kingdom of the blessed, hell, eternity, creation, etc.; or even if he deals with things of which there are examples in experience – e.g. death, envy and all vices, also love, fame, and the like – he tries, by means of imagination . . . to go beyond the limits of experience and to present them to sense with a completeness of which there is no example in nature'.[35]

The result of such artistry is that it arouses 'more thought than can be expressed in a concept determined by words' – thought that is 'ineffable' and that is therefore felt rather than clearly conceived. If such thought could be said plainly and exhausted rationally it would be neither aesthetic nor beautiful.

In the space of approximately three pages Kant reiterates some ten times his assertion that aesthetic ideas, in the form of what we usually would call symbols and metaphors, have a capacity to add to a concept 'much ineffable thought'. Because such thought cannot be contained in concepts it also cannot, in Kant's view, exist for the sake of either pure or practical reason.[36] Yet, even though art does not directly serve understanding or reason, it can hardly be said that the mind caught up in the sort of art described here by Kant is resting in passive contemplation, as it is said to be when in the presence of free and pure beauty. What it experiences is not freedom from any serious conceptual or moral engagement but freedom for 'thinking more', which in poetry, for instance, can actually provide 'food for the understanding' and life to concepts.[37]

So highly does Kant value this thought-enriched and thought-enriching function of art that he believes that the work of art will become dull and spiritless unless its form disposes us to reflection by existing in 'more or less close combination with moral ideas'. This means that in the higher arts the free play of the cognitive faculties carries on 'serious business'.[38]

By now it should not take much imagination to see that, as Kant describes the realm of the aesthetic, the strict dichotomy between free, unconditioned beauty on the one hand and dependent beauty on the other does not stand up. In effect it becomes a description of two more or less hypothetical poles at opposite ends of a continuum. Kant neither uses the distinction consistently nor sets it aside; instead he constantly modifies it in the process of applying it to particular cases, implicitly acknowledging degrees of aesthetic purity. And though Kant is no better equipped than a theorist like Gilson to describe the ends and effects of art in what might be termed integralist (as opposed to purist) terms, his exposition repeatedly suggests that the response we have to beauty and sublimity is in fact deeply conditioned by factors that are not themselves aesthetic.

What remains to be shown more clearly is that the genuinely aesthetic qualities of objects and artifacts so conditioned are themselves in some measure modified as a result. If this can be demonstrated, then it will be evident that such things as 'commodity' and even 'firmness' can be relevant to 'delight', thereby becoming mediately aesthetic. It also will be plain that our quarrel with the purist account of the nature of the aesthetic cannot be dismissed as merely a verbal dispute. That various kinds of aestheticon can have, in turn, both immediate and mediate relevance to such spheres as religion and morality will then become a distinct possibility to be explored further as our study unfolds.

The Aesthetic Milieu in View of the Religious

Even if it is true that Kant did not entirely know what to make of his distinction between free and dependent beauty or, rather, made of it different things at different times, his exposition of the notion assists our own endeavor. For, as we have seen, not only does he shed light on the traits of the aesthetic but he also inadvertently illuminates a variety of ways in which, to different degrees, the aesthetic is conditioned by the non-aesthetic.

Our claim that non-aesthetic factors affect aesthetic perception can be made still more plausible if it can be shown that some of the aesthetic predicates we use to describe aesthetica at either pole – the free or the dependent – are modified in meaning or aptness under the pressure of non-aesthetic considerations. To that end we will perform two thought-experiments using our familiar examples of aesthetica.

First of all let us suppose that, due to difficulties with the 'light ring', the back-up project called *Arsat* has been launched (a prospect that is presently in doubt).[39] As it circles above the globe everyone can see the beauty its designer had hoped for. Some hikers on a lengthy wilderness trek, however, momentarily mistake it for a strange and astonishing new comet or supernova in the night sky. That is, they see it (as Kant would have supposed) in the light of the thought that it is natural in origin.

But Kant evidently was wrong to assume that distinctly aesthetic judgment would be unaffected by this thought. Seen as a natural phenomenon, the object manifests such otherworldly radiance that if our hikers were Romantics they would not hesitate to call it sublime. Being of a different era, they call it 'awesome'. Their comments and perceptions change, however, when they recall the predicted launch of *Arsat*. Upon realizing that this heavenly body is in fact a work of art, they suddenly see it as having a quite different aesthetic aura. Now it looks daring and innovative, or (conceivably) even pretentious – but no longer sublime, which carries with it connotations of mystery, magnitude, and power more appropriate to supernovae than to satellites, however artistic. This indicates that the hikers' aesthetic estimate of the supposed beauty or sublimity of *Arsat* was conditioned all along – conditioned by ideas and associations not aesthetic in themselves, and pertinent to nature rather than to human artifice.[40]

As for the response of *Arsat*'s designer, he is happy to report that he enjoys the object in actuality just as he had anticipated in conception, relishing the beautiful lines of this 'star in the sky, . . . born of human hands, a mad dream'. With this quotation again before us, however, we see that even for Pierre Comte the dream is about *art* and not about sheer form. Art is envisioned here as emblem: as a 'mad' rivaling or surpassing of nature. Take away its status as artifact 'born of human hands' and immediately for Comte (as well as for countless others) the 'star' in the sky makes a very different aesthetic impression. Apparently, even at its purest, art is a manifestation and interpretation of the 'artworld' of human culture.[41]

A second thought-experiment will make it clear in the case of conditioned aesthetica as well that precisely our aesthetic perceptions and descriptions are conditioned by initially non-aesthetic considerations. Suppose we are on extended holiday and, after a tour of the cathedrals of the *Ile-de-France*, have flown on to Florida where we soon find ourselves at Disney World. Let us imagine, then, that much to our surprise there is a new addition called 'Medieval World', where we enter a thoroughly medieval-looking 'town' in the midst of which stands an exact replica of Chartres Cathedral. Soon we are informed that, though this building is visually indistinguishable from Chartres, it is constructed of lightweight and economical synthetic materials originally developed for use in space stations.

The replica exactly replicates the sense-impressions produced by Chartres. Most traditional and modern aesthetics would suppose, therefore, that it would be aesthetically identical. But in the setting imagined here it does not, after all, convey to us the same aesthetic experience – the same 'look' and 'feel' – as Chartres. This is because the aesthetic effect derives from more than meets the eye. The aesthetic object is constituted not just by *what* is seen but by *how* it is seen – that is, by what it is seen *as* – which depends partly on its whole milieu, including the contexts of perception and various things that we know or think we know. In this case we know, for instance, that the replica has not stood firmly for eight hundred years, that it does not exist in continuity with a genuinely medieval history and community, and that it is not dedicated to any god evocative of religious adoration.

From our response to the original edifice we also can deduce that, whether or not we consider ourselves religious, the height of religious aspiration and the weight of religious responsibility are felt in the very structure of the authentic cathedral, which often has been termed sublime. This is why it would never occur to us to call the pseudo-cathedral sublime.

What this means is that the aesthetic 'delight' taken in 'dependent' art like that of a cathedral is itself very much conditioned by one's cognizance of the building's actual 'firmness' and its evident religious 'commodity'. To a lesser extent non-aesthetic factors are at work as well in the aesthetic appreciation of apparently 'unconditioned' aesthetica such as *Arsat* and works of nature.

This being so, one cannot be satisfied to say with Etienne Gilson that the 'end' of a significant object of art or beauty is anything so simple as delight or pleasure, and especially not if this pleasure or delight is understood in purist terms. In the case of a work like Chartres one need not choose between aesthetic delight and religious devotion. It is more plausible to suppose that the edifice – even as art – exists for countless reasons, all more or less unified by aesthetic form and culminating in devoted delight or delighted devotion.

More generally this means that when we are describing the traits of aesthetica that have any appreciable depth or complexity, we only engender misconceptions if we say simply that they exist to delight or to be valued for their own sake. At the very least we should say that their value is *not only* cognitive, religious, moral, or sensual and that they exist *in part* to delight, which is good in its own right. This makes it clear that there is no *a priori* reason to segregate all aesthetic goods from religious ones and acknowledges that aesthetic goods are multiple and complex.

Ever since the time of Socrates we have recognized, of course, that something can be both good in itself and good for something else. What has seldom been realized is that, in the sphere of aesthetics proper, certain goods of art and of the aesthetic cannot be attained without incorporating what is *not* artistic or aesthetic – be it historical, moral, or religious. This material is then transformed in the aesthetic milieu. It is not annihilated but made new:

not only new as an otherwise unattainable aesthetic product and effect but also new as an otherwise unavailable historical reality or moral insight or religious expression. Thus, in being good for religion, aesthetica give to it some of what they alone are good for in themselves. Religion, in return, gives to aesthetica what it alone can give, though even this is thereby changed.

If, then, it is a whole perceptual milieu that is aesthetic and not just an isolated object, and if that milieu can contain religious elements, how are we to tell when to call something aesthetic and when to call it religious? If the context is such that one attends from (or looks through) those features of the object that could only be called aesthetic and attends to (or focuses on) those features that could only be called religious, then the object of perception normally is called religious. If the reverse is true, the object (or event or process) is called aesthetic. In the context of a Vespers service a Mozart setting of the Psalm 'Laudate Dominum' normally is heard as (aesthetically) religious, whereas in a concert hall it normally is heard as (religiously) aesthetic. In one context the listener is focally aware of elements that in the other context become subsidiary.

In either case, however, the specific qualities of the medium affect the message; the specific style affects the substance; the specific form affects the content. Since this is true only when distinctly aesthetic elements are present, we can say that the milieu itself is in some way aesthetic whenever particular qualities of medium, style, and form affect message, substance, or content. Everything within an aesthetic milieu, moreover, is of either immediate or mediate aesthetic relevance. And since everything religious could in some context be at least mediately aesthetic, everything religious is in principle susceptible to aesthetic treatment and transformation.

If nothing that is shaped aesthetically remains precisely the same, it is plain that religious meanings conveyed within an aesthetic milieu can never fully be captured apart from that milieu, which itself is never completely fixed. For this reason, among others, we now are pressed to say more about the dynamics and purposes of the aesthetic transformations of religious meaning. Our inquiry into this topic can best be carried out by focusing on the meaningful making associated with art.

4
Artistic Makings and Religious Meanings

Art and Impurity

The true, the good, the beautiful; thought, action, passion; theory, praxis, creativity: if we confine the aesthetic to but one of these venerable categories, it is sure to remain pure. At the same time it is sure to be of limited relevance to religion and theology and, one might add, to the self and the human community. If in reality, however, the aesthetic is not thus constrained – if it actually interanimates and consorts with other things in such a way that all are in some measure changed by their mutual relations – then it may be accused of promiscuity and the order of things may appear to be threatened. But in the end that order as regularly conceived may be but a logical possibility that bears little resemblance to what we know most deeply of science and cognition, morality and religion, or beauty and art.

This last point was implicit in our demonstration that few (if any) aesthetica are perfectly pure and free in the Kantian sense. It is true that in attending to sense, form, and process we can discern relatively pure aesthetic qualities the very perception of which captures our 'disinterested' interest – an interest virtually independent of any cognitive, utilitarian, religious, or moral benefits that also may accompany or accrue to the experience. The reverberant, crashing chord that at length fades away to nothing at the end of the Beatles' song 'A Day in the Life', thereby bringing the *Sgt Pepper* album to a stunning close, plainly has a timbre, texture, and contour that simply as such are of intrinsic interest. Yet these relatively pure aesthetic qualities gain in complexity and meaning when heard as the coda to a song that alternately parodies the absurdities of life and death – war, suicide, the 'daily grind' – and invites an anonymous 'you' into a kind of nirvanic fullness/nothingness associated with 'turning on' (presumably to drugs, to eros, to expanded consciousness). The aesthetic character of the

77

musical moment changes as it becomes ingredient in a 'criticism of life' and in a particular image of life's possibilities at the brink of nihilism.

In view of the importance of such emergent aesthetic qualities, we can recognize that it will not do to continue speaking of the more complex aesthetica merely as impure or dependent, thereby implying that they are somehow deficient. Rather we should refer to these aesthetica as integral and interdependent. They integrate simpler kinds of aesthetic and non-aesthetic perceptions into a more complex gestalt. And their unique aesthetic effects are interdependent with, and mutually transformative of, perceptions that are religious, moral, social, and so forth.[1]

In its own way religion too involves integral and transformative experience and hence (in one sense at least) 'impurity'. But just how various kinds of aesthetic and religious experience are correlated, and how they are affected by their interdependence, are matters we have not yet had a chance to explore in depth. The principal reasons for religion to take aesthetic form at all likewise have barely been glimpsed so far, although we have hinted that some of the usual concepts of religion would need to be altered in view of our changing image of the aesthetic and the artistic.

As we undertake to examine these issues here, the most promising approach will be to study the making of religious and aesthetic meaning in the medium of art *per se*. In particular we will want to see how the means and ends of art are made religiously meaningful. Beginning with a proposal concerning how best to define and conceive of art, we subsequently will inquire into the makings of art and the religious meanings that are thereby made. What our analysis implies about the nature of religion itself, and about the specific varieties of religious experience and expression, is something we will pursue in the chapter to follow.

Concepts and Definitions of Art

Works of art – some of them, at any rate – are among the few things that human beings ever make solely with the intention of providing aesthetic delight. Perhaps because of this unique connection between artistic production and aesthetic appreciation, aesthetics in many circles has been more or less synonymous with philosophy of art.[2] Even among non-philosophers the objects and experiences that today epitomize what is meant by the word 'aesthetic' are ones associated with the arts, and especially with fine arts such as ballet, music, painting, sculpture, poetry, drama, and (perhaps less frequently) architecture.

Just as we commonly think about aesthetics chiefly in connection with art, we also commonly think of art *qua* art mainly in connection with its aesthetic features, typically regarded as beautiful or expressive. One sees this quite clearly in a definition of art proposed by Monroe Beardsley: 'An artwork', he says, 'is something produced with the intention of giving it the capacity to satisfy the aesthetic interest'.[3] This suggests that it is precisely the intentionally aesthetic design of an artifact that distinguishes it as art. Most modern thinkers take this for granted. 'A bicycle shed is a building; Lincoln Cathedral is a piece of architecture', writes Nikolaus Pevsner; 'the term architecture applies only to buildings designed with a view to aesthetic appeal'.[4] Architecture, he implies, is building that is artistic, and it can be called artistic and hence architectural if, and only if, it is aesthetic.

In attempting both to complicate and refine such concepts of art, we will want to reaffirm the intrinsically aesthetic nature of those things we think of as artistic. Otherwise the efforts we have made to explicate the traits of aesthetica might have little application to works of art as such. In the preceding discussion of Chartres Cathedral and other aesthetica, however, we argued against any purist notion of what Beardsley and Pevsner would term (respectively) aesthetic 'interest' or aesthetic 'appeal'. Only in this way could we lay the groundwork for an understanding of art that would recognize its aesthetic character without thereby automatically minimizing its potential religious or moral import.

Our challenge now is to formulate an overall concept and working definition of art that will seem relatively consistent with experiences and ideas of art found at times and places different from our own and that, even while non-purist in nature and thus open to religious meanings, also will seem plausible in terms of modern thought. Unless we can do this, we will have no criteria for deciding which features of religion are artistic or how anything significant to art in particular might be religious.

This part of our task, like so many others, is complex enough to require a degree of patience and fortitude. The very idea of trying to bring together certain modern ideas of art with those of other times and places is somewhat daunting. For one thing, 'art' in the modern era means above all 'fine art'. Yet our idea that poetry, music, painting, sculpture, and drama all are 'fine' arts pre-eminently concerned with the 'beautiful', the 'aesthetic', or the uniquely 'expressive' comes to us mostly from the Enlightenment, via the Romantics. So, too, does the now common distinction between fine arts and applied crafts.

Such distinctions are imprecise and fluid; an art considered 'fine' at one time (as gardening often was in the eighteenth century) may not be considered an art at all at some other time. Furthermore, our own particular modes of classifying the arts are alien to many of the eras and societies whose artifacts we are proud to place in our most illustrious art collections and museums. Even in the West, the fundamental distinction prior to the Enlightenment was always between liberal (or 'free') arts and servile (or 'mechanical') ones; that is, between arts requiring mental effort alone and those requiring physical effort as well. Seldom did the former include any of the arts that eventually would be considered 'fine'. Even the 'music' studied as part of the medieval quadrivium was concerned with theory rather than with the craft of music-making.[5]

This is not at all to imply that what Enlightenment thinkers such as Batteux achieved in reconceiving and reclassifying the arts was negligible, although it was in fact anticipated in some respects by the Aristotelian division between imitative productive arts (which afford pleasure and beauty) and original productive arts (which are utilitarian). The Enlightenment, we can say with some justification, made it possible fully to recognize and isolate what we now regard as the distinctively artistic – and specifically aesthetic – elements within a wide range of human skills and products.

Yet one can argue that the typical Enlightenment and modern view of an art like painting as something that simply 'lays down its own rule' and confines itself to aesthetic effects of great purity is finally no less problematical than the Enlightenment's preoccupa-tion with the idea that imitation (as *'mimesis'* was translated) is fundamental to the fine arts – an idea that has long since been set aside. André Malraux points out that we all now identify as artworks a wide array of products from cultures and histories remote from our own, relying on such things as photographs to help us construct a virtual 'museum without walls'. Under the influence of the Enlightenment, we may think, as Malraux himself does, that we can look on such heterogeneous works as *art* only if we conceptually 'frame' them in such a way as to screen out what we might know or learn of their original cultic and social function, symbolic status, or historical context.[6] In that case we see them primarily in relation to other artworks; their history becomes the history of style alone.

Such a narrow, non-communal, and ahistorical understanding of art, when pursued with logical consistency, is both aesthetically and morally suspect. Aesthetically it leads to the conclusion (with which Malraux himself flirts) that the more one-dimensional and pristine the milieu in which one perceives an artifact, the better one can appreciate it as *art* – a conclusion that our analysis in the preceding chapters fails to support. Morally it can easily suggest the imperialist notion that one can most profitably use the meaningful products of an 'other' world, perhaps Sumerian or Ugandan, if one does not reckon with their intended status and purpose, whether political, personal, or ritual. This lets one side-step the possibility, or perhaps obligation, of dealing with the claims and criteria of other cultures. One can choose instead to extract and import the only thing one can imagine would be of 'timeless' value: the aesthetic and artistic essence.

There is good reason to believe – if not on the basis of theories put forward so far, then on the basis of the related ideas of anthropologists such as Clifford Geertz – that such a concept of art is untrue to the way arts actually function in historical and world cultures, and for the most part even in our own.[7] In any case, there is no necessity for our vision of art to be blinkered in the way Malraux believes is inevitable for the appreciation of art proper. For if one traces the Western term 'art' to its roots, one discovers various senses and connotations of the term that would by no means lead to such a restricted understanding of the nature of art, either past or present. Two of these in particular warrant our attention: first, the concept of art as knowledgeable and skilful making; and, second, the quite different concept of art as something specially suited to religious vision and prophecy.

The etymology of 'art' is traceable to the Latin *ars*, itself a translation of the Greek *techne*. At least in Plato the latter word has to do neither with the creative process nor with its end product. It designates instead the practical skill and know-how that someone in any of the recognized professions such as law, medicine, and the crafts needs to possess.[8] As such it can be ascribed to a horse-trainer as well as to a painter. Aristotle differs only slightly from Plato on this point, in that he uses *techne* to refer both to know-how and to the actual exercise of that know-how in production. Art, he says, 'is identical with the characteristic of producing under the guidance of true reason'.[9]

A concept of art as broad as this might be expected to include everything we presently think of as art, since it obviously includes much that we do not. But this is not the case. Among the Greeks true poetry (along with its ever-present companion music) was not originally thought to be truly art, because it was considered to be dependent not on know-how, skill, and rules but on the irrational inspiration of the gods and muses. It was visionary and prophetic, speaking of higher things and often in behalf of higher powers. It also was *'psychagogic'*, with a mysterious ability to influence the mind and spirit.

Beginning with Plato, however, poetry is compared (sometimes unfavorably) to the arts proper. In Aristotle, moreover, it becomes a genuine art: a form of *mimesis*, or representation; and it resembles other 'imitative' arts in being subject to certain rules or guidelines. Interestingly enough, the effect of this inclusion of poetry among the arts is mixed. On the one hand, poetry loses some of its associations with inspiration and prophecy. On the other hand, the other imitative arts begin to seem *less* a matter of sheer skill and technique; for the mimetic making (poiesis) that they entail is now seen to rely partially on native gifts and inspiration as well as on *techne*.

Even this short detour into history reveals that activities and products regarded today as artistic were long ago associated both with the powers of the prophet and seer and also with the skills of the informed maker. In antiquity these ideas and functions of art existed alongside, and in some tension with, other features of art such as its connection with representation, with the creation of beauty, and with pleasing instruction. To these images of art and of its functions the modern, Enlightened world has added most notably the ideas of aesthetic autonomy, of self-expression, and of non-discursive or symbolic expressiveness – to which the post-modernist has further added such ideas as textuality or intertextuality.

What must not escape our attention is that the prophetic and visionary dimension of the arts, despite being played down in most modernist theory *per se*, actually thrives in the modern era. It flourishes in Romanticism, of course, and also in a number of modern creations such as Messiaen's *Quartet for the End of Time*,

Schoenberg's *Moses and Aaron*, Kandinsky's cryptically encoded abstractions, and Joyce's secular epiphanies. Art of this sort is centrally concerned with presenting possibilities of existence and with interpreting life and death, humanity and divinity. Similarly, art that is centrally concerned with informed capability and skilful production persists not only throughout the Middle Ages and the Renaissance but also in the work and pedagogy of contemporary composers like Paul Hindemith and painters like Joseph Albers, and in fact almost everywhere that the making of art is taught. Both of these aspects of art ambiguously come together, moreover, in a post-modern work like John Adams's opera *Nixon in China*, with Alice Goodman's carefully crafted yet often consciously prosaic libretto that locates the auspicious and historic within the ordinary and quirky happenings of the merely historical.

Without as yet deciding which of all these features are most pertinent to a workable definition of art, we can see quite plainly that any general concept of art that screens out the wide range of its ends and means, from the religious and moral to the knowledgeable and productive, is unacceptably restrictive. In trying to form a more flexible and perceptive overall conception of art, it may be useful to picture the products of art as occupying a kind of territory or region. Surveying this region as a whole, we see that it is extremely varied and vaguely defined. Yet within its boundaries there are a number of landmarks: the Parthenon, the Taj Mahal, Mozart's *Jupiter* Symphony, Stravinsky's *Rite of Spring*, Rembrandt's self-portraits, Sophocles's *Oedipus the King*, Hokusai's color prints, the novels of Charles Dickens, the lyric poems of Emily Dickinson, the dances of Isadora Duncan. We may not value these works equally or even believe that works so different in kind can be appreciated for the same reasons. Nonetheless we do really identify such things as art and they help guide our conceptions of what else should count as art, and indeed as excellent art.

Near, or just beyond, the rather indefinite and shifting borders of the region of art are things that are not always thought of as art *per se*: artifacts like the Golden Gate Bridge, Stonehenge, various graffiti in the Paris Metro, the hymn 'Ein Feste Burg', Walt Disney's animated cartoon version of *Pinocchio*, Ennio Morricone's soundtrack to the film *The Mission*, the *Monty Python* television series, bonsai horticulture, Hummel figurines, origami birds and flowers, Zen rock gardens, Arabic calligraphy.

The labels often given to many of these art-like things are meant to distinguish them from art proper: applied (versus fine), minor (versus major), low (versus high), popular (versus elite), pleasant (versus beautiful), or decorative, commercial, uninspired, or tasteless. But the main characteristics and values of art are not in fact directly correlated with these conventional divisions and labels. There may be more in common between the not-so-'fine' art of a Zen rock garden and the certifiably fine abstract art of the Rothko Chapel than there is between, say, two works that are both 'fine' and that even employ the same medium – almost any sculpture by David Smith compared with almost any by Rodin, for instance. Likewise the *Oresteia* of Aeschylus may finally have more in common with many Holy Week liturgies, which we rarely think of as art at all, than it does with an arty musical like Andrew Lloyd Webber's *Phantom of the Opera*, even though opera itself did, of course, draw inspiration from Greek drama and the latter's use of music and choreography.

If not all members of the class 'art' have the same make-up or purpose, it should be evident that not all works within or near the boundaries of art proper will be valued for the same reasons. Some may be valued more for prophecy and disclosure, others for craftmanship and know-how; some may be valued for their passion and expressiveness, others for their formal design and self-contained beauty. Any particular art, moreover, may function differently for different audiences and in different epochs.

The relevance of this point to discussions of religion and art is considerable. To begin with, the fact that our conventional divisions among arts have inherent limitations means that the large number of 'lesser' arts found in and around religion cannot automatically be dismissed from serious analyses of the relations between art and religion. Hymns as a whole do not rank high as art, yet Ralph Vaughan Williams's setting of the hymn 'For All the Saints' is no less artful in its way than many a *Lied* by Schumann or Wolf. And even minor works may cumulatively make a major impact.

At the same time, the sheer variety within art means that when we try to conceive of art in religious terms, we must take care to specify which sort of art we mean. If we want to follow the modern Protestant theologian Paul Tillich and say that art is an expression of ultimate concern, we must ask whose ultimate concern it expresses and whether the Great Pyramid is closer to the Pharoah's concern or to the workers'; we might ask ourselves, too, whether the expression of ultimate concern cannot more readily be attributed to Michelangelo's art than to Fragonard's.[10] If we want to join the modern Catholic theologian Karl Rahner in referring to the poet as potential priest, we must take care to specify whose priest and which kind of poet.[11] Finally, even if we share Hans Küng's enthusiasm for Romano Guardini's claim that art functions eschatologically, so that the tree beautifully painted on canvas 'is not sealed in its unreality, but rouses the hope . . . that the world as it ought to be will at some time actually arise' – a hope, in short, for a new heaven and a new earth –[12] we nonetheless will need to temper our judgment in specific cases. If the tree is a Van Gogh cypress or a Friedrich fir, this may be so; if it forms part of the background in a Gainsborough portrait of The Honourable Mrs Graham, one may well wonder.

At this point we cannot avoid the question: Is there anything that binds together these different kinds and instances of art? Must our general conception of art finally be incoherent? Our observations up to now certainly do not encourage us to hope for a tidy or all-encompassing *definition* of art. On the contrary, they lend considerable credibility to the now well-known argument stemming from Wittgenstein that, because genres and concepts of art change, one never can specify any conditions that are necessary and sufficient for us to be able to say that 'x is a work of art'. Descriptive uses of the term 'art', this argument goes, reveal only 'family resemblances' among the things described; whereas when we use the term 'art' in a prescriptive or honorific fashion, this serves to call our attention to properties deemed praiseworthy without, however, isolating anything essential to art in general.[13]

Nevertheless, as even this argument admits, there really are family resemblances among the things we call art; and we and our institutions do continually make decisions about what belongs in the art 'family'. Even though one sometimes is forced, especially when reckoning with avant-garde movements, to retreat to the idea that in some sense 'art is what counts as art', it still is true that not everything counts as art.[14] Some sort of concept of art organizes our thoughts and perceptions, and some kind of working definition therefore seems at once in order and unavoidable for any extensive study in aesthetics.

What connects most ideas and expectations of what we presently call art is a quite general understanding at least implicit within the various ancient and modern theories that we have been seeking to bring together. This is the understanding that art entails knowledgeable, skilful, or inspired making; that an art always exhibits intrinsically appreciable – that is, aesthetic – qualities not duplicated by the workings of sheerly abstract thought or exhausted by mere utility; and that, finally, certain products of art are among the things we find most human or most divine. These are works apart from which life would be mute where it most wants to speak. Without them it also would be diminished in spirit and vitality, and perhaps in wisdom and power. Most societies have at least intimated some such beliefs about things we ourselves label 'art'.

Now, no definition of art can encompass all this. A definition must be generally applicable, which means that it must in some ways also be minimal – if not quite so vacuous as the facetious Greek definition of a human being as a featherless biped. Nevertheless, a definition of art need not *rule* out what it *leaves* out, as so many modernist ones do. And in fact a relatively plausible and informative definition can be formulated if we combine the modern notion of art as eminently aesthetic with the ancient yet persistent ideal of art as know-how and informed making – taking care as we do so not to exclude the possibility that simultaneously much art also might be beautiful, expressive, representational, or prophetic.

For our purposes art can best be defined as any and all of the creative skills, informed practices, and primary products manifest in the making of publicly recognizable aesthetica. A surrealist like André Breton minimizes one dimension of artistry when he suppresses technique and skill by drawing on dream-like processes or employing 'automatic' or stream-of-consciousness methods. He still can be considered an artist, however, because the choice to work in this fashion is informed, the execution may well display creativity or a sort of inspiration, and the product can be publicly recognized – and potentially appreciated – as significantly aesthetic. A dreamer, by contrast, is not inherently an artist. The aesthetic or imaginative qualities of dreaming cannot directly be estimated and appreciated by any public. If the dream is narrated, as Joseph's dreams are in the book of Genesis, it is the narrative and not the dream that is the art, just as it is the story of Joseph's life and not the life itself that is literally artistic. By the same token, a supremely knowledgeable and powerful god that did not actually create anything, perhaps leaving the task to a demiurge, would be no artist; whereas one that made a cosmos that as a whole could be recognized as beautiful or sublime would be very much an artist, and indeed the greatest of all.

In all of these cases we see that art cannot on the whole be divorced from the possibility of publics and products. Art thus is something fundamentally communal and interpersonal, though often pursued and enjoyed in private. This is part of its being the sort of thing that can take perceptible or intersubjectively imaginable form. As we later will see, this has important religious and moral implications.

To avoid confusion, it should be noted that some of the socially consequential practices and products we call 'arts' are not subject to our definition, being aesthetic strictly in an incidental way. The con artist, for example, does not practice art in our sense. Other arts, such as embalming or gunmaking, produce aesthetic qualities that, however appreciable, nonetheless contribute relatively little to the traits for which the products of the art are primarily valued. Well-made guns are not in the end much like well-made plays, and gunmaking therefore is not basically an art of the kind defined here.

Yet there are still other secondarily artistic spheres in which the aesthetic elements, however subsidiary in awareness, are essential to one's ability to make or perceive vividly and meaningfully what is of paramount interest. The Easter liturgy of the Russian Orthodox Church, for instance, would be immeasurably impoverished without its knowledgeably produced and richly aesthetic qualities, all of which remain subsidiary in one's attention. The makers of liturgy thus are significantly, though still not primarily, artists and should be recognized as akin to religious dramatists or painters; the participant in liturgy likewise is a kind of performer, albeit sometimes unpractised or inept.

In such a study as this it is important to ask, finally, whether theology itself can be an art in the sense defined here. This possibility is raised, for instance, by Gordon Kaufman's thesis that theology is an exercise of 'imagination', the particular goal of which is 'the construction of a concept of God which shows the meaning and significance of God for our own time and place', thereby 'bringing all of life and the world into relation with God'.[15]

To this the most reasonable reply is that, insofar as the means and ends of theology are largely intellectual and conceptual (as they characteristically are) then its constructive, imaginative work is not basically or even mediately aesthetic. Here there is making, but without aesthetically embodied meaning. This explains why theology in its intellectual forms cannot in itself fully succeed in its goal of 'bringing all of life and the world into relation with God' and why it must exist in complementary and dialectical relation not only with praxis but also with those richly aesthetic arts that can bring these relations imaginatively to life. Although certain works such as Augustine's *Confessions* and Dante's *Divine Comedy* are at once vividly aesthetic and rigorously theological, they are exceptional, and valued as such.

Having explored the idea of art in general and formulated a definition applicable to the arts of religion as well as to the arts as a whole, we need to supply a correlative definition of the work of art in particular. For, as our map of the region of art suggests, it is the artwork that figures most prominently in present-day aesthetics.

We will consider a work of art to be anything that is at least partially artificial in origin, that reflects creativity, skill, or know-how, and that in large measure is, or could be, something appreciated by a public attentive to aesthetic factors such as form and style, and responsive to aesthetic effects such as those we regard as intrinsically interesting, expressive, or beautiful.[16] It should be noticed that implicit within our definition of the work of art is the presumption that something may be more or less artistic, more or less fine, more or less inventive, skilful, expressive, unified, or formally finished. Thus, while neither a parable nor a prayer is likely to be fine art – art that maximizes effects toward the 'pure' end of the aesthetic continuum – both certainly can be artistic, as can sermons and vestments.

As we already have implied, for many Christian groups the liturgy itself functions as the dominant work of art in their midst: a kind of religious *Gesamtkunstwerk*. Although not all Christians would agree with the claim that the Mass is 'the pattern and source towards which all art is striving', it is not surprising when Joseph Jungmann endorses this view in his classic study *The Mass of the Roman Rite*, where he also asserts that the Mass can be called 'the central artistic achievement of Christian culture'.[17] We would add, furthermore, that during the Reformation even the sparsely anti-ritualistic ceremony of Zwingli's service of the Lord's Supper exhibited impressive aesthetic and artistic qualities by virtue of what has been described as its 'monumental simplicity and stillness'.[18]

It must be said, however, that the art of the liturgy (and of other ritual) depends to an exceptional degree on values and meanings shared primarily by a particular group. Moreover, this is not an art that in most instances is usefully considered to be *only* art, or art that is 'fine'. Even for those to whom its language is native, its aesthetic features are appreciable chiefly in relation to goals that extend far beyond anything aesthetic in itself; and while High Mass frequently includes certain elements of sound, sight, space, and setting 'the very perception of which gives delight', these do not permeate and integrate the whole in the degree to which they do in Mozart's *Don Giovanni* or Wagner's *Parsifal*, for instance, or even in quasi-ritualistic conglomerate events such as Woodstock or the Cannes Film Festival. In this respect, at least, the Christian liturgy cannot after all be regarded as 'the pattern and source toward which all art is striving'.

And what of the Bible? Is it literature – that is, a work of verbal art? Despite the fact that the Bible is not in every major part aesthetically rewarding enough to make it mainly and thoroughly a work of literary art, its aesthetic qualities, such as its use of symbol and story and of poetic and narrative structures, are significant enough for it to be considered, secondarily, an artistic work. In fact the Bible cannot fully be appreciated for what it is apart from sensitivity to its aesthetic traits. This has been recognized in varying degrees over the centuries, and increasingly in the past two decades.[19]

Nevertheless, in speaking of the Bible as literary and aesthetic, we do not mean to imply that we can simply ignore the various designs it has on readers, including its intent to change lives and to show what is true and just. Here, if anywhere, one sees the manifold dangers of accepting a theory like that of Roman Jakobson, which describes the specifically poetic/aesthetic function of language as nothing but the focus on the text or utterance (or 'message') 'for its own sake'.[20] The extent to which the formal and stylistic features of works of art occupy the foreground of our attention varies widely, as do the purposes served by what Jakobson terms the aesthetic 'message'. Consequently there is no reason to join the disciples of Jakobson who make the *a priori* assumption that insofar as a work is literary it 'is not about the real world or life, but about itself'.[21] We may not be able to imagine or conceive any unified and perfectly 'real' world; but a literary parable or gospel without significant ontological or referential implications is no parable or gospel as all;[22] and a *Lear* which said or implied nothing about tragic possibilities and realities would not have the particular literary qualities for which Shakespeare's play is most treasured.

There remain three lesser points requiring clarification. First, in some instances the 'artificial' and 'made' aspect of art may derive as much from arrangement and display as from fabrication. Such making is evident in the landscaping of many a cloister and in the very siting of churches such as those on the hilltops at Durham, Vézelay, or Laon, the strategic locations of which doubtless have practical and political advantages as well as aesthetic.

Second, on the basis of our integralist notion of the aesthetic, we can see that what makes something appreciably aesthetic and therefore potentially artistic may not always be anything directly perceived by the senses, though it must have some imaginative appeal. Art today includes such 'pieces' as Robert Rauschenberg's *Erased DeKooning Drawing*, which is just what it says it is; a 'performance' of John Cage's composition entitled *4'33"*, during which the pianist sits before the keyboard for the specified time without playing a note; and Duchamp's notorious *Fountain* – a plain urinal signed 'R. Mutt' and offered for exhibition. In such cases the perceptual objects themselves are not of particular aesthetic interest or informed by artistic know-how; but the gestures, acts, and 'statements' of which they are necessary concomitants may be.[23] Such art, when successful, is not altogether unlike the baffling art of the Zen koan or that of the prophet Ezekiel when he dramatically eats a scroll or lays seige to a miniature brick model he has made of Jerusalem.

Last, we should note that, while anything artistic must in some sense be made knowingly, even if it is meant to include elements of chance, it need not be made with the conscious and express intention of producing an *aesthetic object* or an *aesthetic effect per se*. Otherwise neither Durham Cathedral nor the paleolithic figure dubbed the *Venus of Willendorf* could legitimately be thought of as art, having been made in the absence of any idea directly corresponding to our notion of the aesthetic.

Equipped now with the concepts and definitions of art and artistry that are open to possibilities ranging from aesthetically embodied prophecy or religious vision to aesthetically formed expression and skilful representation, we can examine with greater care some of the basic means by which artistic making can become religiously meaningful. As an intermediate step, we will pause to contemplate one important respect in which much art plainly verges on religion – namely, in its surplus of sense and meaning.

Interlude: The 'More' within Art

In comments addressed to an audience at the Museum of Modern Art in New York, Paul Tillich once asserted: 'The artist brings to our senses and through them to our whole being something of the depth of our world and of ourselves, something of the mystery of being. When we are grasped by a work of art things appear to us which were unknown before – possibilities of being, unthought-of powers, hidden in the depth of life which take hold of us'.[24]

There is reason to doubt that Tillich's claim about the visionary, revelatory capacity of art is equally applicable to all artworks, or was meant to be. Yet Tillich certainly judged it applicable to certain works that he himself had found most meaningful. As chaplain in the trenches during World War I, he took his mind off all the 'mud, blood, and death' by thumbing through magazines available at the field bookstore, some of which contained reproductions of famous works of art that to him were as yet unfamiliar. These he pored over by the light of candle and lantern during lulls in the bitter fighting at places like Verdun. One painting that especially 'comforted' him in battle was Botticelli's *Madonna and Child with Singing Angels* (Plate 2). Shortly after the war had ended, he went to the Kaiser Friedrich Museum in Berlin where he viewed the painting itself for the first time. 'I felt a state approaching ecstasy', he writes:

> In the beauty of the painting there was Beauty itself. It shone through the colors of the paint as the light of day shines through the stained-glass windows of a medieval church.
>
> As I stood there, bathed in the beauty its painter had envisioned so long ago, something of the divine source of all things came through to me. I turned away shaken.

Writing many years later, Tillich declared: 'That moment has affected my whole life, given me the keys for the interpretation of human existence, brought vital joy and spiritual truth'.[25]

This is a large and perhaps extravagant claim. Yet even the sophisticated and worldly-wise Jacques Barzun, in the midst of arguing that 'art is irremediably of this world, not of the next', avers that anyone deeply experienced in art 'will testify from first-hand knowledge that great art has the power of transfiguring the aspect of the world, while also mysteriously recasting in new shapes the substance of the self'. It is enough to gaze at the west front of Chartres Cathedral, he says, 'to know that something unique and unaccountable is acting formatively and beneficially on something within'. Indeed: 'The experience of great art disturbs one like a deep anxiety for another, like a near-escape from death . . . : it is a massive blow from which one recovers slowly and which leaves one changed in ways that only gradually come to light'.[26]

Immediately we are returned to the realm of Kant's 'aesthetic ideas', ideas that allow one to 'think more' than concepts can contain. Clearly we should add, however, that perhaps some art allows one not only to think more but also to feel more, and that in both of these ways together it manages to mean more, possibly even letting one be and become more.

The 'more' in each instance is what Paul Ricoeur has termed a 'surplus'.[27] It is at times analogous to, or actually part of, the surplus that is perceived as transcendence or depth within certain forms of religious experience.[28] Where does it come from? What are the means by which it enters into the makings of art?

What we will attempt to sketch now is a tentative theory, and a framework within which fuller answers to these questions might further be pursued. This we can do best by focusing on the makings – the constituent ingredients – of the work of art and finally on its meanings, especially where and insofar as they might be religious.

The Makings of Art

'The artist brings to our senses . . .' If Tillich had stopped there, he already would have touched on a distinctive ingredient of art. Only the erotic comes near to the aesthetic in the degree to which qualities of sense figure in the 'making more' that is characteristic of its acts and products. Both bring us to our senses, physically speaking, although in the case of literary art this is largely by means of imagination.

Sense is not yet art. In art the sensory is brought into focus, reshaped, and transfigured, becoming ingredient in what Dewey calls 'integral experience'. Theodor Adorno puts it this way: 'In significant works of art the sensuous shines forth as something spiritual, just as, conversely, the spirit of the work may add sensuous brilliance to an individual detail, however indifferent it may be towards appearance'.[29]

To understand how the sensory aspects of art are integral to its meaningful, 'spiritual' aspects, and hence to the 'more' that art can create and become, we need to recognize that sense and 'spirit' are to some extent already interrelated. Whether in architectural design, interior decoration, or a Turner seascape, what is sensed possesses an incipient or latent 'feel', and often an aura or penumbra of meaning. A sensory input, therefore, is not merely a stimulus leading directly to adaptive response or cognitive processing. In the visual domain, for instance, dark blues tend to seem subdued and in some contexts depressed; circles set off-center within rectangles create a disquieting feeling of imbalance. Open spaces tend to be perceived as emotionally expansive; long and dark ones as mysterious. Thus elemental aesthetic qualities are integral to our immediate experience of form and color (and of sound and movement as well).[30] If in art these incipiently 'expressive' qualities typically contribute to expression in a fuller sense, and so begin to engage what Tillich terms our 'whole being', this is in no small measure due to the fact that the very apprehension of such aesthetica already entails more of our being than sheer physiology. What we normally regard as a purely visual or auditory 'feel' is registered integrally, by body and mind together. A jagged, 'nervous' line looks nervous to me and not just to my eyes.[31]

Not all of our most basic aesthetic perceptions, either in life or in art, have to do with the five discrete senses. The aesthetic qualities of temporal passage – its 'tempo' and 'weight' – cannot be located in any one sense or for that matter in any one faculty, such as memory. Within time, moreover, we experience not an undifferentiated flow of unrelated and undirected events but, as Dewey says, a rhythmic pattern that includes more or less complete experiences in which anticipation leads through tension and conflict to some kind of transformation, resolution, and denouement. This too we sense, though not with our five senses; and the sensation is at once heightened and (to use Dewey's word) 'consummated' in temporal arts such as music and drama. In addition, gestalt psychology informs us that in all our perceptual activity we seek and even impose structure: we 'read' biomorphic and theomorphic shapes into the scatterings of stars and forever hear a rhythmic tick-tock in the unvarying tick tick of the clock. Again, however, the discernment of such structure is not a function of any of the five senses *per se*, although it joins with the other senses we have mentioned to constitute an intrinsic part of our aesthetic perception of things and their relations. Without our sense of, and desire for, meaningful patterns and structures, form in art would remain for us essentially insignificant or literally unformed.

Accompanying all this is one's largely unconscious and global 'proprioceptive' sense of the overall coherence and felt unity of the body itself: of the togetherness of its parts, and of their belonging with and to *oneself*. As Oliver Sacks documents in his popular writings, this sense, which is so pervasive that it can hardly be recognized apart from a disease that causes its arrest, is altogether integral to vital and meaningful existence. Indeed, in those rare cases in which a person for years at a stretch cannot feel *one* in body and must make a conscious effort to identify this arm or that leg as his or her own, the result is a pervasive sense of being not only dis-embodied but also dis-spirited, as though one were 'cored', or 'pithed'.[32] Perhaps it is not too conjectural to think that the kinesthetic forms and effects of arts such as dance, sculpture, and music extend and enhance our sense of bodily belonging, and thereby our sense of inspired wholeness.

In any case, it would appear that as art makes either delicate or intense contact with the outer aesthetic fibers of the web of awareness, it can send vibrations through to inner fibers, so to speak, where the sensory and aesthetic connects with a different and more complex kind of sense, which we call meaning or significance. This transition from an essentially nonconceptual aesthetic sense to a larger and more complex sense or meaning is in effect the process whereby the more or less purely aesthetic within art becomes interdependent with, and transformative of, initially non-aesthetic perceptions. Such a process would seem to be essential to the means by which art is able to 'transfigure' some aspect of the world, as Barzun asserts; it also must be why some works of art can, in Tillich's words, bring 'to our whole being something of the depth of our world and of ourselves, something of a mystery of being'.

The thesis that art has the capacity both to transfigure the world's appearance and to engage us 'wholly' will seem grossly inflated, however, unless art's commerce with the bodily, sensory, and affective side of our aesthetic senses can be seen definitely to involve some sort of genuine commerce with thought and reason in particular; for we would scarcely be 'whole' without our rationality, and thought plays some part in any construal of the world. That there is ample basis for such interaction between art and the reflective mind is what we now must try to show, without forgetting also to look for what would make art's mode of interaction distinctive or unique.

Familiar as we now are with certain modern views of art, the possibility will of course occur to us that reason and thought, when called on by art, are simply invited to engage in what Kant terms 'free play'. What else, we might ask, could our rational mind possibly do with a modern dance choreographed by Robert Joffrey or a jazz improvisation by Miles Davis? Even granting that artistic making can be guided partly by intelligence and that some arts obviously are representational, symbolic, and even instructive, it still might be the case that art itself is not directed in a fundamental or distinctive way toward shaping how we conceive of the world and ourselves.

We can, for instance, admire Brueghel's painting *Landscape with the Fall of Icarus* (Musées Royaux des Beaux-Arts, Brussels) without believing that its depiction of the consequences of an act of hubris and of the heedless oblivion of the rest of humanity significantly deepens or modifies our understanding of these things. And Tillich's ascribing revelatory depths to Botticelli's *Madonna and Child with Singing Angels* (Berlin-Dahlem Museum, Berlin) might have no actual effect on his *understanding* of what he supposes has been revealed.

Maybe we take pleasure in making and beholding such pictures chiefly because, as Aristotle says, we are creatures that enjoy *mimesis*. Or, if that is not all there is to it, perhaps their effect nonetheless is quite ineffable and irrational. Wolfgang Iser therefore might be quite right to claim that the work of art provides an experience that constitutes a 'dynamic happening' rather than any sort of explanation. This experience, he asserts, cannot begin to be defined 'in terms of other meanings that one knows' or related to other ideas of the world.[33]

Disputing so radical a separation between the aesthetic and the cognitive or reasonable, we earlier had recourse to a critique and reconstruction of Kant's notions about the power of aesthetic ideas to permit and prompt us to 'think more'; and now we might appeal to the whole tradition in which the words and works of poet and artist are allied with soothsaying and the most penetrating philosophy. But it is not as though Kant or the ancients or we ourselves have explained very satisfactorily how sensory and imaginal embodiments such as those that the arts provide can manage to reflect or affect rationality and understanding. Our theory will rest on firmer grounding, therefore, if it can be shown that embodiment and imagination are from the start involved in the workings even of the rational mind and that rational understanding also asks for imaginative extrapolation and development.

In his recent study *The Body in the Mind*, Mark Johnson has brought the ongoing discussion of these matters to a new and potentially fruitful stage.[34] What Johnson argues is not just that sensory impressions provide raw data necessary for thought and knowledge, which empiricists of all stripes would say. His central claim is that bodily states, processes, and perceptions continually supply the tacit basis for abstract mental operations and for the very meaningfulness of concepts and propositions.

This is not to say that our minds, in depending on our bodily experience, always work with vivid, fully developed imagery. In fact, Johnson notes, 'there is a growing body of experimental evidence in support of the thesis that there is a distinctive image-schematic level of cognitive processing that must be distinguished from rich images or mental picturing'.[35] Schemata active at this level of cognition have traits less vivid than mental pictures but more vivid than abstract concepts and propositions.

Recurrent and aesthetically spare image-schemata such as those of force, balance, and containment can be projected and elaborated from one perceptual modality to another, and hence from the bodily sphere to the social, economic, or philosophical. They seem to function (though Johnson does not explicitly say so) somewhat in the manner of the oval shapes that, marked with a line or two, serve children perfectly well as pictures of fearsome or friendly 'faces', thereby helping them learn to face fears and friends. What counts here is not the precise form and its design but the imaginative acts the image enables: the meanings it helps discover or create. In the case of schemata, this is accomplished through a metaphoric process. Applying a schema of bodily equilibrium, one could think or recognize: 'I must weigh the gains against the losses'; 'That is a dizzying prospect'; or 'Justice necessarily seeks a balance between the rights of the few and the needs of the many'.

Metaphorically projected in this way, schemata allow us to have a world, a whole whose parts are understood and felt to be related.[36] This is a world the fullest understanding of which involves not just intellect and empirical reasoning in a narrow sense but, rather, *'our whole being* – our bodily capacities and skills, our values, our moods and attitudes, our entire cultural tradition, . . . our aesthetic sensibilities, and so forth'. In relation to such a world, meaning and meaningfulness have ultimately to do with something as broad as 'the meaning of someone's life'.[37]

If we are hoping that Johnson himself will go on to say how or whether understanding at its most encompassing might depend on specifically artistic embodiments that engage our 'whole being', we are bound to be disappointed. For at just this point there is a large lacuna in his theory. Openly indebted to Kant's notions about imagination, Johnson fastens onto the famous statements about the power of aesthetic ideas to provoke us into 'thinking more'. Yet Johnson judges that the chief reason why aesthetic ideas can evoke 'more' from thought is simply that they metaphorically project and elaborate image-schemata. One recalls, however, that image-schemata are no more than minimally aesthetic. And the same can be said of the metaphors that Johnson favors in his examples – half-dead figures like 'time is money' and 'we must weigh our losses'. If we need nothing more than such schemata and metaphors in order to obtain the fullest possible understanding and to have a meaningful life and world, then art as such must mainly be needed or wanted for something else.

Doubtless we do need and want art for other things; but if we supplement Johnson's theory with a few insights drawn from another philosopher of imagination, we may discover a vantage point from which to see how art can contribute to understanding as well, and in fact to a kind of understanding intrinsically valuable to religious life and reflection.

In recent years Mary Warnock has attempted to reaffirm the thesis, dear to the Romantics among others, that there is an intimate connection between reason and the emotions, and between both of these and imagination, religious and aesthetic.[38] This has led her to the following conclusion regarding imagination:

> There is a power in the human mind which is at work in our everyday perception of the world, and is also at work in our thoughts about what is absent; which enables us to see the world, whether present or absent as significant, and also to present this vision to others, for them to share or reject. And this power, though it gives us 'thought-imbued' perception (it 'keeps the thought alive in the perception'), is not only intellectual. Its impetus comes from the emotions as much as from the reason, from the heart as much as from the head.[39]

If philosophy begins in wonder, as Aristotle said, then this aspect of imagination is one of the wonders with which it might do well to begin again, and at this very point. Warnock is as aware as anyone that the terminology she has no choice but to use is in many ways unsatisfactory. Talk of 'heart' and 'head' borders on cliché and suffers from imprecision. Dividing up mentality and life into 'reason', 'emotion', 'imagination', and so forth likewise leaves much to be desired, falsely implying that these are quite distinct faculties, which is something Warnock's theory explicitly denies. Yet the unavoidable crudeness of the language need not obscure the main point of wonder, which is that what comes to us in one form of experience or mode of thought is related to what comes to us in another – perhaps something only fictive or hypothetical – and that through imagination we can make of these things something more: new relations and new meanings having shareable 'significance' that, partly in being experienced intersubjectively, seems not so much made up as discovered or revealed.

In her accounts of imagination Warnock does not attempt to develop a theory of body and meaning as Johnson does. Yet she includes in imaginative construction what Johnson for the most part omits: art and religion. She also, and by no means accidentally, includes 'significance' and emotion (or feeling), which Johnson both needs and slights. What is important about feeling in this context is that if there is to be anything like 'significance' or what Johnson calls 'meaningfulness', and if that meaningfulness is to be understood, then it must at the same time be felt. One cannot find something – and especially something like 'life' – meaningful without feeling it to be so. Without the presence or possibility of feeling, moreover, there can be no art, or indeed religion; for these depend on our having or wanting a world in which something matters; and, apart from feeling, there is no 'mattering'.

Coming back to the issue of art and the question of its makings, we now can say that what art makes of both bodily and rational sense is, at a minimum, something that is felt to matter. In art, moreover, that which is felt to matter is understood and valued intersubjectively. At least potentially it is made communal 'property', and indeed a kind of gift. Far more than the private perceptions of ordinary life or the often incoherent forms of civic and public interchange – and with far greater skill and understanding than the usual efforts at expression – the forms of art make palpably and imaginatively available to us moments and emblems of appreciable life. They provide signs and embodiments of dimensions of human feeling and thought that understanding must in some way acknowledge and grasp – schematically, conceptually, and imaginatively – if it is to make an adequate accounting of the world we ourselves find most meaningful to comprehend.

Clearly Warnock's and Johnson's studies, as well as the theories we have presented on our own, indicate that there is no contradiction in linking thought to the highly concrete sensory and imaginal aspect of the aesthetic in art, or in life either. Thought is already found within the milieu of perception; and, if the drift of Johnson's argument is right, thought itself can be meaningful and inquisitive only as it continually relies on graphic translations of our elemental sensory and bodily awarenesses.

Image-schemata, in any case, are shared by both art and abstract thought. Art builds on these schemata metaphorically and imaginatively by constructing complex and subtle surfaces, forms, and fictions never before experienced exactly in this way, or known previously to the body itself. Reason, for its part, moves beyond image-schemata by building intellectual structures exhibiting a kind of precision, logic, and critical acumen for which full embodiment would be both unnecessary and impossible. Yet art cannot elaborate genuinely meaningful forms or imaginary worlds, let alone worlds and meanings that are felt to matter, without drawing on reason's powers, and on more of reason than schemata themselves can contain or the body alone can give. Analogously, reason cannot adequately ponder or conceive the world that human beings experience 'wholly', and that they most want to understand philosophically or religiously, without drawing on a more replete and refined aesthetic rendering of the qualities of experience than schemata transmit and than body and sense consistently present. Accordingly, it would seem that by and large aesthetic/artistic construals and constructions of our world(s) exist in dialogical relation to the constructs of conceptual and propositional thought. The element of overt play, fiction, and fantasy is of course higher in the aesthetic mode than in the conceptual (whether philosophical or theological). And, happily, not all art is especially thought-provoking. Nevertheless, where art in general appears to differ most from abstract thought is not in some total lack of concern for either reflection or truth but rather in the degree to which it has us think by means of aesthetically rich images, forms, and representations.

It is true that art is not the only sphere in which thought combines with aesthetic perception. In some measure this constantly occurs in daily life; and scientists and mathematicians not infrequently testify to an aesthetic component within their own thought. What is exceptional about art is the extent to which, at the same time that the sensory and imaginal is focused on and even gloried in, the deeply felt and keenly pondered elements of body and mind all can be drawn into the artwork's aesthetic milieu.

As we have begun to see, the mind has much to gain by this. So perhaps does the body, and even the 'heart', the seat of thoughtful affection and effective will that Warnock says we cannot forget. We will describe more fully why and how this is so in the last section of this chapter, where we also will try to fill out our explanation of how art, in mattering to us 'wholly', can do so specifically in ways that are of significance to religion.

For the sake of convenience and clarity, our discussion of these topics will center on a description of three different means by which art as defined in this study generally engages '*body*, *mind*, and *heart*', and through these something that might in religious terms be called the integral '*soul*'. Many of the points we will make along the way, especially regarding artistic expression and representation, will be fleshed out in the subsequent chapter, where we will consider not so much the commonality as the variety within art's ways of being religious and, indeed, Christian.

Artistic Imagination and Religious Meaning

Apparently it is important to the ways in which art can matter religiously that for the most part, as T. S. Eliot says, 'the author of a work of imagination is trying to affect us wholly, as human beings, whether he knows it or not; and we are affected by it, as human beings, whether we intend to be or not'.[40] Within the Jewish and Christian traditions, at least, one is commanded to love God with all of one's heart, soul, mind, and strength, and to love one's neighbor as oneself. It is not difficult to see that within this framework artistic imagination would have a special capacity for religious meaning due to its ability to touch one 'wholly'. In doing so it could affect the relation of heart, soul, and mind to the vital elements – human, natural, and divine – of what one regards as an ultimately meaningful Whole. This is true, moreover, even if post-modern theorists are correct in claiming that the self (or soul) as a whole, along with the very idea of an ultimately meaningful Whole beyond the self, is a kind of fiction; for it is this 'fiction' that certain forms of religion use in order to motivate loving relations and to undermine fictions they consider truly dangerous, such as the delusory denial that we are in fact responsible beings whose life is a gift and whose very existence is in relation.

To speak at all of religious and artistic meaning is admittedly to put a certain strain on language and thought. The words 'meaning' and 'meaningful' are notoriously difficult to pin down, and especially so in matters of art and religion. In the wake of the work of analytic philosophers like Wittgenstein, Ryle, Austin, Quine, and Searle, it is clear, however, that meaning generally has a great deal to do not just with the sense and reference of signs and symbols but also with their use and with the actions they perform. And everyone will agree that meaning of every kind pertains to relations. Something has meaning only in relation to something else and for someone. A meaning that is intended or 'given' must somehow be embodied or encoded in a perceptible form if it is to be received or 'taken'; and it will be 'taken', received, or realized by some person or group only when the elements of the embodiment or code are understood, along with the way the embodied form or code is being used. Such understanding usually depends on at least minimal cognizance of the social and historical context of the maker/sender, and inevitably is influenced as well by the situation and pre-understandings of the respondent/receiver. All this is involved in the making of meaning, the act of making out the meaning, and finally the act of evaluating what to make of the meaning.[41]

To the foregoing observations about meaning – observations relevant to later phases of our study as well as to the present – the theologian needs to add that from a Christian perspective the relations and meanings that in the end matter most have primarily to do with self and others, God and world. These meanings cannot completely be identified or realized apart from linguistic expression and symbolic embodiment. Yet they have a kind of significance beyond what can plainly be said or precisely conceived. If Tillich is right, they are most meaningfully discerned and enacted through the activity and receptivity of one's 'whole being' (inasmuch as one can ever be whole), which is the being and becoming of the integral 'soul'.

This returns us to the topic of art, since it suggests that, given the overall nature of artistic expression and of the concerns basic to religious meaning, religion may have no option but to become in part aesthetic and artistic. Among our symbolic and expressive forms, those that are markedly artistic seem best able to affect us in the totality of our being.

Nevertheless, to establish that art actually can be religious, we must do more than show merely that it can affect us wholly. One might, after all, express or apprehend something with one's whole being that was wholly antithetical or wholly antagonistic to anything religious or to the particular religion one would want to embrace. Some further criterion is needed to determine that art typically or even occasionally has religious import. Using the Christian tradition and its theology as our primary frame of reference, we will feel some confidence that we have located religious meaning within an aspect of art if this aspect can be shown to be positively connected with what Christians regard as ultimately meaningful, and hence meaningful with respect to relations deemed ultimately significant to and before God; and certainly if it can be apprehended and appreciated in terms of the particular identity and values of the Christian tradition in its major manifestations.

With these clarifications in mind, we are prepared to consider more carefully the ways in which art as we have defined and conceived it characteristically addresses and engages us in such a fashion as to have potential for religious meaning. Three clusters of artistic traits will be of particular interest here: (1) that art is made in such a way as to be appreciably aesthetic and often beautiful; (2) that it is made skilfully, knowledgeably, and creatively by human agents; and (3) that it is made in forms that can express, fictively represent, and imaginatively transform 'worlds' in a revelatory or prophetic way. With respect to each of these features of art, we will spell out how the relevant traits address and engage what we will figuratively speak of as *body*, *mind*, and *'heart'* – understood here as distinguishable but inseparable 'parts' or functions of the self. And in the same context we will indicate how each cluster of artistic traits can matter religiously, affecting the well-being of the *'soul'*, or the self as a whole, and the life of the soul's religious community.

First, then, let us consider the fact that art is to a notable extent directly and appreciably aesthetic, with qualities that interest and delight in one's very perception of them. When Tillich speaks of his response to the Botticelli *Madonna and Child with Singing Angels*, his words indicate that he is struck by beauty that, as others would say, is its own excuse for being. In such art the beautifully integrated qualities of line, color, proportion, luminosity, and balance relate to the viewer's own bodily sense of balance, integrity, and well being (or possibly the lack thereof). Thus the work's relatively pure aesthetic elements undoubtedly are linked to the sorts of image-schemata that Johnson says our minds use to translate the body's awareness of dynamic forms and relations into rational understandings. In responding to art, however, the body/mind apprehends far more than image-schemata alone can mediate or graphically interpret.

The *body* benefits from this encounter with aesthetic embodiment by finding in the work of art an extension and evocation of its own capacities, pleasures, and sensibilities. The artwork's sensuous and innately expressive qualities encourage one, in fact, to relate to the work itself less as an object than as a figurative body, close attention to which heightens the actual body's sensitivity and sense of vitality, thereby creating a kind of bodily ecstasy that exceeds the bounds of ordinary physical sense and sensation, just as the imagined and artificial world of the artwork typically exceeds the bounds of the real as charted in existing language and thought.

The rational *mind* benefits as well because anything that heightens the body's awareness and the acuity of its perceptions either generates more subtle and adequate schemata or interprets them more fully, thereby increasing the facility and adequacy of understanding. Moreover, as the mind contemplates the intrinsically appreciable and innately expressive qualities of art, it is pushed up against what is not rational and sometimes not even meaningful: the 'simply itself' that appears in the most purely aesthetic moment and in the radiance of the sensory. The presence of this dimension of art generates a mysterious ambiguity and depth within whatever is artistically meaningful. This tends to disturb prefabricated order and pre-established meaning, and thereby to push reason both to transcend itself and acknowledge its own limits.

Finally the *'heart'*, or the union of 'affect' and 'will', gains from the sheerly aesthetic in art by enjoying something that it wills only to be as it is and that nonetheless enriches the heart's own feeling through a range and complexity of expression rarely found in daily life. Through art something new to feeling is immediately generated, even though this also may bring about a discovery of a feeling that had been suppressed or forgotten. The young person listening to Prokofiev's *Peter and the Wolf* will often feel unspeakable terror at the deep and omininous sound of the horns even before realizing that they are the WOLF; and while this is a terror that is strangely familiar, it also is indeed strange, and different from anything else.

In so wholly involving us, even these relatively pure aesthetic qualities potentially matter religiously to the *'soul'* and its religious community, or specifically the Church. This is evident in several ways. To begin with, Christian theologians have always respected the power of aesthetic forms to move the heart and will, the recalcitrance of which is regarded as a major stumbling block to the soul's cooperating with the will of God. Moreover, there is the ancient idea that beauty in particular is at least analogously divine, which gives the arts of the purely beautiful a kind of divine right to exist. Even were that not true, it would appear that aesthetic excellence is one of the goods to be faithfully treasured by human beings, and in fact gratefully enjoyed as part of the earthly *shalom* ordained for them by God.[42] A beautiful secular work such as a pastoral landscape by Claude Lorrain can therefore be received by a Christian as a delight both earthly and blessed – a remnant of the original goodness of the created order and a foretaste of the final beatitude for which Christians wait and hope.[43] Finally, since the whole of a work of art can be good or beautiful in spite of passages of ugliness or even horror, the Christian can find even within purely aesthetic form an image and token of Atonement and

Salvation, which many theologians would say constitute in part God's recreation of the good possibilities within the fallen and fragmented order of creation.[44]

Specifically within the soul's community known as the Church, the God-given goodness of even the beautifully sensory and purely aesthetic aspect of art means, for example, that a piece of aesthetically excellent but ostensibly secular instrumental music, if not indelibly associated with trivial or ungodly things, can have a rightful place in a service of worship. Such music's beauty can be received as a gracious gift; and the more-than-rational aesthetic order of the music can unsettle all merely finite calculation and determinate meaning, appearing as a sign and sound of mystery that finally is beyond comprehension. At times, indeed, it may function sacramentally – as an outward and visible sign of an inward and spiritual grace.

None of this is to deny that, like every other good, aesthetic excellence is subject to abuse that is harmful to the soul and its corporate life. If severed from its place in right relations and if sought as a substitute for that which grounds all meanings and goods, sheerly aesthetic delight becomes (as Augustine would be quick to point out) a form of cupidity: an aestheticism that corresponds to gluttony and carnality in the realm of the appetites. This may be especially apparent within the context of the life of the Church, where one also must reckon with the reality that not all religiously moving and aesthetically appealing art is equally good in church, and not every work potentially good for church use is also good for every liturgical season or service, or with every other kind of art so used. That is to say, because Christian liturgy has an aesthetic order of its own, the incorporation of works of art into the liturgy is itself an art the malpractice of which can be spiritually as well as aesthetically harmful.

We want now to consider the second cluster of artistic features, which have to do with the fact that art's appreciably aesthetic qualities are intimately associated with making and artifice, and so with human knowledge, skill, and creativity. What this means is that the fabric and fabrication of art inevitably are interwoven with human purposes and with culture as a whole. Unlike the driftwood found on the beach, the work of art as human sign and act manifests aesthetically what in most of our experience is manifest by human beings themselves: feelings, meanings, and understandings. Artistry, moreover, employs devices encountered in human life at large: fictions and fantasies, images and stories, gestures and ideas. All of these, regardless of content, in some way exhibit humanity and reflect human abilities.

For the *body* as such, the fact that the work is humanly produced and is implicitly 'humane' itself means that the artistic embodiment to which the body so immediately responds has a presence rather like that of a person. And since the personal embodiment in art is not one's own, the body's response is more than merely narcissistic.

Just as the work of art is experienced by the body as a figurative body, so – because it is understood as the product of knowledge, skill, and creativity – it is experienced by the *mind* as a figurative mind. In art, furthermore, the community of mind is extended because through the work one indirectly meets not only the mentality of some one person but also, since no person is an isolated entity, the mentality of a whole culture whose values and ideas are reflected and in some degree created in the knowledgeably made work. Given that ideas themselves cannot fully be understood apart from their cultural and experiential matrix, such an artistic extension and sharing of mind is of incalculable value to the quality of reflection itself. At the same time it generates a genuine sense of wonder before human capacities and skills.

For the '*heart*', meanwhile, the fact that art is a human product means that the feelings it finds expressed there are not ones it simply puts there itself, reading them into the form. It is appropriate that, on the first page of the score of Beethoven's great *Missa Solemnis* in D Major, the composer wrote: 'From the heart – may it go again to the heart'. Recent criticism reminds us, to be sure, that what one finds as human presence in art is also an alluring and deceptive sort of absence. And what is therein given and made present may make its own surreptitious demands. Yet to ignore the dimension of human presence and intention in art, as some critics advise, would be to sever the tenuous but heart-felt sense of mutual belonging (and mutual strife) that art makes possible.

It is not hard to see that, quite apart from their connection with skill and creativity, the humanity and intentionality of art could be religiously meaningful, and hence meaningful to the '*soul*'. Certainly it is clear from Tillich's description of his profoundly religious response to the *Madonna and Child with Singing Angels* that he is keenly aware of this painting as a product of human making; for he refers to its beauty as something 'its painter had envisioned so long ago'. Yet the skill of the maker is not in itself what is foremost in his mind. This becomes evident when Tillich goes on to compare the beauty of the painting to that of the stained glass in a medieval church. By associating the Renaissance painting with the art of the Church in ages past, Tillich finds himself, in a moment of intense privacy, related nonetheless to humanity across the centuries and indeed to the community of saints. Extrapolating from this and similar experiences, the theologian can say that the arts on the whole engender a moral sense of relation within the human community, fragmentary and strained though it may be. And the Church's own arts help create and sustain the Church itself – the ecclesia or assembly that sees itself also as the body of Christ.

Naturally this feature of art also has its negative side. The same artistic powers that can serve to unite us within and through our diversity are susceptible to being used to symbolize and reinforce divisions not only of church but also of clan, class, gender, and power. Art as we know it exists in the world after the Fall and, more particularly, after Babel. Its restorative powers depend on grace as well as on works.

We have already said, moreover, that the traits associated with art's 'humanity' are simultaneously related to distinctly human accomplishment: that is, with know-how and creativity. And since Christians as a whole are skeptical about the efficacy of strictly human works, it might appear that there would be little in this regard to edify the soul, individually or in community. Humanists might indeed rejoice in powers of the human maker; but can these be affirmed theologically?

It is true that when art becomes purely a virtuosic display, it has little to commend it religiously or morally; but then it also is weak as art. It is true as well that, especially since the Renaissance, our keen awareness of the glories of artistic creativity and skill has resulted in recurrent cults of the artist and genius, which amount to a kind of apotheosis of the human creator. Not surprisingly artists themselves, including great artists like Picasso, sometimes have encouraged such idolatry. Even so, the Christian theologian need not be embarrassed to say outright that skilful and know-ledgeable artistic making in principle is morally and religiously good, exemplifying an important feature of humanity's having been made in the image of God. Indeed such creativity, though secondary and by no means *ex nihilo*, may provide one of our clearest glimpses into the kind of creativity Christians can rightly attribute to God. Especially might this be true if we follow process theology in interpreting God's creative activity as both essential to the nature of God and yet restricted by the limitations of the materials with which God has to work at any given moment in history.

In looking at the traits of art connected first with its being aesthetic in nature and second with its being humanly, creatively, and skilfully made, we have found several major ways in which art affects us in body, mind, and heart and becomes religiously significant for the whole soul and its religious community. We need, last, to locate the religious implications of the fact that imaginative art has powers that sometimes are experienced by the whole self as visionary, revelatory, or prophetic.

We can start by recalling that the 'realities' of art include those that, as Warnock notes, would appear to our physical senses to be entirely absent from the work itself. As one listens to Bach's Goldberg Variations, all that the ear as sensory organ hears is sound. But what the imagination hears in the sound, and what it hears the sound *as*, is more than sound. It has shape and organization, movement and direction, vitality and purpose. Again, even the abstract forms and the felt qualities of each variation – the serene gracefulness of the opening 'Aria' and the muscular vigor of the fifteenth, canonical variation – are in a sense fictive. They are made up, or rather made out of, what the ear discerns. But what they are made into is something more, and more significant.

Quite often, in fact, the work of art seems to comprise or gather into itself a kind of world, both like and unlike our own.[45] Writing of the last movement of J. S. Bach's Partita II in D Minor for solo violin, Johannes Brahms declares: 'The *Chaconne* is for me one of the most wonderful, unfathomable pieces of music. On one stave, for a small instrument, the man writes a whole world of the deepest thoughts and most powerful feelings'.[46] Similarly, on the frontispiece of his edition of the Goldberg Variations, Ralph Kirkpatrick places the following quotation:

There is something in it of Divinity more than the ear discovers: it is an Hieroglyphical and shadowed lesson of the whole World, and creatures of God; such a melody to the ear, as the whole World, well understood, would afford the understanding. In brief, it is a sensible fit of that harmony which intellectually sounds in the ears of God.

These are, of course, the very words of Sir Thomas Browne that we have had occasion to quote before. What we want now to notice is that, as these quotations both suggest, a work that we might encounter as a figure of the body or of the human mind and heart can also body forth something that metaphorically stands as a cosmos – sometimes, indeed, as a sacred cosmos, and thus as what the body, mind, and heart together as 'soul' could sense, know, and love, were they indeed made in the image of a god who is able at will to invent worlds and become incarnate in them. Such art comes as a vision and perhaps revelation, its artifices and fictions revealing what may strike us as real but virtually unsayable features of our own world, with its mysterious order and inescapable disorder; with its created order and lurking chaos.

This artistic capacity to envision, and in vision to transfigure this world or some hypothetical counterpart, evidently responds uniquely to an abiding human need. That is the need to discover, imagine, and come to grips with a world that can be thought and felt to matter, both in its goodness and beauty and in its evil and horror. The fact that art can in various ways address this need is one thing that distinguishes it from mere play or sport, which even at their most exciting and involving are rarely said to be deeply meaningful or revealing. Art, too, has its games, thrills, and spectacles. Art, too, provides moments of sheer escape from a life that threatens to become unbearably hard or abusively boring. But we need art for more than that. Precisely because we are embodied, thinking, passionate beings who want meaning and meaningfulness, truth and emotional satisfaction, we cannot be engaged wholly except through forms that imaginatively encompass and orient us within something like a world: something, moreover, as purposeful in its apparent purposelessness as we hope and trust life itself can be.

The *body* gains from artistic world-making because it is partly through the fiction of a world and its embodiment that the body itself is able to speak to the mind of which it is a part and which it partly transcends. The world of the body, in short, is mediated in part by the worlds of art, which become the body's self-disclosure.

The *mind* gains from art's imagined worlds because, although they prompt it to 'think more', its thinking does not exhaust them.

Because the worlds of art represent things felt to matter (even while distanced from immediate concerns) and amounting to more than what is strictly logical, quantifiable, and measurable, the mind that thinks through the alternate worlds of works of art reconsiders even this present world in terms of qualities and values and purposes. If the mind's processes of reasoning remain as before, the sense of things with which they begin and to which they finally must appeal is changed. In addition the blurring of the lines of distinction between real and unreal in art causes the mind to re-examine its assumptions about what makes for reality and unreality. In all these ways the artistic affects and expands our sense of truth itself, giving rise to what Kant calls 'thinking more'.

From this the *heart* itself benefits; for the worlds it is given in art are ones to which willing and feeling belong. Where the worlds of art and of actuality converge, and yet in converging do not conform to the heart's desire, there it becomes the heart's will to transform or be transformed. Art then can become prophetic in mode, showing what is unjust or senseless, and possibly what is required in response. In this way as in others, art potentially can render, in Barzun's words, a 'massive blow' that 'leaves one changed'. For the heart, the world of the prophetic work is morally or politically or perhaps religiously charged.

Because a world so charged is the sort of world that one enters or inhabits religiously, we can conclude that the worlds of artistic imagination can at times serve to reveal the realities significant to religion and *soul*. Nothing less is implied in Tillich's assertion that through the beauty of the Botticelli painting 'something of the divine source of all things' came through to him, and in a way that affected his whole life. If the theologian objects to anyone's making such a claim with respect to art, arguing instead that it is God and not art that reveals, then there are two counter-arguments that theological aesthetics might make. First, since Scripture is counted by most Christians as in some way revealed, and since a significant portion of Scripture is artistic, then it follows that art can play a part in divine revelation. Second, it seems plain that however illuminated the human mind may be by what some theologians term 'special' revelation, one still is human and usually responds most fully to those media that speak most vividly to the human being as a whole. And since nothing – even if revealed – is meaningful unless discerned and in some way understood, it makes sense that the meaning even of 'special' revelation should be mediated in part by aesthetic and artistic forms that can engage one wholly.

Our discussion of the visionary and prophetic dimension of the arts indicates that, like religion as a whole, art is widely engaged in the transformation of life and world and, indirectly, of what we have referred to as the embodied soul. Even if one concludes that the world revealed and envisioned through the deepest works of artistic imagination is the world that somehow or in some way was there all along, one nevertheless must recognize that it was not already there in just that way for oneself or for the human community. Mimesis in art is always in some degree metamorphosis. From this it follows that through artistic imagination and metaphoric representation our human world and religion itself undergo continual transformation and reformation. While what the Church terms the 'Word of God' calls into question the absolute validity of any human expression and vision, there is no reason why that 'Word' cannot sound – and in a distinctive tone – in the prophetic, visionary, and revelatory artistic expressions found within the community of Christian faith. It also may sound from without. The art that has the greatest religious significance is not necessarily the art of institutional religion but rather that art which happens to discern what religion in its institutional or personal forms needs most to see.

What we have ended up claiming, then, is that at points religion takes the form of art, and art the form of religion; that whatever is considered ultimate in being and meaning can speak through both forms, and can call both into question; and, finally, that even outside the realm of formal religion, art in the various aspects we have discussed can become religiously significant, though without some of the meanings supplied by the institutional religious milieu. Through many such arts the health and wholeness of the self and of the human community come into question; yet they also come into a condition of new possibility.

Having established the general potential of art and artistry for becoming religiously meaningful, we next will try to describe more adequately the conditions under which this can occur. After looking more closely at the nature of religion *per se*, we will give special consideration to the different ways in which aesthetica express and partially create the variety within religious experience.

5

Varieties of Religious Aesthetic Experience

Religion and its Varieties

Just as most societies throughout history have managed to produce and appreciate artistic and aesthetic things without any concepts closely corresponding to our modern ideas of fine art and aesthetic experience, so have they managed to practise religion without making use of the equally modern idea of religion as such – that is, the idea of religion as a general phenomenon that takes particular forms. Religion in this sense is, as recent writers have stressed, a 'child of the Enlightenment' conceived in the scholar's study.[1] Moreover, religion so conceived is not itself the object of devotion and faith. When following a particular religious path, even the self-consciously religious person is not seeking some sort of generic religious experience any more than a connoisseur looking at Donatello's *David* is in search of aesthetic experience in general.

We need not conclude from this, as some scholars do, that by and large we would be better off not to talk about 'religion' and 'religions'.[2] The abstract concept of religion, like that of art, helps one to place, comprehend, and attend appropriately to distinctive kinds of objects, processes, and experiences. Yet, like the term 'art', the term 'religion' applies to a wide range of heterogeneous phenomena and so resists neat and precise definition. Most scholars now realize that the uniquely modern search for the one true essence of religion is misguided. Some of what we call religions emphasize belief, others emphasize practice; some are theistic or indeed polytheistic, others are indifferent to the gods; some pursue immortality, others earthly prosperity; some seek mystical union, others spiritual communion; some are inclined to be theoretical, others to be ethical; some stress values or acts that are personal and solitary, others stress ones that are corporate and social; some religions are hierarchical, others egalitarian; some worry about guilt, others about shame; some concentrate on salvation, others on 'etiquette' and right relations. The extent of this variety is so great as to be almost impossible fully to take into account; even William James in his classic study *The Varieties of Religious Experience* (1902) ends up discussing mainly varieties of personal spirituality, and of these mostly the Western, modern, and vaguely mystical. It could be argued, in fact, that the varieties of religious experience are as many as the varieties of religious expression.

Nevertheless, as we also found in the case of art, we do discover family resemblances and recurrent patterns among the various things we regularly describe as 'religious'. On the basis of these resemblances and patterns we can venture a general characterization of religion for which we can claim relative adequacy: On the whole religion is concerned with living life well, in its totality; and religions in various ways not only project a vision of what 'living well' means but also recognize that life overall, and in various particulars, tends to fall short of well-being and well-doing. Consequently religions are in the business of transformation and rectification. To that end they provide special kinds of communities and leadership, and often they affect the shape and direction not just of individual lives but also of society at large. By means of sacred stories, symbols, doctrines, and rituals, religions convey a sense of what matters most in life and in the cosmos as a whole; and by celebrating and recalling exemplary lives and thoughts of saints and sages they promote specific actions and attitudes among their followers. In all this they characteristically invoke the necessary aid of – and evoke the praise and honor to be rendered to – certain undergirding or overarching powers and realities that go beyond anything that immediately meets the senses or that can entirely be figured out. These powers and realities are regarded as mysterious, numinous, or divine; as awe-inspiring, holy, or sacred.

Moving from the level of general characterization to the level of a quasi-formal or 'working' definition we can say that with respect to its experiential dimension, religion constitutes the individual's and group's total response to what is apprehended as the sacred or transcendent realities, or reality, on which we and our world ultimately depend.[3] Second, with respect to its structure and function, religion can be said to constitute what Clifford Geertz terms a cultural and symbolic system that 'tunes human actions to an envisaged cosmic order and projects images of cosmic order onto the plane of human experience',[4] in the hope that life can be made bearable, responsible, and meaningful. Again we must stipulate, however, that for an envisioned order to function *religiously* it must be seen as somehow sacred or holy, or as otherwise transcending the merely mundane.[5]

What we have been proposing, then, is a pluralistic, integralist, and non-purist understanding of religion and religious experience. Such an understanding not only accords with, but also is positively required by, the integralist understanding of aesthetica, art, and imagination for which we have been arguing all along.

By rejecting religious as well as aesthetic purism we can persist in taking seriously the idea that part of religious experience simply *is* a kind of artistic and aesthetic experience. If in various Hindu traditions, for instance, Lord Krishna is said to dwell wherever his devotees sing,[6] then we need not regard such singing merely as an outward expression of something 'more important', such as belief. We also can take at face value the observation that the central act of much popular Hindu worship is seeing – and being 'seen' by – the image of the deity present in the sanctum of the temple, often at times of day when it is beautifully adorned with fresh flowers and when the curtain is drawn back to allow the image to be fully visible.[7] Unlike the religious purist, we feel no necessity to treat such a sight as just a *token* or *illustration* of genuine devotion. While religious singing and seeing always exist in relation to other dimensions of religion, they too really are part of religion, and potentially as much of religion as anything else is.

This means, however, that we cannot feel satisfied with the seemingly unexceptional assertion that, in the words of a recent author, 'religion and art have been related to each other for a long time'.[8] If one holds that in part religion is art, and art partly religion, such a statement seems misleading; for the part of art that is religion is not something one can say is *related to* religion. This is like saying that between my daughter and my family there is a relation. A family consists in relations between its members; but the related members are not *related to* the family; they *compose* the family. So too does art in various forms combine with much that is not art to compose the family of phenomena we call religion.

If a significant part of art and aesthetica is a significant part of religion, and if religion and art both are varied in expression and experience, then the immense variety within religiously significant art and aesthetica is likely to constitute a significant part of the variety within religion.[9] At the same time, given that aesthetic experience even in its multiple religious modes has its own qualities that cannot entirely be reduced to or translated into other modalities, it would appear that certain varieties of *religious* experience can only be registered through acquaintance with certain varieties of *aesthetic* experience. And since religious aesthetic experience enters the shareable world only through modes of expression, it is in fact both the expression and the experience of religion in its aesthetic varieties that now will be our concern.

Although once again we must restrict our discussion to the Christian tradition, at least it can be said that this tradition as a whole has never been accused of lacking variety. Indeed, so great is its variety that we will only be able to hint at the range of aesthetic expression that is in keeping with various aspects of the tradition. Even so, it now will be possible for us to explain to ourselves with somewhat greater precision what it means for one religious tradition – one 'variety' of religion – to be in itself variously expressed by aesthetic means. First, however, we must confront the fact that frequently it is not variety that leaps to mind when people think of Christian aesthetic values; it is monotony – a monotonously pristine, ethereal, 'angelic', or perhaps even ascetic approach to aesthetic expression. We therefore begin with several observations about this way of picturing Christian aesthetic expression and aesthetic experience (aesthesis).

Imagining Christianity Aesthetically

One of the most highly regarded dance critics of the nineteenth century, Théophile Gautier, once contrasted two dancers in the following way:

> Mlle Taglioni is a Christian dancer, if one may make use of such an expression in regard to an art proscribed by the Catholic faith: she flies like a spirit in the midst of transparent clouds of white muslin with which she loves to surround herself; she resembles a happy angel who scarcely bends the petals of celestial flowers with the tips of her pink toes. Fanny [Elssler] is a quite pagan dancer; she reminds one of the muse Terpsichore, tambourine in hand, her tunic, exposing her thigh, caught up with a golden clasp; when she bends freely from her hips, throwing back her

swooning, voluptuous arms, we seem to see one of those
beautiful figures from Herculaneum or Pompeii. . . .[10]

It is interesting to set alongside this characterization of a 'Christian'
versus a 'pagan' style the complaints that John of Salisbury,
writing in the twelfth century, lodged against what he clearly took
to be an unchristian style of singing in Christian worship:

Music [now] sullies the Divine Service, for in the very sight of
God, in the sacred recesses of the sanctuary itself, the singers
attempt, with the lewdness of a lascivious singing voice and a
singularly foppish manner, to feminize all their spellbound little
followers with the girlish way they render the notes and end the
phrases. . . . Indeed, such is their glibness in running up and
down the scale . . . – [and] to such an extent are the high or even
the highest notes mixed together with the low or lowest ones –
that the ears are almost completely divested of their critical
power, and the intellect, which pleasurableness of so much
sweetness has caressed insensate, is impotent to judge the
merits of the things heard. Indeed, when such practices go too
far, they can more easily occasion titillation between the legs
than a sense of devotion in the brain.[11]

Even allowing for the likelihood that various issues are being
addressed and possibly confused in this condemnation of a manner of singing, it is clear that John of Salisbury shares at least one
major assumption in common with Gautier and countless other
people – the assumption that properly Christian aesthetic expression has to do with what is 'higher' and indeed transcendent and
therefore cannot or should not appeal too much to feelings that are
emphatically bodily and particularly sexual.

'Transcendence', in the sense of something far different from
what ordinarily is experienced as real or possible, is indeed a major
Christian motif, being especially ascribed to God. Moreover, because transcendence when translated into experience always entails a change in perception and in the perceiver, it gives rise to the
companion motif of transformation, or conversion. The ethereal-
ized spirituality or 'angelism' implicit in the views of Christianity
just now cited, however, gives us but one rendition of these
Christian themes. Our aim now is to show something of the
genuine variety within Christian aesthetic experience by analyzing

in the next two sections four different forms of the aesthetic expression of divine transcendence and then, finally, various ways in which from a Christian perspective aesthetic experience appears to be involved in human transformation. This will enable us to see how aesthetic expressions and perceptions contribute to the kind of variety in religious experience that is both common to Christian life and practice in general and also generative and symptomatic of sectarian differences.

Christian Aesthesis and Divine Transcendence (1)

To transcend is literally to climb across – not to ascend or descend, but to cross over and go beyond. From what we already have said about the Christian tradition, it should be clear that the one supremely transcendent reality envisioned in Christian thought and experience is God. But what does God cross over? In what way and to what extent does God go beyond? And how can this be expressed and experienced by creatures whose own capacity for transcendence is limited both by their finitude and by their persistent failing/falling?

Christian experience and teaching suggest that divine transcendence occurs in numerous different modes – in relation to time, place, knowledge, morality, and so forth. Here we will propose that it also appears in at least four major forms, which we will term negative transcendence, radical transcendence, proximate transcendence, and immanent transcendence. As we will see, each of these forms of transcendence is expressed and experienced in various ways, some of which are aesthetic and all of which potentially make for new possibilities of transcendence within human life: possibilities we later will consider under the rubric 'human transformation'. In this section we examine the aesthetic expression of negative and then radical transcendence.

Most Christian theologians are inclined to say that divine transcendence actually exists not only in many modes but in all possible modes, because God as maker of all things visible and invisible is essentially and infinitely beyond anything we know or experience, including time, place, materiality, and thought. But if God is totally beyond us, then God may be 'experienced' by us chiefly as a kind of Holy Void. When this perception predominates in one's response to the divine, one is on the route of negative theology and is entering the way of darkness, silence, and emptiness in religious experience.

The sense of God's transcendence as Infinite Difference, Hiddenness, and Darkness rarely occupies the center of Christian devotion or worship and certainly cannot be restricted to any one Christian group. One reason, perhaps, is that such transcendence is literally unimaginable and inexpressible. And yet at least its possibility can be expressed, as well as something of its import. Furthermore, it appears that much that is expressed with respect to this negatively experienced transcendence may take significantly aesthetic form. For the language eliciting acknowledgement of and response to the literally Inexpressible and Incomprehensible Other must in large part be that of paradox and catachresis, the meaning of which is felt or intuited aesthetically rather than strictly thought out. Such is the figurative language of Pseudo-Dionysius when he speaks of the luminous, 'superessential darkness' that is God, and of Meister Eckhart when he preaches: 'The final goal of being is the darkness or the unknowability of the hidden divinity, which is that light that shines "but the darkness has not comprehended it"'.[12]

Beyond such figures of speech, the aesthetic forms that can serve to call to human awareness the One that can never literally be called to mind include dark, vacant cells for meditation and rugged, forbidding terrain such as that surrounding the monastery of St-Martin-du-Canigou in France. They also include numbingly repetitive chants or amazingly lengthy and logically redundant catalogs of what God is *not*, such as are found in apophatic mysticism. Likewise great Stillness or Otherness may be pointed to through music that borders on silence or chaos, as in passages of Penderecki's *Magnificat* (1974) and *Requiem* (1987). Then there is painting of the sort encountered in Anselm Kiefer's enormous and controversial *Osiris and Isis* (1985–7), which presents us with the charred remnants of sacred and political power. Here a vast pyramid, strangely surmounted by a burnt-out circuit board from which copper wiring extends in every direction, appears in its ravaged condition to be neither safe nor amenable to any ordinary mode of restoration or demolition (Plate 3). Through such aesthetica, positive perceptions can be challenged, the world made to appear as nothing inherently holy and abiding, and nonetheless something More signalled by what is taken to be only a sign and neither presence nor genuine mediator.

It is scarcely surprising that Christians for whom the experience of negative transcendence is compelling or predominant often resonate with modern Jewish works such as Arnold Schoenberg's great unfinished opera *Moses and Aaron*, in which one hears the strange and alienating half-singing (*Sprechgesang*) of Moses as he strives without success to utter the truth of the infinite, unperceived, inconceivable God. Significantly, Moses's 'truth' of the Incomprehensible One largely goes unheeded. Meanwhile Aaron (a tenor) sings in a relatively lyrical *bel canto* style as he caters to the popular demand for palpable, accessible gods. The arts of unutterable transcendence are seldom popular.

We should note, last, that in our day it is not uncommon for the *via negativa* and its aesthetic expression to pass over into the outright negation of theology and of the supposed reality of God as well. At such times the experience of transcendence becomes an experience of God's eclipse, absence, or death. That it could remain religious at all may seem strange; yet those on this tortuous path suggest that the deconstruction of Logos and God may leave a trace of something beyond even God – something that always is on the other side of what can be said or seen and that is evoked aesthetically in absurd play and parody, in redoubled paradox, and in carnivalesque transgression of the ordinary.[13] We have testimony that such a vision of negative or paradoxical transcendence can be evoked through the enigmatic parables of Borges. That it could claim to find itself sparked or inspired by the parables of Jesus as well is surpassingly strange, yet also is true.[14]

Having considered the aesthetic expression of the Christian and Post-Christian response in which divine transcendence is experienced chiefly as that which is Divine Negation, Otherness, or even finally Absence, we now can reflect on expression and experience in which transcendence seems a step closer to the world we humanly know. This is a transcendence that is radical and yet communicative, as though it were an electric charge that could arc across an infinite gulf between heaven and earth.

The conviction that God can in some way be known and experienced positively is not, of course, unusual among Christians. Indeed the majority of Christian theologians assert that, although God as known to God's own self must be essentially unknown and incomprehensible to human beings, God chooses in acts and events of self-communication, and especially in the Incarnation, to relate to humanity truly and trustably, and in some manner appropriate to our limitations. Just how transcendent God continues to be even after such self-revelation is, however, a matter about which Christians differ greatly both in theory and experience. And in fact the God revealed in Christ and Scripture remains in other ways and times radically transcendent for many Christians. Although every Christian tradition in some fashion recognizes more than one form of transcendence, Christians in the Reformed line (mainly Calvinist) are among those in whose experience radical transcendence predominates.

For that branch of Reformation piety and theology known as the Reformed, it seems the case that religious awareness, though not consigned to silence and darkness, is most often confronted by a God of Unlikeness before whom one stands struck, if not by awe, then by a sense of the incapacity of anything finite to bear or contain the infinite. To be sure, one still may believe that certain things of divine import and all things necessary for salvation are made plain in Christ, in Holy Writ, and by the testimony of the Spirit. Yet even in the more rationalist Reformed churches, it is widely acknowledged that God's ways and truths are far from rational by our standards; God's infinite goodness, moreover, is deemed quite unapproachable from our side.

Yet when a radically transcendent God wills to be encountered, it will come to pass. And in the eyes of the Reformed tradition God is able to make use of aesthetic forms, among others, to mediate or prepare for divine self-disclosure. In seventeenth-century England, for instance, Anglicans influenced deeply by Calvinism formulated expressly biblical poetics that repeatedly affirmed that in the Bible one has exemplary art, and art with the overwhelming capacity to reveal God's providential power, law, judgment, love, and grace. The Holy Spirit is seen, in short, as a transcendently magnificent poet. And though God is a 'direct' God, as John Donne says, and often would be understood literally, God also is 'a figurative, a metaphoricall God too' whose tropes and allegories put profane authors to shame.[15]

Of course when human beings themselves seek to employ the rich rhetorical resources of Scripture in their own writing and preaching there is, from a Reformed viewpoint, a distinct danger of conceit – in the usual sense rather than the rhetorical one. The Puritan and early Calvinist sermon tended therefore to be artless and sober despite achieving at times a remarkable degree of rhetorical skill and appeal.[16] And the Baroque style of the English metaphysical poets, many Calvinist in theology, was of religious value because it had the capacity ultimately to reveal its own incapacity, thus potentially functioning – paradoxically – as a vehicle of religious receptivity. Thus the early Anglican lyric of the seventeenth century exists by and large as what has been called a 'self-consuming artifact' – a work which, 'by conveying those who experience it to a point where they are beyond the aid that discursive or rational forms can offer', becomes 'the vehicle of its own abandonment', and potentially of the corresponding aban-donment of self to the action of grace necessary for salvation.[17]

Self-effacement, if not self-abasement, is even more evident in the aesthetics of the Puritan meeting house in New England. Such a building makes visible the conviction that human effort cannot bring the divine closer. The very plainness and simplicity of form testifies that these (and other) Calvinist houses really are not meant to be 'houses of God'; that nothing made with hands can house divinity or can properly become a focus of God's presence. For we ourselves, as Calvin insisted and as the poetry of George Herbert reiterates, are made to be the real Temple of God, and we have nothing to offer of our own but our impoverishment. At the same time, the physical barrenness of the interior of the building, typically devoid of images of any kind, has the value of permitting one to attend chiefly to the divine Word, with the gathered people themselves as the true Church.

It is indeed the Word, delivered literally from on high, that dominates the aesthetics of communication within the traditional setting of Reformed worship. Certainly there is no dance or drama. Nor is there a great interest in what is seen (or tasted) in communion now that 'Real Presence' is spiritualized or even converted into Zwinglian memorialism. In any event, communion is celebrated less frequently and ceremoniously than in Catholic, Lutheran, or later Anglican traditions.

Traditionally the one sensuous art that the Reformed tradition employs extensively is also aural and thus intangible – namely music, the physical medium of which conveniently self-destructs rather than remaining as a potential distraction and temptation. The religious significance attached to this art should not be underestimated. George Herbert spoke for many Calvinists in and out of the Church of England when he commented that the times when he felt closest to heaven were during prayer and while hearing the music in Salisbury Cathedral.[18] Many a Calvinist could say with Luther: 'After theology I give music the highest place and highest honor'.[19] Even so, much more than Lutherans, Calvinists typically insist here too on an art of 'less' rather than 'more'; of poverty rather than abundance. Whereas Luther borrowed secular melodies, unwilling – as he said – to let the Devil have all the good tunes, Calvinist songs (ordinarily Psalms) were from the beginning austere and unmistakably 'sacred' in style: originally sung in unison and unaccompanied.

Finally we must stress that when the Reformed religious aesthetic sensibility extends beyond the church itself, it continues to acknowledge and proclaim the radical transcendence of God. The Calvinist typically sees nature and its orderly beauty as directly subject to God's will, as providing a proper theatre for divine action, and as declaring the glory of the Creator – possibly even supplying, as Jonathan Edwards thought, images and shadows of divine things. But this God, while working through nature for providential purposes as well as for purposes of chastisement, is not present *in* nature, but 'above' it. Nature serves mainly as the stage for history, which turns out to be sacred drama at its highest: the comedy of salvation, with the tragic sub-plot of damnation. Mindful of this grand plot, Reformed Christians seek to organize life as a whole, creating orderly social structures, works, and habitations. This impulse seems tacitly to assume a divine will-to-order, possibly anticipating the Great Housecleaning of the Last Judgment.

Thus, all in all, Reformed piety affirms the power and activity of a radically transcendent God. This is a God who graciously chooses to communicate through particular forms – even aesthetic. Although in principle reserving the right to grace and bless everything equally, the God of radical transcendence makes most use of what is plain and humble and pure, in sense, form, and imagination.

Up to now we have concentrated on kinds of Christian religiosity frequently regarded as alien either to the definite experience of transcendence, as in the case of negative theology, or to the truly aesthetic expression and proclamation of transcendence, as in the case of Reformed Christianity. Having seen that in actuality there is in each case, after all, such experience, expression, or proclamation (and hence an aesthetic befitting transcendence or its shadow) we can turn to the rather more obvious possibilities of aesthetic expression afforded by divine transcendence experienced as proximate and as immanent.

Christian Aesthesis and Divine Transcendence (2)

Any form of Christianity that extends across different epochs and cultures is bound to exhibit considerable internal variety, as do the religious predilections of individual Christians with any given tradition and at any given moment in time. It must again be emphasized, therefore, that every tradition is in some way and to some degree open to various of the forms of religious experience we are examining. Yet the balance and emphasis differs among traditions. Just as we can say that the theology and experience of the Reformed tradition tends to place special emphasis upon a sense of God's radical transcendence, so can we also say that the pervasive sacramentalism of Catholicism, including that of the Eastern Orthodox and Anglo-Catholic traditions, fosters an especially keen sense of what we will call proximate or 'near' transcendence. As we will see, an equally proximate but quite different sort of transcendence is experienced in the kind of Evangelical Christianity exemplified in much of the worship of Black Free Church and Pentecostal congregations in the United States. In both contexts the experience of transcendence by its very nature exhibits and is shaped by distinctive kinds of aesthetic expression.

Hardly anyone would deny that in Catholicism there is a commitment to preserving a sense of the transcendence and mystery of God, whose essential unknowability is emphasized by theologians from Augustine through Thomas Aquinas to Karl Rahner. Yet this is a transcendence that draws near to us in a number of ways. It supports and illuminates our God-given capacity for reason, so that reason itself, while unable to understand the inner nature of God, can show that God exists. And through grace it precedes, meets, and uplifts our efforts at goodness, so that righteousness is not merely 'imputed' to us, as Luther thought, but is also actualized in us. Moreover, in this understanding of the Transcendent, it is susceptible to being described and represented truthfully, albeit not univocally, in the language and art of analogy.

Equally important from the standpoint of aesthetics, the Incarnation is here typically taken to mean that bodily, physical mediation of the holy is not to be scorned. The Orthodox theologian John of Damascus speaks for a significant part of the entire Catholic tradition when, in responding to any and all iconoclasts, he declares: 'Perhaps you are sublime and able to transcend what is

material . . . but I, since I am a human being and bear a body, want
to deal with holy things and behold them in a bodily manner'.[20]

Not surprisingly, in the Catholic understanding of proximate
transcendence there is great emphasis on the sacraments. What is
significant about this is not just that Christ is affirmed to be really
present in the consecrated elements of the Eucharist, which
Lutherans (among others) also would affirm. It is also that the
sacraments as such are greater in number and more diverse in
function than among Protestants. Even more, it is the fact that
there is a general sense of sacramentality that extends to other
things of this world whereby God's presence is mediated.[21]

It is to be expected, therefore, that the Catholic liturgy of the
Eucharist would regularly make use of abundant aesthetic means
of mediation: bells and incense, gestures and processions, poetic or
(formerly) archaic language, vocal and instrumental music, and
often impressive architecture. Even if many of these aesthetica
never draw attention to themselves individually, they collectively
and cumulatively create a rich sensory and imaginative milieu that
contributes to one's awareness of sacramental presence.

One may claim, of course, that none of this counts except the
Eucharist itself and that Christ's presence depends not at all on the
incense and music and lofty space. Yet, as even a theology of
objective Real Presence will admit, Christ's presence is not effica-
cious for the partaker unless one is properly receptive. If the
prospective communicant despairs of ever approaching God, communion may be declined; if the communicant is proud, or alien-
ated from the larger community of the Church, the heart may be
hardened. The aesthetic milieu of the Mass works against these
attitudes. God must be very great and awe-inspiring to warrant
such extraordinary art and ceremony; one therefore is humbled in
God's presence. Yet the rank upon rank of significantly aesthetic
forms associated with the Eucharist create the sense that approach
is indeed possible from both sides – God's and ours – and in many
ways, and from varying degrees of distance, all in community.

Beyond this, we would argue that the whole range of religious
mediation recognized by the Catholic tradition – mediation accomplished not only by liturgical acts but also by a host of saints and
angels, by the Blessed Virgin, by the persons of the Trinity, by the
clergy and the sacraments they administer, and implicitly by all of
sacred history – this mediation is itself in significant measure
aesthetically mediated to the believer and worshipper. That is to say:

In the experience of the devout the reality and value of acknowledged religious mediators, visible and invisible, is to a significant
extent made more proximate and 'immediate' by means of aesthetic modes of expression, including sounds and sights, smells and
colors, shapes and rhythms, stories and metaphors, images and
spaces.

This suggests that, whereas in its theoretical statements the
Western Church generally has justified its arts on pedagogical
grounds, pointing out their usefulness for the poor, the uneducated, and the spiritually immature, the truth seems to be that in
practice the arts (broadly conceived) have helped grant to all the
faithful, in varying degrees, access to the Church at its very heart,
and to a God who wills to approach and be approached.

Of course not all Catholic aesthetica that serve this function do
so in the same way. Even within monasticism there is both art that
purges and pares away and art that fills up and spills over – the
Cistercian versus the Cluniac, for instance. Likewise there is
accessible art such as a folk-like 'Alleluia' from Taizé and difficult
art such as a highly melismatic twelfth-century 'Alleluia' from
Notre Dame de Paris. Then, too, there is 'chaste' art of the sort
clearly preferred by John of Salisbury; and there is the worldly,
corporeal religiosity of Rubens and much of the Baroque. Throughout, however, the sense of sacramentality and of the potential
proximity of the divine persists to a remarkable extent.

It is characteristic of Eastern Catholicism, however, that the
greatest possible tension is created and sustained between utmost
transcendence and utmost proximity. Among the Orthodox the
liturgical singing, for instance, is traditionally austere in that it
normally restricts itself to chant; and yet the chant as sung is
frequently ecstatic and voluminous, lifting one into the very
presence of the Most High and reminding one that in this tradition
we ourselves are to be transfigured and ultimately divinized.

Again, in Orthodox churches the cosmic, majestic Christ –
impassive emperor of the universe – typically stares out from
mosaics where he appears as the awesome yet inescapable Presence of the God declared not later than the fourth century to be
incomprehensible, glorious, and fearful. And in the liturgy the
laity, having been excluded from the offertory procession, look on
as spectators in what is described as a theatre wherein the holiest
of dramas takes place. They look not into the sanctuary itself, nor
upon the acts of consecration, but upon the Iconostasis, which

screens off the sanctuary *per se*. Nevertheless the numinous and awe-inspiring comes close. In the rite the Bishop slowly processes in plain view, 'acting the part' of Christ. Above, the usual dome stands as the image of heaven, yet plainly resting on architectural members that connect it with 'earth'. The Eucharistic elements, considered to be the very body and blood of Christ, finally are indeed shared. And by then the icons of Mary, the Saints, and Christ – although stiff, hieratic, and 'un-natural' in appearance – have long since been kissed and venerated by the faithful. The holiest of the holy comes nearer than near through the power of God and the art of vision and enactment.[22]

We observe, last, that in Catholicism as a whole the aesthetic acknowledgement and expression of divine proximity and presence extends to the realm of nature. Although the natural world itself is in no part God, it perpetually participates in the being of God; for nothing can so much as exist without deriving its principle of existence from the divine source of all being. By the same token (especially in the neo-Platonic strains of Catholicism) all light and all beauty in nature as well as in art share in some way (sometimes said to be literal, sometimes analogical) in the light and beauty of God. Thus, however dimly, they reflect God's glory and point beyond themselves to the Invisible Light and Beauty that can be seen directly only in the spiritual Beatific Vision.

As we noted early on, however, this is not the only form of religiosity in which the Transcendent becomes proximate. Quite different theological assumptions and religious experiences of transcendence are apparently at work within Free Church Protestantism, and especially in lower income Black congregations in America that clergy in the Black community often describe as being 'mass' rather than 'class' in character.[23] Three features of this alternative tradition stand out as important to note in relation to questions of transcendence and aesthetic form.

First, proximate transcendence experienced in the context of such African American churches is not so connected with the mediating status and apparatus of the institutional church *per se* as it is with a sense of the power of the Holy Spirit and of the Living Christ to operate freely, outside existing human structures of power and legitimation. The peculiar authority of the Black church is thus in part the authority to allow spiritual and aesthetic freedom – within definite bounds – and so to let the Spirit move as it wills:

ALL   Every time I feel the spirit
Moving in my heart I will pray.
Every time I feel the spirit
Moving in my heart I will pray.

SOLO Upon the mountain my Lord spoke,
Out of His mouth came fire and smoke.
In the valley on my knees,
Asked my Lord, Have mercy, please.

This spirit-filled freedom does not always lead to modes of singing or expression that would be judged decent and decorous by standards of other communities, particularly the White (and often the Black) middle and upper classes. Charles Wesley's fifth rule for singing hymns, of which he and his brother John wrote almost six thousand, was this: 'Sing modestly. Do not bawl'. Methodists in the main, however, have not been afraid of lively tunes drawn from secular sources, with dotted notes and springy rhythms. And many Black Methodists, especially, have not been afraid to 'bawl' when the Spirit moves them. The fact is that the large measure of uninhibited, spirit-moved improvisation found in jazz, for example, finds its way naturally into most aspects of this worship, from the loose 'order of worship' to the spontaneous congregational responses of 'Amen!' and 'Praise the Lord!' Preaching itself becomes a venture into territory not entirely charted ahead of time even by the Good Book.[24] Frequently improvisatory, it is marked by striking and often colloquial images, vivid narratives, powerful cadences, and a tone charged with emotion. The God celebrated in this religious aesthetic is the One who liberates and saves, delivering Daniel from the fiery furnace, Israel from Egypt's land, and prayer and praise from the shackles of rigid propriety.

The second point we would make is that the transcendent God experienced in this tradition is usually not just proximate but also participative and quite anthropomorphic: jubilant, angry, passionate, tender. It is fitting, therefore, that here the differences separating sacred style from secular can be narrow indeed, with God's love and the love shown to God both seeming close to human love in general. In short, 'our' style and 'God's' style are not radically different. One dresses differently for church and keeps certain kinds of language and behavior out of places of worship. It is not a question of being irreverent. Yet in contemporary Black gospel music, for example, there are virtually no musical instruments automatically ruled out of worship; and Aretha Franklin, the 'Queen of Soul', sings in much the same style whether in church or in concert. From the point of view of many of her church listeners (though by no means all), it would seem that a God who frowned on this would be a God unwilling to get divine hands dirty working alongside human beings frequently sweaty and down-trodden. Instead of staying 'above it all', this God comes as the Jesus who eats and mixes with sinners; who even as Lord suffers with and for his servants. No wonder the aesthetic styles suitable to this sort of transcendence tend to be earthy, eclectic, and generally uninhibited.

The third point is presumed by what we already have said: The aesthetic predominant in a great many African American churches is largely popular and egalitarian. This does not mean that there are no standards of quality. Good singers, like good preachers, are recognized and praised; their gifts are counted as gifts from God. It does mean, however, that here aesthetica expressive of God's close way of being transcendent have an immediacy and accessibility that is itself a vehicle and sign of the immediacy and accessibility of God's own saving power and grace.

Even so, relatively few Christians in this tradition go so far as to regard the human and the earthly as always and already in some sense divine. This outlook is more characteristic of those respon-sive to our fourth and final variety of transcendence – namely, immanent transcendence. Among such Christians, who give voice to a recurrent but subordinate motif within many different Christ-ian traditions, God is primarily experienced not as a reality near or present *to* us but as the extraordinary and miraculous reality ever present and immanent *in* us and in all other things, which intimately share in the very life of God. Even here, however, it is not claimed that anything on earth can contain the divine com-pletely; rather, there is a sense that all things both contain and are contained by what always is more than merely finite and temporal.

In Martin Luther's writings this sense occasionally is expressed with great passion (and perplexity):

> God is substantially present everywhere, in and through all creatures, in all their parts and places, so that the world is full of God and He fills all, but without His being encompassed and surrounded by it. . . . These are all exceedingly incomprehensible matters; yet they are articles of our faith and are attended clearly and mightily in Holy Writ. . . . For how can reason tolerate it that

the Divine majesty is so small that it can be substantially present in a grain, on a grain, over a grain, through a grain, within and without, and that, although it is a single majesty, it nevertheless is entirely in each grain separately? ... And that the same Majesty is so large that neither this world nor a thousand worlds can encompass it and say: 'Behold, there it is!'[25]

The references to God's substantial presence in, on, over, and through a grain recall Luther's insistence that in the sacrament Christ's body and blood are present in, with, and under the elements. But now, if only implicitly, it is the whole world that is the sacrament. Transcendent immanentalism of this kind is really sacramentalism pushed to the limit. But in contrast to much neo-Platonic sacramentalism, there is no hint that in the created order we see just a vestige or imprint of God's presence; and in contrast to the views of Thomas Aquinas, there is no suggestion that God's governance of and presence in the world proceeds through an immense hierarchy of beings and powers.

In the modern period, as influences from the Orient, from Western Romanticism, from the new physics, and from process theologies and philosophies all combine in new ways, the immanental side of the transcendent comes to the fore in much Christian spirituality, thought, and worship. God is experienced as being related to us and the world as we are to our bodies. Or God becomes the Christ within. This experience, which normally stops short of pantheism, finds itself often embracing what has been called panentheism.[26]

The Catholic poet Gerard Manley Hopkins expresses something of this sense of immanent transcendence in the sonnet that opens with the declaration: 'The world is charged with the grandeur of God' – a perception related to Hopkins's assertion elsewhere that 'All things are charged with love, are charged with God and if we know how to touch them give off sparks and take fire, yield drops and flow, ring and tell of him'.[27] It is characteristic of the aesthetic of immanent transcendence to discover the radically extraordinary within the ordinary – as Sylvia Plath does in her lyric 'Black Rook in Rainy Weather', or as others do in natural phenomena seen as beautiful, sublime, or perhaps (to our minds) terrible. Thus one also proceeds to find the supernatural within the natural, as in much of Wordsworth and in the fierce, rugged poetry of the American Robinson Jeffers. Musically the *Missa Gaia*, or *Earth Mass*

(1981), of Paul Winter and his consort follows such a path by blending Franciscan piety with a renewed sense of the earth as itself holy.

As we already have indicated, however, immanent transcendence does not have only to do with nature. The photography in the classic yet popular collection *The Family of Man* is so arranged as to suggest to many viewers that the human too is somehow holy in its very acts of love, work, and strife. In a quite different vein, moreover, there is art that, moving within one mode such as the proximate, suddenly breaks into the immanent. In the *Sanctus* of Bach's Mass in B Minor the contrapuntal setting of the phrase 'Heaven and earth are full of your glory' so shines and overflows with the musical manifestation of divine plenitude that in the experience of many a listener heaven and earth seem to converge, revealing the ultimate reality of their ecstatic union/communion. .

So it is that transcendence in its immanent form, as in the others we have examined, inevitably is connected with transformation. Any aesthetic mediation of a sense of the transcendent constitutes, in fact, a transfiguration of ordinary perception. It amplifies or diminishes, gives more than what is expected or undercuts all expectations, radically affirms or radically negates. In these diverse ways it works as well toward the transformation of those it engages and affects 'wholly'. Our treatment of the varieties of religious aesthetic experience therefore needs in conclusion to consider briefly the role of aesthetica in human transformation *per se*.

Christian Aesthesis and Human Transformation

At a number of points we already have seen that the different ways in which divine transcendence is experienced and expressed aesthetically are correlated with different ways in which human nature and its own possibilities are envisioned. Indeed, in every tradition the characteristic aesthetic strategies for expressing something of the reality of the divine depend partly on how that tradition assumes human beings need to be altered so as to respond appropriately to what in some sense transcends themselves.

· The Calvinist tradition, for example, most often looks for aesthetic strategies that will make us conscious of our inherent inadequacy in contrast with God's glory, which nonetheless condescends to us in grace. Eastern Orthodoxy especially cultivates arts that will usher us into the presence of numinous mystery and move us toward our own transfiguration in the image of God. The process panentheist (of whatever affiliation) cherishes aesthetica that can open us to new possibilities for cooperating with God to create a future in which we can truly though limitedly share, thanks to that One in whom we live and move and have our being.

We must emphasize, though, that religious experience even in its aesthetic mediations is concerned with more than the private divine-human relation. Consequently arts occupied exclusively with sheerly personal experience cannot carry the full burden of aesthesis relevant to the requirements of religion, and specifically of Christianity.

Moreover, to the extent to which Christianity calls for the moral and religious transformation of society, it calls in part for arts that will in some fashion help the continual reformation and trans-formation of the Christian's own necessarily limited vision of society and world, along with the world's vision of itself. Not all such arts will be Christian. Nor can they be if Christianity is always in need of ongoing and partially external critique – albeit a critique to which perhaps only Christians and their God will know the most fitting response. In any case, some of the human and social transformations advocated by Christians – transformations such as those entailed in the promotion of peace, responsible freedom, mutual respect, and justice – are ones that many non-Christians likewise hope for and work toward. In these areas, surely, not all arts and aesthetica valued by Christians need to be specifically Christian themselves. What they must be is genuinely transforma-tive, and in a way potentially consonant with what Christians would call the will of God, which for many Christians is as mysterious as it is authoritative.

There are at least four possible objections, however, to the claim that aesthetica can be transformative, or at any rate transformative in ways possibly valued by Christians. These objections we will address in such a fashion as to indicate that any adequate Christian valuation of aesthetica must allow for varieties within both aesthe-tic and religious experience, and hence within experience that is religiously aesthetic.

Objection One: As has often been observed, whatever is reli-gious naturally 'serves as an agent of closure, shutting off human investigation, criticism, and effort in deference to the authority of

the more-than-human, the supernatural, the other-worldly'. Therefore religion, and certainly religious art, merely reinforces existing
'systems of authority' and 'canons of order'.[28]

Response: Whose religion? Always? The objection, to be sure,
says something important about religion; but it voices a half-truth.
Even the most conservative religion may reform rather than
confirm humans in relation to some of their most destructive
habits, which if unchecked would indeed silence all criticism and
invoke certain closure: acts of violence, rage, and pride, for
instance. In any event a powerfully creative though institutionally
certified work like Michelangelo's *Last Judgment* hardly calls for
purely passive deference to any presumed authority on earth. It is
too ambiguous and polyvalent, undermining any sense of absolute
security for anyone, yet holding out signs of ambiguous promise as
well. Recall the disputes over whether Christ's arm is raised in
judgment or benediction – and this in the chapel of the Pope! If any
work is unsettling, this one is. And yet plainly it is Christian. In any
case, there is reason to believe that the very idea of the truly
transcendent, when expressed powerfully through rituals and arts
as well as ideas, can sometimes undermine confidence in any one
institution or person as absolutely authoritative.

Objection Two: Perhaps what you mean to say, then, is that
truly 'authentic versions of art and religion' are ones that 'restruc-
ture everything and by doing so come up with new possibilities,
new beginnings, and new ends'. Thus they contribute 'to the
breaking down of the conservative authority of the present already
existing community'. Their 'true value' thus is 'their fertility, not
their utility'.[29]

If so, however, you will have to be more critical of popular
religious art in general, which is a tissue of clichés, challenging no
one and changing nothing. Even Black spirituals in the days of
slavery reinforced the status quo on earth by promising a better life
up yonder.[30]

Response: The first half of your objection provides a refreshing
alternative to the stereotypical concept of religion assumed in your
first objection and unfortunately reiterated rather mindlessly by a
great many of the better theorists since Karl Marx. But you confuse
the experience of seeing things freshly and anew with that of
restructuring everything. Some features of authentic religion and
art lead to restructuring; some lead to renewed appreciation of

what exists, and so to reconciliation or rejoicing. Both are authentic.

As for your point about the moral and religious anemia of popular arts, it is somewhat blunted by the fact that this claim has itself become a cliché. First, it is not self-evident that even *authentic* religious life has no room or need for mere simplicity or indeed sentimentality. Second, it most assuredly is not the case that a work that is popular and accessible automatically lacks transformative power. American Black spirituals did sometimes function as instruments of solace (and hence at times unwittingly as tools of the oppressor), but some of the same songs became theme songs of this-worldly liberation. Furthermore, the popular religious songs of the civil rights movement in the United States of the 1960s turned positively and healthily subversive as Christianity undertook a critique of itself and of society.

Objection Three: Despite what may seem to have been implied in Objection Two, and what you yourself perhaps assume, neither the best art nor the worst is a faithful imitation or copy of some external reality; it is an alternative or artificial reality indeterminately related to any world outside itself. This makes art pleasing but not directly useful. Actually the disengagement, distanciation, and transformation native to art *prevent it* from being a reliable or lasting means of constructive change. Even the civil rights songs 'worked' only because the main burden was carried by moral and political reflection and action.

Response: There is no way to tell for sure what exactly changes whom and for how long. Similar questions are raised about psychotherapy, but it would be hard to claim that therapy is not in general an instrument of change. If you are wanting to say that art is most effective in conjunction with other human activities and imaginings, then we are very much in agreement. But no human idea or work is inherently 'reliable', in the sense of copying The Truth or The Law. The notion of mimesis, in the sense of an exact or direct imitation of 'reality', has become both unpopular and untenable following the otherwise quite different studies by Gombrich, Foucault, Derrida, and others. Even photographs and photographers distort as they select, record, and transmit. Ideas and systems likewise have built-in distortions the extent and kind of which we cannot easily or perfectly assess, lacking as we do any immediate access to Absolute Truth. Christianity, needless to say, may well endorse the imitation of Christ in one's life, and the true inspiration of Scriptures. Yet in most Christian experience – especially when significantly aesthetic – what is at issue even in inspiration is not any sort of literal duplication of Divine Thought; this would threaten the very transcendence testified to in the religious tradition.

One does want one's religious expression to be in some way *faithful*, however. So the question is: What kind of expression in the spheres of religion and art can count as faithful – that is, faithful to what concerns us most deeply and matters to us 'wholly'? Presumably there is more than one such mode of expression. But surely one such mode might be the sort that comes to mind if the author of this text, shifting from the persona of scholar to the persona of 'person', asks a 'personal' and indeed 'existential' question:

How can I best give a faithful account of what it meant to me to watch my brother narrowly escape death from a long, sliding fall down a snow-packed mountain slope? I instinctively search for a story line, a narrative thread. I look for images and metaphors: for what it was *like*. Slowly I begin to be able to say to myself and to others: 'It was as though . . .' As though what? Well, from where I myself had come to a momentary halt in my uncertain descent down the snowfield – where I could see the icy slope steepen sharply before me and drop at length down to the rocks below – from there, when just to the side and ahead of me my brother slipped and began to slide fast away and down toward the boulders – from there and from that moment it was as though I were watching another being, whom I hardly knew any more, swiftly succumbing to a fatal disease to which I was at the moment somehow immune. I suddenly hardly knew him, possibly because he seemed about to die, and death was to me something unknown. Then he was still alive, standing at a distant edge of the snowfield, and I knew him again but could not know what had just happened until I could say what it was *like*. It was like *that*. And what it *meant* to me I did not quite know or fully feel until I knew that *likeness*.

'Likeness' in this case is 'faithfulness'; but it is not duplication, the illusion of which is duplicity. Instead it is a transformation that forms experience into something meaningful. Perhaps it is this sort of transformative creation and faithful mediation that the aesthetica of religion provide, becoming at once body and sign of that elusive transcendence which is experienced as both near and distant, present and absent. What religious arts say about self and world and God cannot be directly inspected for literal accuracy. Neither they nor the other primary languages of faithfulness are basically literal, after all. Yet, together with closely related exploratory expositions in systematic thought and metaphysical speculation, our religious images, metaphors, and narratives construct and construe a pattern that seems at once faithful and meaningful: true to what has been most valued by ourselves and an ongoing community, as well as by those elsewhere who seem companionable or gifted explorers of the same terrain. Between aesthetic imagination, rational reflection, and communal or intercommunal authentication, there is a degree of risky reliability that seems appropriate to a religion said to venture forth by faith.

Objection Four: So really what you are talking about here is trusting in aesthetic creativity and sensitivity, among other things, to play a significant role in the transformation of lives and human culture. But if you have emphasized anything in this chapter, it is that aesthetic sensibilities vary even in their religious modes and that what you have termed 'transcendence' is therefore experienced differently through different kinds of religious aesthetic expression. This seems to put you in the precarious position of saying that moral and religious transformation is somehow connected with aesthetic taste. As some of us suspected all along, you seem to be headed toward just the sort of religious aestheticism you claim you have wanted to avoid.

Response: Your worries about 'taste' are clearly related to your earlier worries about the reliability of aesthetic modes of human transformation. Though other people might express these worries rather differently, they are widespread enough to deserve a response ampler than a few sentences. In the next chapter, therefore, we will take up explicitly the matter of taste. Then we will come back to the issue of standards. Wherever we come out, it will not be in a place where an aesthete – or a dogmatist either – would feel at ease.

6

Sin and Bad Taste: Aesthetic Criteria in the Realm of Religion

Antinomy

Although our analysis in the preceding chapters should have left little doubt that religious experience and aesthetic response often coalesce, it seems obvious to most reflective religion scholars and theologians that the specific aesthetic tastes of a given person or social group are by nature of little or no concern to religion. Within the Christian tradition, for instance, 'bad taste' is not considered a deadly or even venial sin. Nor is it generally condemned as a hindrance to sanctification or spiritual maturity. Impeccable taste, moreover, is hardly deemed to be one of the 'fruits of the spirit'. Saintliness and the so-called Christian virtues seem to have little to do with the appreciation of the subtler beauties of art and nature. The beatitudes certainly do not mention people with 'good taste' among the blessed. Instead, the poor and outcast, whose taste has often been regarded as extremely questionable, are the ones named to inherit the Kingdom. The rich – the traditional patrons of art and culture – are said to have their reward already.

Yet it also could be argued, even apart from the particular evidence presented in our study, that aesthetic sensitivity and judgment is so integral to the moral and religious life that people whose aesthetic sense is dull or perverse are in an unenviable position. The possibility that bad taste may be a *moral* liability is suggested in fact by the quite traditional notion that sin – which is not only wrong but also profoundly ugly – looks alluring to the unwary, whereas virtue – which is not only right but also profoundly beautiful – frequently appears drab at first sight. It follows that failure to distinguish genuine beauty from counterfeit can lead to moral error. Moral and aesthetic discernment often go hand in hand.

136

THE FAR SIDE By GARY LARSON

The Far Side Copyright 1986 Universal Press Syndicate

That there is an equally intimate connection between the distinctly *religious* realm and the aesthetic is indicated by the fact that, as we have repeatedly pointed out, the aesthetic plays a crucial role in primary forms of religious experience and expression: sacred narratives, rituals, and so forth. We have seen that the Christian liturgy, for instance, is often described as a kind of drama, which by definition entails artistry. The parables and other Scripture likewise have been shown to have literary qualities essential to their religious meaning and function. As described in the Pentateuch and elsewhere, hierophanies such as the burning bush and the blast of the invisible trumpet on Mount Sinai have vivid sensuous and aesthetic qualities. Some theologians would even say that the whole of human and cosmic history is a kind of strange and awesome comedy or tragi-comedy, which presumably bodes ill for people lacking a sense of the dramatic and comic. Seen in this light, 'bad taste' – the failure to discern and respond appropriately to qualities that are aesthetic – again seems at least potentially sinful, a mark of depravity as well as of deprivation.

What has just been sketched is a kind of antinomy: that aesthetic taste does not and cannot matter greatly to a religion like Christianity and yet turns out to matter very much. If there is to be any hope of resolving this antinomy, it will be necessary once more to leave terrain that is familiar to religious studies and to undertake a short but fundamental critique of the concept of 'taste' – one that can then be linked to a rudimentary analysis of the role of aesthetic criteria within religion itself. This done, we will be able to address the specific question of the religious relevance of taste as well as the still more specific question of the religious implications and consequences of *bad* taste.

For the purposes of our inquiry, it will be useful as well as convenient to continue to use Christianity as a test case. In comparison with Zen Buddhism, for example, Christianity seems relatively unconcerned with cultivating what we normally think of as taste. Thus, if aesthetic taste can be shown to be relevant to Christian concerns, its relevance in some form or other to the concerns of different religious traditions should seem probable indeed.

Elements of Taste

It was not until nearly the eighteenth century that the English word 'taste', like the French *'goût'* and the Italian *'gusto'*, began to be used to denote cultivated aesthetic sensibility.[1] Art and taste as we now think of them are both in fact concepts largely fashioned in the Enlightenment period.[2] Obviously, then, we cannot expect to find them perfectly suited to describe either early Christian concerns and concepts or those of the present moment. We can, however, hope to formulate a contemporary version of the idea of taste that will illuminate features of aesthetic and religious experience that are rarely recognized.

Were we simply to follow Kant – and it is Kant who has had the most followers in this field – we might say that taste (*der Geschmack*) is the faculty of judging what is beautiful.[3] Kant's faculty psychology is no longer widely accepted, however, and the beautiful (at least as traditionally conceived) surely is not the only form of aesthetic excellence nor, therefore, the only thing for taste to judge. Furthermore, it is not self-evident that judgment in the strict sense is the only thing for which aesthetic taste is required or employed.

Frank Sibley, in an influential modern article entitled 'Aesthetic Concepts', circumvents these particular difficulties by describing taste as 'an ability to *notice* or *see* or *tell* that things have certain [aesthetic] qualities'.[4] Yet, useful as this may be, it does no more than hint at the variety of capacities and functions frequently subsumed under the concept of taste.

Somewhat fuller indications of the complexity of the constitution of taste, if not of its function, are to be found in the writings of Kant's eighteenth-century predecessors. In Edmund Burke's influential book on the sublime and the beautiful, he observes:

> What is called taste . . . is not [simple], but is partly made up of a perception of the primary pleasures of sense, of the secondary pleasures of the imagination, and of the conclusions of the reasoning faculty, concerning the various relations of these, and concerning the human passions, manners, and actions. All this is requisite to form taste.[5]

David Hume's classic essay 'Of the Standard of Taste' also points to the variety of factors contributing to taste, in this case by arguing that the arbiters and exemplars of taste are people who must combine in themselves a cluster of traits: good sense, delicacy, freedom from prejudice, and a thorough acquaintance with a variety of arts and species of beauty.[6]

From these brief but representative characterizations of taste it seems reasonable to conclude that what we call 'taste' involves such things as sensibility, reflection, and judgment or – in Roger Scruton's recent and somewhat different scheme – experience, preference, and thought.[7] To say this, however, is still not to say much about the functions and kinds of taste. This is not surprising, since most of the above theorists assume that, however complex the constitution of taste, it has but one basic form and one basic purpose: to recognize or judge what is aesthetically excellent. But this assumption is questionable indeed. Consequently, we need to attempt now a different sort of analysis. Again we will discuss three basic elements of aesthetic taste, but in our framework each element is at once a part of some more encompassing form of taste and also in itself a particular form of taste. The three basic elements or forms of aesthetic taste are ones we will call apperception, appraisal, and appreciation.

The term *apperception* denotes the mental process that not only raises subconscious or indistinct impressions to the level of attention but also forms them into a coherent imaginative and intellectual order – a distinct phenomenon.[8] As the activity by which we 'take in' and attend to the aesthetic features of an object, apperception involves imagination and (often) thought as well as sensation and emotion. Thus, while sensory perception is necessary for aesthetic apperception, it is not sufficient. If a dog were to sit in front of a Victrola in the manner once depicted on HMV/RCA products, it would be able to perceive the sounds of Schubert's *'Gretchen am Spinnrade'*, for instance, but surely could never apperceive the music, the song. Despite the fact that most dogs have preferences, including a dislike for almost anything played fortissimo, they have no taste.

Appraisal constitutes the self-consciously critical and evaluative aspect of taste by which one seeks to ascertain the aesthetic excellence of a work or object. There can be no appraisal that is not grounded in apperception; no genuine judgments of taste are second-hand. Although informal appraisal spontaneously (and possibly instantaneously) accompanies and influences almost all apperception, appraisal in the fullest sense involves a conscious judgment of aesthetic status. This judgment goes beyond apperception and is different from the expression of personal likes or dislikes. Thus, to say that Bach's *Art of the Fugue* is the summit of musical counterpoint is not to say that one has a taste for it, but that it is admirable as art and so could be admired by people with good taste.

The third aspect of taste, *appreciation*, has directly to do with private response and personal evaluation. As in the older sense of 'setting a price', appreciation in this technical sense can involve depreciation. Furthermore, like appraisal, it can entail reflection and even deliberation, since something of the kind seems necessary even to be sure of what one personally likes or dislikes. At the same time, appreciation is always intimately connected with apperception; for when one apperceives a work as dreamlike or agitated, comic or tragic, exciting or disturbing, one invariably does or does not find oneself personally 'attuned to' and 'resonating with' the work. Nevertheless, we can in reflection separate purely personal response from both apperception and considered appraisal. My fond childhood memories of the Rocky Mountain region may color my personal response to the movie Western *Shane*, but these memories can be 'bracketed' if I am called on to say whether I think the movie is good. Again, a highly qualified juror suffering from a throbbing headache may not personally enjoy a single work submitted for a show; or the works may all be in a style that the juror, though feeling perfectly well, does not personally enjoy, or can enjoy only when in a certain mood. Under these conditions an appraisal can still be perceptive, although not finely tuned, because the basic quality of the work can be recognized without being personally valued.[9] If the work is good it may evoke a positive *impulse*, even though the response and actual pleasure is blocked; or it may elicit the kind of detached admiration that many of us have for beautiful people who are not 'our type'. In any case, positive appraisal always assumes that a work *could* be positively appreciated by people with good taste.

From this analysis it should be clear that apperception, appraisal, and appreciation all are constituents of taste in its most encompassing form: Taste, with a capital T. Beyond that, however, we can also say that, singly and in various combinations, they themselves constitute forms of taste.

This theoretical claim can best be supported by three examples. Suppose, first, that an established painter has become so tired, pressed for time, and anxious about living beyond his means that he takes virtually no pleasure in some of the art he makes, although his training and his excellent 'eye' enable him to recognize when the work is of high enough quality to be exhibited and offered for sale. His is a jaded taste, but taste nonetheless. Retaining certain powers of aesthetic apperception and appraisal, it is almost devoid of the element of active appreciation.

Meanwhile the harried dealer to whom the artist consigns much of his work may not immediately take the time to enjoy the artist's latest painting or to appraise its aesthetic worth, being more concerned about where it can be stored. Nevertheless, the dealer sees almost at a glance that the new work has been influenced slightly by two other artists whose work he handles and sells in quantity. The dealer's apperceptual acumen, although divorced both from active appreciation and from the actual appraisal, must likewise be considered a kind of taste, cultivated by practice and honed by necessity. We can thus agree with Sibley that the very ability to see or notice certain aesthetic qualities is a matter of taste.[10]

Finally, suppose an unassuming and inexperienced schoolgirl drops by the gallery on her way home from her Saturday drawing lesson. Without claiming to know much about art, she admits to the dealer that she has a special liking for the five assorted pieces that have been set aside in the back room. 'Are they being returned to the artists because they wouldn't sell?' she asks. 'Aren't they any good?' The dealer, realizing that these have just been chosen by a major museum for a travelling exhibition, sees at once that the girl's personal preferences reflect remarkably good taste. Although certainly not formed into public judgments, or what we have termed appraisals, they show a gift not only for apperception but also for appreciation – which is more than can be said for the tastes of the artist mentioned above, whose work as it happens is not among the pieces being reserved for the museum show.

What we have given are examples of what common linguistic practice acknowledges to be the plurality of the forms and functions of taste. Even this relatively simple step marks a significant break with the Kantian tradition and has far-reaching implications. We can, to be sure, agree with Kant that to judge that an object is aesthetically excellent is not merely to like and appreciate it; it is implicitly and in principle to make some claim about its aesthetic value within the human community and about the communicability of the pleasure to which it gives rise. Furthermore, we concur with Kant's view that aesthetic appraisal is logically separable from the apperception of the beautiful object and from the appreciative act of taking pleasure in the object – an act we have declined to consider essential to appraisal.[11] But in our view these different *elements* of taste also represent different (and sometimes independent) *forms* of taste, each with a different function. We can easily entertain the possibility, therefore, that each form is a factor in helping to define different human communities and contributes to different human activities and values, some of which may be moral and religious as well as aesthetic. If so, Kant's formalism, tied as it is to one particular aspect of what we would term Taste (with a capital T), would be an inadequate foundation for aesthetics as a whole, as would his search for *a priori* conditions that would permit taste to make subjective *universal* judgments. It may be that the very effort to make such judgments is too private to begin with, and presumptuous in the end.

If our departure from the Kantian position provides a basis for a new understanding of the religious relevance of taste, this is in large part because it allows us to reconsider who has taste (good or bad) and what uses taste can possibly have. It is to the possible uses of taste in the realm of religion that we next turn our attention.

Taste in the Realm of Religion

Without doubt there is such a thing as Christian art – not merely art made by Christians. Mozart's 'Ave Verum Corpus' and Van Eyck's Ghent Altarpiece are both art and both Christian. But is there such a thing as Christian taste? Does the good Christian necessarily seek to have good taste? What, after all, is the relevance of taste to Christian life and values? To indicate how such questions might begin to be answered, we need to determine how taste in its different forms might function in relation to values and activities clearly pertinent to religion and to Christianity as such.

To the extent that religion, and specifically Christianity, is concerned with all of life, everything in principle has some sort of religious relevance. Yet many things are in fact either neutral or peripheral to Christian concerns, and others that are commendable, such as various forms of 'self-improvement', are matters of personal preference and choice as opposed to moral or religious obligation. One's taste in what is neither proscribed nor prescribed belongs, presumably, to the sphere of what Martin Luther terms 'the freedom of a Christian'.[12] Thus, in the classic Pauline example, whether or not one eats the food offered to idols makes no difference as long as it does not lead another person to fall. Paul's conclusion is this: 'Whether you eat or drink, or whatever you do, do all to the glory of God'.[13]

Accordingly, one conventional Christian position on art and taste might be rendered: You are free to make and appreciate things that are artistic and beautiful if you do so by way of glorifying God. This benign but feeble principle is transformed into something considerably more powerful if the theologian can show that the exercise of aesthetic taste is not only permitted but also imperative if one is to be responsive and responsible in certain areas essential to morality and religion. To that end, it would be useful to establish that aesthetic taste is in one or more ways intrinsic to 'glorifying and enjoying God' – if we may adapt the paraphrase of Paul found in the Westminster Catechisms.

The idea that aesthetic taste and artistic activity can indeed glorify God is both venerable and persistent. Seventeen hundred years after Paul, J. S. Bach closed even his humblest exercise books with the words *'Soli Deo Gloria'*. Two and a half centuries later, Alice Walker dedicated *The Color Purple* in this way: *'To the Spirit*: Without whose assistance/Neither this book/Nor I/Would have been written'.[14] The next year Lionel Richie concluded the liner notes to his Grammy Award album, *Can't Slow Down*, with a similar gesture. After naming and thanking each of seventy-five people for their help, he wrote, 'and most of all, to my co-writer, THE GOOD MASTER, thank you'.[15]

To be sure, there are differences here. One cannot imagine a Black womanist like Alice Walker dedicating her work to 'THE GOOD MASTER'. And we can hardly ignore the possibility that a God with any taste at all might worry about being given credit for some of what is marketed as divinely inspired. But these very distinctions of quality and kind must be utterly inconsequential unless taste does in fact matter to religion as one major ingredient in the glorification and enjoyment of God. According to our analysis, the ways in which taste matters to religion basically fall into two categories: the broadly moral and the specifically religious.

The morality of aesthetic taste has in itself more than one aspect. The least impressive, perhaps, is manifest in analogies between the aesthetic and the moral. Here one finds Kant's claim that the beautiful, which of course one judges by means of taste, is a symbol of the morally good. Thus not only does taste *per se* involve a truly common sense, a *sensus communis aestheticus*, that shows one's ties to the whole human community, but the very act of estimating the beautiful induces one to value something for its own sake – as an end in itself – which is likewise what is required for the moral life.[16] A watered down version of the analogy between taste and moral judgment can be seen in Roger Scruton's suggestion that the cultivation of taste means developing a sense of the appropriate, which in a different guise is as important to morality as are rules of right and wrong.[17] More interestingly, Marcia Cavell argues that the ability to reason morally grows out of

1. Chartres Cathedral: Nave viewed from the west.

2. Sandro Botticelli: Madonna and Child with Singing Angels, ca. 1477.

3. Anselm Kiefer: Osiris and Isis, 1985–7.

Et in _ car _ na _ tus est   de spi _ _ ri _ tu

san _ _ _ cto   ex Ma _ ri _ a vir _ gi _ ne _ et

ho _ mo fa _ ctus est,   et ho _ mo fa _ _

_ _ _ _ _ _ _ _ _ _ _ _ _

_ _ _ ctus est,   fa _ _ _ _ _ _ _

_ _ _ ctus est,   fa _ _ _ _

_ _ _ _ _ _ _ _ _   ctus est,

4. Wolfgang Amadeus Mozart. Excerpt from soprano solo line, 'Et Incarnatus Est', Mass in C Minor, K. 427.

a sensitivity to the immediate and particular, and entails an ability to experience the familiar in unfamiliar ways – all of which is required in the act of interpreting art and hence in the use of taste.[18]

Cavell's line of reasoning recalls, in turn, John Dewey's contention that the experience of art opens up new possibilities 'of human relations not to be found in rule and precept, admonition and administration'.[19] The taste needed to apperceive, appraise, and appreciate art would therefore appear to be a moral asset. By this point, however, we clearly have gone beyond mere analogies between aesthetic taste and moral sense to an assertion of positive connection. The same plainly is true when a theologian such as Stanley Hauerwas claims that one's capacity to live a moral life is correlated with one's capacity to tell and hear significant narratives,[20] or when James Gustafson insists on the significance of fictions in moral formation even while refusing simply to conflate the aesthetic and the moral.[21]

What is often overlooked even by some of the theorists making such claims is that, for the aesthetic to have the impact on the moral in the ways just mentioned, the aesthetic and the moral in these instances must be intimately related indeed; in fact, at this level they cannot clearly be separated or completely distinguished. Whether in a civil rights song like 'We Shall Overcome' or in a novel like *Huckleberry Finn*, the combination of the aesthetic and the moral constitutes a genuine compound, not simply a loose mixture that would allow the moral insight to be separated neatly and fully extracted from the aesthetic milieu. Mere mixtures are easy enough to sort out, even on Kant's theory; for we have seen that, despite Kant's formalism, Kant himself recognized that in the arts beauty is often 'dependent', being combined with concepts and interests – including those of morality.[22] What he did not see is that the con-fusion of the aesthetic and the moral can create a new whole in which complex aesthetic qualities affect and reflect moral perceptions and insights. But it is just this that shows that morality necessarily depends in part on aesthetic discernment, on taste: taste as apperception, enabling us to recognize moral implications in aesthetic forms; as appraisal, enabling us to estimate the morally good (or bad) within the beautiful (or ugly); and as appreciation, enabling us personally to value the aesthetically manifest good or to reject the bad, and hence to be disposed to act.

That said, we need to notice a final aspect of the morality of taste, which consists in the fact that, because aesthetic excellence *per se* is good for life and generative of human community, it is a moral good in itself. As we have previously noted, Nicholas Wolterstorff points to this in theological language by saying that aesthetic delight is 'a component within and a species of that joy which belongs to the shalom God has ordained as the goal of [personal and communal] existence'. Therefore, he claims, 'it becomes a matter of responsible action to help make available, to ourselves *and others*, the experience of aesthetic delight'.[23] Clearly the form of taste we have termed 'appreciation' is necessary if this morally good potential for delightful community is to be realized. In this respect as in others, taste would plainly be part of the glorification and enjoyment of God that is possible through the moral life.

Turning from the broadly moral to the specifically religious functions of aesthetic taste, we see that the latter can be traced along similar lines. First, one discovers an analogy between aesthetic experience and the experience of the holy or divine. John Dewey gives a modern version of this analogy when, in writing of what he describes as the 'religious feeling that accompanies intense esthetic perception', he says that through art 'we are, as it were, introduced into a world beyond this world which is nevertheless the deeper reality of the world in which we live in our ordinary experiences'.[24] Dewey thus pictures experience of the aesthetic 'beyond' as like, but not identical with, encounter with the holy or divine – and hence as providing a sort of secular sacrality. We have seen, furthermore, that certain kinds of neo-Platonism emphasize that the sensible beauty that one can apperceive through taste is analogous to the divine beauty that can be known through the intellect or religious affections; one's love of the former can lead therefore to love of the latter, and aesthetic taste can in this way be transformed into its spiritual analogue.[25]

Beyond the perception of analogies is the whole range of experiences in which aesthetic awareness becomes intrinsically and inseparably part of religious response. This often occurs in the Mass or in the singing of Psalms, and may happen in a country baptism on a Sunday morning at the river with a hovering mockingbird serving as Paraclete. Even if one could somehow attend strictly to whatever sheerly aesthetic qualities one might apperceive in such things, one would by no means fathom the aesthetic and artistic richness that they have when apperceived as also religious. Conversely, whatever the religious meaning one might derive from some purely non-aesthetic apperception of the same events and works – and they would not in truth be the same when thus apperceived – it would not begin to match the religious meaning that emerges when the aesthetic is also attended to.

Certainly for Jonathan Edwards in eighteenth-century America, salvific knowledge of God required the heart and the religious affections, which he thought must be sensible to divine beauty and its shadowed image in nature and art.[26] For much of the Romantic tradition, whether in the arts or in theologies like that of Schleiermacher, the most profound aesthetic experience was religious, and religion was also inescapably aesthetic.[27] Similarly, in our own day, Hans Urs von Balthasar has emphasized the intrinsically aesthetic character of divine revelation both in the form it takes and in the response it evokes,[28] while Paul Tillich and his followers have found the concern of art ultimately to be religious, with art potentially serving a sacramental function.[29]

The Tillichian position may be the closest that modern theology comes to saying that the aesthetically excellent, and the apperception thereof, is fundamentally religious in and of itself – which is a third mode of linking aesthetic taste and religion. In the past, however, one side of neo-Platonic theology had said that very thing, by stressing that earthly beauty participates in the divine and shares God's beauty not only in name and by way of analogy but also in reality, however dimly so.[30] Hence, just as the beautiful is already in a sense moral, it may also already be incipiently religious.

What is seldom if ever explicitly stated by any of these theorists is the logical deduction that, if at least part of what we consider to be aesthetic is analogous to, ingredient in, or an instance of what we regard as distinctly religious, and if aesthetica cannot even be recognized – let alone appraised or appreciated – apart from taste, then taste has a unique place in religion itself. It must be seen as an intrinsic part of adequately or inadequately glorifying and enjoying God. It is this conclusion that makes all the difference to understanding aesthetic taste as a part of religion.[31]

Having sketched the basic outlines of the moral and religious functions of aesthetic taste, we have reached a stage at which it is imperative to consider how to regard certain aesthetic tastes or lack thereof as truly good or bad, which means also considering what place communities of taste play within the community of saints.

Against the Antinomy

If our analysis so far is fundamentally sound, aesthetic taste should be understood as an intrinsic part of morality and religion. Accordingly, bad taste would seem to be a moral and religious liability. But for this to be so, and for us to specify in what way, we must be able to argue that certain acts or dispositions of taste are genuinely better than others. Unfortunately, nothing seems more subjective than taste, and nothing is more subject to dispute, despite the Roman adage *de gustibus non disputandum est*, which suggests that such disputes have no real grounds. We must ask, therefore, whether the subjectivity and disputability of taste does not in fact undermine the notion that taste can in some sense be good or bad rather than merely pleasing or displeasing to particular people. Our answer to this question will clear away the last obstacle to our resolving the antinomy with which we began.

With respect to the subjectivity of taste, it must here suffice to say that, even if taste is indeed rooted in subjectivity, it is not in this regard fundamentally different from moral or religious sense; consequently, whatever gives credibility to apperceptions and evaluations of a religious and moral sort may well give credibility to aesthetic response. Certainly this is true if those philosophers and theologians are right who maintain that aesthetic forms can yield insights into that which is both subjectively real and objectively mysterious: into our experience of ourselves as free and purposive agents, for instance, and into our experience of the world itself as somehow instilled with purpose and with value that both transcends and is immanent within the here and now. Even Kant eventually suggested that, for all its subjectivity, taste points toward the 'supersensible' ground of reality that he called the noumenal.[32] In any case, many philosophers reject the sharp split between objective and subjective that would relegate taste to the sheerly subjective sphere.

Even so, we still face the problem of radical discrepencies among judgments and responses having to do with taste. Kant attempted to solve the problem by an *a priori* deduction that pronounced judgments of taste to be at once subjective and universal. As we earlier implied, however, Kant's idea of taste, or of what we have termed our capacity for aesthetic appraisal, is at once excessively private and presumptuous. It is too private because Kant considers the judgment of taste to be purely individual, made without any actual consideration of the views and experiences of others. He alleges, moreover, that a judgment of taste is impossible apart from personal appreciation – which means that one could not even recognize that there is aesthetic value in things that others set store by unless these are things that one also appreciates personally and for oneself. Kant's concept of taste is at the same time presumptuous, because he claims that the genuine judgments of taste are unconditional verdicts with which everyone *ought* to agree, and ideally *would* agree, although entirely on the basis of their private experience.

It seems far more reasonable to conclude that all evaluations involving aesthetic taste are to some extent communal both in formation and application rather than completely private and/or universal. When claiming aesthetic excellence for any work of art or nature, one rationally cannot and need not claim that everyone ought to find the same thing excellent. One is not commanding all people everywhere to take pleasure in what one finds aesthetically excellent, but commending it to others on the basis of a conviction (subject to modification) that some and perhaps many significant groups of people with good taste would appreciate it to a high degree, or would come to do so in time.[33] Even then, one knows that the degree of appreciation can be expected to fluctuate as communities of taste change. Such fluctuations are observable in relation to nearly all works of art, from *Don Quixote* and Gothic architecture to Impressionist painting and the films of Ingmar Bergman. The idea of a perfectly stable classic is an illusion.

Nonetheless, the idea of a classic is not itself illusory, and neither is the idea that there can be relatively adequate appreciation and appraisal of any work or object having aesthetic excellence. This is because the aesthetic standards of a community are rooted in human nature, which for all its variety and mutability maintains certain fundamental desires and needs that persist through change. A community of taste shares standards and understandings that make mutual experience and internal dialogue possible. Yet its standards also reflect in a particular way values potentially perceptible and intelligible beyond that community. People outside a given community of taste can with training and experience at least come to share the apperceptions, if not all the appreciations, of members within that community who have good taste. The 'outsider' with good taste actually may even come to appraise and appreciate a community's prized works more or less as an 'insider' would. Even when a work or aesthetic object appeals to desires or needs relatively peculiar to a particular community of taste, the reason for its appeal may be apperceived and its traits partially appreciated by 'outsiders' who are acquainted with structurally or functionally equivalent works within their own communities of taste. This inter-communal interaction of tastes clearly is evident in the mutual influence of African and American visual and musical styles, part of which can be seen in the Western artistic fascination with African masks and the African use of Western materials (such as anodized nails) within traditional forms. Cross-communal influence can be heard in jazz or, for that matter, in Paul Simon's award-winning album *Graceland*. In each large community, artistic taste is expanded, challenged, and changed by tastes from outside.

Taste as it is here conceived is thus dynamic rather than static, and communal rather than strictly private. It also appears in kinds and degrees. *Good taste, therefore, cannot be solely the possession of any one community, and certainly not only of the culturally elite.* Instead, good taste is manifest in many kinds of response and in many objects and styles that, even when foreign to the elite of society and culture, are in keeping with standards of excellence that other groups and individuals with good taste might eventually recognize and come to appreciate.

Having clarified the rudimentary but essential points of our theory of aesthetic appraisal and appreciation, we are within sight of the resolution of the antinomy with which we begin: the self-contradictory claim that taste does not and cannot matter to a religion like Christianity and yet turns out to matter anyway. This antinomy hinges on the conjunction of mutually incompatible notions of taste, some of which we can now jettison. Taste cannot matter greatly to Christianity if taste is supposed to be needed only to appraise aesthetic quality, which in turn is defined strictly by the preferences of the social and intellectual elite; yet neither can taste matter much to Christianity if all judgments and acts involving taste are equally bad or good; nor, finally, can taste matter religiously if aesthetic excellence is completely autonomous, bestowing purely self-contained and amoral delight. But these ideas of taste are ones we have rejected explicitly, thereby implicitly rejecting the antinomy itself. What is left is the fact that, for all the reasons we have earlier enumerated, taste (as reconceived here) is important to Christian life and practice.

With our antinomy not only held at bay but sent away, we now can deal directly with the question of how and in what ways *bad* taste is actually *sinful*. As we do so, however, the ghost of the antinomy will accompany us; because some of the ways in which taste becomes sinful recall the misunderstandings of taste and religion expressed in the antinomy itself.

Sinful Taste

For better or for worse, bad taste holds a certain fascination, rather like the sins depicted in Dante's *Inferno*. Accordingly, this last portion of our study will describe several basic kinds of sinful taste, each of which might deserve a circle in Hell or, if repented, a corresponding terrace on Mount Purgatory.

For the sake of simplicity, we will confine ourselves to four major categories of sinful taste: that of the aesthete, the philistine, the intolerant, and the indiscriminate. As we try to see why these involve sin, we will do well to think of what James Gustafson describes as the facets of human fault, all of which are acknowledged in some way by Dante himself.

According to Gustafson, the kinds of fault into which Christian theology has had insight are basically these four:

> the experience of misplaced confidence (the traditional problem of 'idolatry'), the experience of misplaced valuations of objects of desire (the traditional problem of wrongly ordered love), the experience of erroneous perceptions of the relations of things to each other and of our understanding of things (the traditional problem of 'corrupt' rationality), and the experience of unfulfilled obligations and duties (the traditional problem of disobedience).[34]

Gustafson explains that what makes these faults sinful is that 'persons have a measure of accountability to God' for each.

Is bad taste a fault, in any of the above senses? If not, it cannot be a sin. If so, is bad taste a fault for which persons have a measure of accountability to God? If they do not, then it still is not a sin, however regrettable it may be. Unless the fault of bad taste is somehow *my* fault, it is not my sin; I may have missed the mark, but it was not a mark I could be expected to hit.

That certain forms and functions of aesthetic taste are indeed faults, and faults for which a Christian might well believe we can be held responsible, should become evident in our analysis of forms of sinful taste embodied in four types of people.

Our first concern is with the aesthete, the person whose chief goal is not glorifying and enjoying God but glorying in the aesthetic delights of creation (human or divine). Immediately one recalls Kierkegaard's warning against confusing the aesthetic with either the ethical or the religious. Surely, from a Christian point of view, this is a blameworthy fault, and actually a form of idolatory. In addition, it may lead to a shirking of duties and obligations in the world of moral and religious practice.

It could be argued that our condemnation of aestheticism is actually tantamount to a condemnation not of any form of taste *per se* but of the very inclination to link taste with religion and morality in the manner of the present study. It is clearly the case that one must guard against naively equating aesthetic sensitivity with morality and religion. George Steiner painfully reminds us that those who oversaw the Nazi death camps 'were avid connoisseurs and, in some instances, performers of Bach and Mozart'. 'We know of personnel in the bureaucracy of the torturers and of the ovens', he writes, 'who cultivated a knowledge of Goethe, a love of Rilke'. On this basis he concludes that 'obvious qualities of literate response, of aesthetic feeling, can coexist with barbaric, politically sadistic behavior'.[35] One form of aestheticism, then, is the idolatry of aesthetic experience *per se*, and a second is the theoretical assimilation of the religious and moral to the aesthetic, on the assumption that art and beauty are intrinsically and inevitably redemptive.

There is another and equally sinful form of aestheticism, however, which is the intense appreciation and high appraisal of only those elements and kinds of art that have little or nothing directly to do with religious and moral values. Thus an aesthete can be so devoted to 'art for art's sake' that he or she simply cannot apperceive the moral and spiritual intensity of works that this person otherwise admires: Beethoven's setting of Schiller's 'Ode to Joy' in the Ninth Symphony, for example, or the *Heiliger Dankgesang* offered in the third movement of the same composer's String Quartet, opus 132. Such a person is lacking in taste and in more than taste, since the taste called for by works like these is wed to morality and religion.

It remains to be said that the aesthete is not found only among devotees of 'elite' arts. In fact, the cult followings of rock stars from the early days of Elvis to the more recent adulation of U2 or Madonna can generate aestheticism of a fervent sort as some fans virtually live to experience the art and to see and perhaps touch the artist.

In contrast to the aesthete, the philistine in the realm of aesthetics does not highly value or personally appreciate anything artistic and aesthetic that cannot be translated into practical, moral, or specifically religious terms. In some cases, in fact, the philistine is deficient in all forms of aesthetic sensitivity. This is clearly a mark of bad taste. But is it sinful? One might doubt that there is any sort of religious obligation to delight in beauty or other forms of aesthetic quality. Yet such a duty is implicit in Wolterstorff's assertion that aesthetic delight is part of the earthly *shalom* that is divinely ordained for human life. It is also expressed in more pungent terms in Walker's *The Color Purple* when Shug says to Celie, 'I think it pisses God off if you walk by the color purple in a field somewhere and don't notice it'.[36] The religious and moral value that the philistine hopes to preserve by retaining and promoting a taste only for the most blatantly moral and religious art is compromised by the impoverishment of the moral and the religious itself. For, as our theory has repeatedly insisted, the moral and the religious are at times inseparably and subtly joined with the aesthetic; and the aesthetically good is already in some sense good morally and religiously, partly by analogy with, but perhaps also as an instance of, the moral and the sacramental.

The third class of sinners in matters of taste is that of the intolerant. The intolerant person, who (like our other sinners) probably associates with a community sharing a similar defect in taste, is keenly aware of aesthetic standards of appraisal, but elevates his or her own standards to the level of absolutes. Intolerance is thus the aesthetic equivalent of the sin of pride, and it can be judged sinful for many of the same reasons that pride can be. It severs human ties and does violence to the freedom, integrity, and selfhood of others.

Intolerance is readily found within the communities of taste associated with the so-called elite arts. A large number of connoisseurs and professionals within all these arts assume that, at least with respect to the art in which they are most knowledgeable or accomplished, much of what transpires at a folk level, and all of what transpires at the level of popular and mass culture, is either abominable or completely trivial. Such judgments are reinforced by the general and often unqualified condemnations of mass culture made by Marxian theorists.[37]

This disdain for the popular has actually been defended in Christian terms by appealing to Kierkegaard's concept that to be Christian is to be allied with the unpopular, and that it is therefore possible to be a Christian only in opposition to others.[38] This maneuver, however, is without warrant. Kierkegaard's point is not to be dismissed lightly, but when the principle is completely generalized, it is questionable both from a theoretical point of view and from the standpoint of Christian morality.[39]

Jesus himself can hardly be said to have been closely allied with the socially and culturally elite, having instead favored the spiritual values of the humble and the poor. To be sure, many such relatively 'uncultured' people exhibit taste that is in some respects questionable, showing little appreciation for 'refined' aesthetic objects. They would never agree with Max Liebermann's dictum that a well-painted head of a cabbage is in itself more valuable than the badly painted head of a Madonna.[40] In fact, they would be more likely not to notice that the latter head was, from one point of view, badly painted. Among the 'masses', however, some viewers might appreciate very much that it was painted at all, and their apperception of the religious meaning of the painting could be extremely keen. Besides, unlike many a jaded connoisseur, they might genuinely appreciate the aesthetic qualities that they do apperceive, and might apperceive with considerable discernment the religious significance of whatever beauties they behold.

As for the widespread inability of the 'masses' to judge the worth of 'elite' art, one cannot afford to forget that conventional good taste has its own limits. Hume could not tolerate the artworks of nations he regarded as 'barbaric', yet many of these works are now prized by art collectors. It is safe to say, in fact, that bad taste in the form of intolerance and provinciality is inherent in much of what has traditionally been thought of as good taste. Thus in eighteenth-century France 'the man of taste was the man who believed in a certain type of civilization, as incarnated in a certain type of man'.[41] That man, needless to say, was either an aristocrat or someone with aristocratic airs. And he would scarcely have been deeply appreciative of the arts of the lower classes, of a number of foreign nations, or indeed of *women* at any level of society.

It is quite a different sort of good taste – ironic but nonetheless appreciative and possibly perceptive – that prompts one modern artist to make the following comment about a very bourgeois movie beloved by the many, though perhaps not by the few:

> *Bambi* has always been one of my favorite movies, especially because of the voice of Bambi's mother: so mature and so resonant and so patient. . . . And Bambi's wonderment at his first rainstorm, do you remember, when the rain drops from leaf to leaf? It's absolutely glorious; it's better than the infant Jesus in a way. It certainly has hit a lot of people.[42]

That it has hit a lot of people hardly proves that *Bambi* is good aesthetically, let alone an improvement on the infant Jesus. But, to repeat, good taste becomes intolerant and therefore morally and aesthetically bad if it refuses even to consider that the popular taste for such a movie may be more than *merely* 'sentimental', and hence may be good in ways that 'elite' taste cannot easily appreciate and appraise.

And yet it surely is not only the elite who sin through aesthetic intolerance. At the conclusion of Flannery O'Connor's story 'Revelation', Mrs Turpin, a self-righteous but hardly sophisticated woman, has a vision in which she sees a motley group of people streaming across a bridge extending upward from the earth toward heaven. Among the people are some she recognizes as like her husband and herself, walking up the bridge with dignity and in good order. Ahead of them, however, are 'whole companies of white-trash . . . and bands of black niggers in white robes, and battalions of freaks and lunatics shouting and clapping and leaping like frogs'. Aesthetically and religiously speaking, the ones Mrs Turpin thought should come last (if at all) have come first.[43] Taste that seems good can be bad, and allegedly bad taste can turn out to be good.

But if this leads one to conclude that really there is nothing good or bad in matters of taste, one is guilty of being indiscriminate, which is the final sin on our short list. Here one can see the shadow of our abandoned antinomy. For one basic supposition behind the half of the antinomy that we ended up rejecting is that taste pertains only to concerns that have no religious or moral standing. And there is no clearer way of embracing and reinforcing this supposition than by arguing that there are no standards of taste at all, so that where taste is concerned all opinions and perceptions are equal. Radical aesthetic relativism severs taste from religion and morality because if taste were tied to them in any way, it would necessarily be tied to notions of right and wrong, righteousness and sin, wholeness and brokenness, freedom and captivity.

Those whose taste incorporates such relativism by indiscriminately embracing all aesthetic phenomena cannot – except perhaps in moments of mystical transcendence – value anything appropriately. They cannot even distinguish between what in their own experience has relatively lasting value and what is just superficially appealing. And because the superficially appealing can be profoundly ugly, and the profoundly ugly can be deeply evil, the indiscriminate are virtually defenseless against the demonic. This is not to say that either bad *art* or bad *taste* is necessarily demonic. It is to say that bad taste in the form of indiscriminate appreciation and judgment is vulnerable and, to the extent to which it is a result of choice, it is also culpable and not merely innocent.

Yet its proximity to innocence makes indiscriminate taste the easiest to forgive. This is true even in the eyes of Flaubert, the most discriminating of people in matters of taste. In his tale 'A Simple Heart', Flaubert tells the story of Felicité, a simple peasant woman whose severely tested fidelities and frustrated loves culminate in love for and attachment to a parrot named Loulou. Loulou is given to Felicité by a derelict on the day the old man dies; after Loulou's own death, the parrot is stuffed and, though eventually worm-eaten, is treasured not only as a constant companion but also as an aid to religious devotion. One feels that there is infinite and immediate forgiveness for the indiscriminate judgment shown by the old and mortally ill Felicité on the last day of her life. On this day, the feast of Corpus Christi, she gives Loulou to be placed alongside other gifts on the altar and – as she herself breathes her last – thinks she can see 'in the opening heavens, a gigantic parrot hovering above her head'.[44] The vision of the Holy Spirit as Loulou, and hence of the Heavenly Dove as Parrot, borders on being aesthetically ludicrous and theologically idolatrous. But, in view of the exemplary humility and love of Felicité, any recognition of the inadequacy of her indiscriminate aesthetic and religious imagination is bound to suggest the inadequacy – as well as mysterious efficacy – of imaginings that would more commonly be deemed acceptable.

From a Christian perspective, the final theological reflection on sinful taste in *all* its forms should, perhaps, have to do with forgiveness. For if taste is as essential to morality and religion as we have said, then Good Taste in its highest, multifaceted form is required for human perfection. But if Good Taste at its best is as encompassing and demanding as we have also said – involving communities as well as individuals, and the discernment of goodness and holiness as well as beauty – then in taste as in other things there is always the imperfection that Christian theologians call sin. Consequently, the ultimate answer to bad taste may not be good taste but Grace.

7

Questioning the Classics: Norms and Canons in Religion and Art

Classics in Question

From the vantage point afforded by our study at this penultimate stage, we are able to see that much of the undeniable substance and variety in ways of being religious – and specifically in ways of being Christian – is directly concerned with forms of experience and expression in which aesthetic discernment, appreciation, and judgment are significantly ingredient. The likely discomfort of a Presbyterian or Baptist at High Mass in a Bavarian Rococo church has to do not just with differing understandings of the Eucharist, for instance, nor merely with the fact that the liturgical actions and surroundings may be unfamiliar, but also with what amounts to a difference in aesthetic sensibilities regarding the appropriate setting and language of worship. There is every reason to take seriously a claim like that of Margaret Miles when she argues that the Protestant Reformers, in supplanting the Catholic emphasis on the visual with an emphasis on the aural (verbal and musical), altered a whole religious sensibility at a perceptual level.[1]

If it is the case that, as we have been insisting, aesthetic form and religious content often are interrelated while being in some degree distinguishable, one cannot dismiss such aesthetic and perceptual considerations as a matter merely of externals, as though faith itself were untouched by them. Miles argues that they can have as great an impact on religion as does theology *per se*. And we saw in our analysis of the varieties of religious aesthetic experience that one's very perception of the nature of the divine and of the potential of the human is deeply conditioned by the forms of religious aesthetic mediation with which one is confronted within and without institutional religion.

We now would venture to argue specifically that a great many of

those things that function normatively and authoritatively for a
particular religious denomination or tradition – the works, acts,
images, narratives, and texts that serve as its *classics* – are markedly
and intrinsically aesthetic, even in groups or traditions that do not
promote the arts as such. Although this is not of course the first
time anyone has proposed such a thesis, the integralist neo-
aesthetics we have espoused and the pluralist theory of taste we
have articulated put us in a position to see the aesthetic dimension
of religious classics and of their various functions in a new light.

The discussion that follows will essentially be concerned with
four basic questions regarding religious aesthetic classics, without
however making any attempt to cover in detail those issues that
already have been treated in depth in separate studies in hermeneutics and literary theory. Here we will ask, first: How is it
possible for an aestheticon such as a work of art to be both
aesthetically and religiously a 'classic', and hence a signal work in
terms of which an artistic and religious tradition each understands
itself and its values? Second: How can one religion acknowledge as
its classics various works that not only differ in kind but also in
some sense compete and conflict with one another, as the classics
of Christian art and theology often do? Third: What is the relationship between classic, counter-classic, and non-classic? And,
fourth: What is entailed in the 'performance' of a particular religion
as itself a 'classic' that both allows and requires a diversity of
performing traditions?

Our answers to these questions, which again will be pursued in
relation to Christianity, will indicate that certain traditional notions
of what it means for something to be religiously authoritative and
classical can and should be questioned and reformulated in the
light of the kind of aesthetics we have been developing here.
Throughout this discussion we will be moving toward what we
will term a critical theological pluralism – endorsing the possibility
of standards of religious and aesthetic value, yet treating all such
standards as subject to varied expression and to ongoing critical
dialogue within and between traditions.

Artworks as Religious Classics

That a classic work of art can also be religious is obvious to
everyone. But many people – Christian theologians in particular –

seem to have had doubts that aesthetica such as classic works of art can be counted among the very highest and most trustworthy forms of religious expression. In other words, they doubt that whatever it is that makes a work a *classic* in the sphere of art could contribute directly to its being a genuine *classic* in the sphere of religion: a first-class work by which the tradition can evaluate, understand, and orient itself.

One expression of such doubts takes the form of condescension: It is all well and good for babes in the faith to feed on the milk that religious arts provide, but the spiritually mature will go on to something more substantial – something that is truly normative, such as one finds in theology and Scripture. Augustine says something like this in Book Ten of the *Confessions* when he approves of the singing of hymns, but primarily so that 'by indulging the ears, weaker spirits may be inspired with feelings of devotion'. In the same context Augustine discretely congratulates himself on having reached a level of spiritual maturity at which he is moved more by the meaning and truth of the words sung than by the actual singing.[2] It evidently does not occur to him that the truth apprehended *as sung* might be in any way deeper or richer than the truth that the mind apprehends on its own.

Writing seven hundred years later, in 1125, Bernard of Clairvaux adopts a similar posture. Allowing that 'material beauty' might need to be used in churches because it is in this way that the devotion of carnal people can be aroused, he argues that those who are supposed to be spiritually superior – the monks at Cluny, in this case – should have no need of the pictures and sculptures that they in fact have all around them: 'So many and so marvelous are the various shapes surrounding us that it is more pleasant to read the marble than the books, and to spend the whole day marvelling over these things rather than meditating on the law of God. Good Lord! If we aren't embarrassed by the silliness of it all, shouldn't we at least be disgusted by the expense?'[3]

Doubtless Augustine and Bernard were making valuable points. But the foundation for their negative bias against what today we term the aesthetic and the artistic is shaky. Indeed, it quite disintegrates if one does not accept the dubious and originally non-Christian idea from the late Classical and Hellenistic world that there is an ontological hierarchy – a great chain or ladder of being – ascent of which requires that the devout spirit and truth-seeking mind progressively leave behind things of body and sense. It is this particular hierarchy and this view of human nature, with its spirit/body split and its accompanying deprecation of the physical world, that prevents any acknowledgement that some-thing so sensory as art could provide a true standard or norm for religious awareness and insight.

Most biblical writings, by contrast, at least presuppose that body and spirit belong and function together. The bread of physical nourishment and the bread of eternal life go together; physical healing is part of spiritual healing. While John's gospel affirms that God is spirit and must be worshipped in spirit and in truth, there is no suggestion there that the singing of hymns, for instance, would not be fully as spiritual an act as some exercise of the mind *per se* would be. Since the writings of the Christian scriptural canon seldom share the Gnostic scorn for the material world, it is not surprising that modern Christian theologians, combining biblical and psychological insights, have developed fruitful ways of pictur-ing 'spiritual' activity and progress that do not radically separate spirit and body.[4] Although none of this exalts art as such, none of it precludes a high estimate of its religious possibilities.

There is, however, another kind of argument that could be brought to bear against our claim that a religious work might in some instances be the classic that it is only by virtue of incorporat-ing aesthetic qualities of the highest sort. This second argument against our thesis is put forward most subtly and forcefully by the contemporary Catholic theologian David Tracy. Interestingly enough, it is he who of all modern theologians makes perhaps the most and best use of the idea of the religious classic and who, in doing so, employs the idea of the artistic classic (though not only the artistic) as a paradigm for thinking about the religious classic.

Since Tracy mentions poems by Gerard Manley Hopkins and John of the Cross as simultaneously artistic and Christian classics, and since he places works by Kierkegaard, Bernini, and Rubens in this category as well, there can be no doubt that in his view the artistic classic can be a Christian classic. Yet Tracy insists that this is extraordinary indeed. And even when it does occur, there clearly is (for Tracy) a question as to whether that which makes a particular work an artistic classic can ever be a major ingredient in making the work a religious classic as well.[5]

Why does Tracy think that the convergence of the religious classic and the artistic classic in one work is so unlikely? The chief reason he gives is that, in his view, the explicitly religious classic struggles intensely with 'subject matter' that its form plainly cannot adequately express: something that we have called transcendence and that he calls the manifestation of 'the whole itself by the power of the whole'. Only through a radically dialectical process of concealing-revealing can the work permit 'a recognition of the event-character of a true manifestation of the whole'. Tracy asks, rhetorically, 'How can we expect a fully adequate [artistic] form, genre or style to express *that*?' Mark's gospel, Tracy hastens to remind us, is an indubitable religious classic, but, despite having literary merit, it is not a literary or artistic classic. Moreover, even in the exceptional cases in which artistic classics are also religious ones, they are not, says Tracy, 'under the same rules of production, identically both at the same time'.[6] Presumably he means by this that the ends or goals informing the making of art specifically are quite distinct from the ends guiding the making of something religiously valuable or normative.

Illuminating as these observations may be, they also are problematical. Is it really the case that there is something inherent in the highest aims and means of artistry that would prevent artistic form from fitting the highest requirements of religious expression? Or is it not the case that a rather high proportion of the greatest works of art are greatly valued by various religions, and that in the West they also are frequently Christian, and powerfully so?

Now Tracy himself makes it plain that he accepts the view of Heidegger and Gadamer that the classics of art disclose truth, and in fact mysteriously conceal even as they reveal, just as religious works must do.[7] And he himself points out that the greatest artistic classics are frequently somewhat 'unsteady' and flawed in form and style, their greatness consisting partly in their capacity to work with, and in spite of, tensions and creative ambiguities.[8] It would seem only reasonable to conclude that these traits would be suited to a religious 'subject' – some aspect of the world and life seen not just in its particularity but also in its unfathomable depth, and so in relation to what is ultimately yet mysteriously significant. This would give the artistic classic a capacity to transform our mundane sense of things and hence to disclose (and simultaneously to conceal, as beyond our grasp and full comprehension) something of the religious 'whole', or the transcendent.

Tracy resists this conclusion, however, apparently because he thinks that for religious purposes the inadequacy of form must almost always be intensified to the point that the work becomes somewhat inartistic. What Tracy thereby ignores is the fact that an inartistic and ineptly de-formed 'form' can lose both the intensity and the power needed to shatter or transform the respondent's normal mode of awareness. He forgets what he at one point seems to realize: that the enormous formal tensions and expressive self-abnegations in late Michelangelo or in late Rembrandt or in many of the 'self-consuming artifacts' of the metaphysical poets all engender striking and moving artistic effects that can and often do serve precisely the purposes that Tracy states are essential to a religious classic.[9] Such formal 'inadequacies' are all the more striking, moving, and at times disturbing *because* they are artistically wrought. Thus these classics of art release tremendous spiritual energy as they reach a limit at which, in probing sacred history or individual experience, they point beyond themselves and push us toward the ultimately inexpressible yet gracefully self-disclosive transcendence within and beyond what we perceive.

That said, we also must point out that, contrary to what Tracy and a number of other theologians seem to assume, the way of formal imperfection is not the only path by which classic art can achieve classic religious status. Indeed, in the ears and eyes of many Christians there is profound religious meaning in the virtual perfection of form exhibited by works such as Thomas Tallis's utterly simple yet beautifully crafted anthem 'If Ye Love Me Keep My Commandments', or in Bach's setting of the Nicene Creed in the Mass in B Minor, or in Michelangelo's Vatican *Pietà*. The formal perfection of such works of art seems itself to mediate, and indirectly to manifest, an infinitely greater perfection, potentially experienced as divine.

We still must reckon, however, with Tracy's claim that when one examines the supposedly rare works that are somehow both artistic and religious classics, one finds that they are not, 'under the same rules of production, identically both at the same time'. To this our reply is that it is quite true that if one's 'rules of production' are exclusively and narrowly artistic (that is, devoted to aesthetic ends of the purest sort), then one cannot produce a classic that by design is also intrinsically religious. Yet in point of fact works can be produced according to intuitive 'rules' and conscious aims that work to wed artistic goals with religious ones. It certainly could be argued on the basis of the neo-aesthetic theories we have been proposing that works such as the book of Job, a number of Psalms, Chartres Cathedral, Dante's *Divine Comedy*, and Fra Angelico's paintings for the Florentine convent of San Marco are the particular aesthetic and religious classics that they are precisely because the peak of their aesthetic excellence actually coincides with, and could not be attained apart from, the peak of their religious vision – and vice versa.

This leads us to, and helps us answer, the final objection that some Christian theologians would lodge against our wanting to consider certain works of art to be Christian classics. According to many theologians (often Protestant and neo-orthodox) it is within the power of art only to show the misery of the human condition in its unredeemed state and so to pose the human 'question' to which Christianity and its theologians provide the religious 'answer'.[10] While art can humble and shake us, it cannot be 'a way of rising toward God'.[11]

There is no denying that art can serve a vital critical and prophetic purpose. Much art of great religious significance probes our humanity in such a way as to reveal that we are, as Augustine would say, a problem to ourselves. Moreover, there is no art that can coerce either God's self-disclosure or human transformation. Yet we have taken pains to demonstrate that if there are indeed things that Christians can regard as religiously 'uplifting', as envisioning redemptive possibilities, or as in some sense revelatory of the transcendent, certain classics of art should be counted among them, and not just the literary classics of the Bible. Dante plainly believed his *Comedy* could corroborate and vividly re-express not just the horrors of human nature but also its highest possibilities – a belief many of his readers fully share. Again, Haydn expressed a conviction that, though his oratorio *The Creation* was being presented in a church against the wishes of its pastor, it would be able to stimulate 'holy feelings', with the result that the people would be more 'uplifted than from listening to [the pastor's] sermons'. One woman observed in response to this music: 'One must shed fond tears over the greatness, the majesty, the goodness of God. The spirit is uplifted. One can only adore and marvel'.[12] There is Handel as well, who with reference to his experience in composing *Messiah* is reported to have exclaimed: 'I did think I did see all Heaven before me and the great God Himself', and who publicly credited Heaven with having in some sense given him the work.[13] To numerous Christians this claim seems somehow credible. All of these works do more than reveal the human predicament and pose the human question. They proclaim or manifest the 'good news' of Christianity itself.

We have every reason to conclude, therefore, that Christian theologians by and large seriously underestimate the extent to which classic artworks, within and without the church, have historically and legitimately functioned for many people as classics of the faith. That these classics have largely been ignored by the theological tradition mainly indicates that they are not first and foremost theology. It does not mean that they are not significant means by which Christians identify and orient themselves. To acknowledge this fully and openly, however, is to alter significantly the usual notions of what we might call the 'canon' of Christian classics. At the same time it raises the question of whether Christian classics, exhibiting as they do such undeniable diversity, can all be said to work together compatibly and harmoniously to build up the faith. It is to this question that we turn next.

The Plurality of Classics and the Conflict of Norms

To include aesthetic works in the canon of Christian classics is entirely consistent with the integralist theories of art and religion which we have supported and presumably advanced. Like other religious classics, these are works of exceptional quality that deeply and repeatedly reward attention and that can be valued similarly over a long period of time by a wide range of perceptive and receptive people.

To claim certain artworks as religious classics, however, is by no means to assume that they exist in perpetual harmony with other Christian classics or that they always give rise to compatible interpretations and evaluations. Indeed, if one considers the tensions and conflicts evident within the supremely normative Christian classic, the Bible, and the plurality of the interpretations and applications of the biblical texts over the course of Christian history, one begins to understand that it is in the nature of any classic, or of any canon of classics (which really the Bible is), to generate conflicting interpretations and to exist in some tension with other classics.

In point of fact, with respect to the classics in general – and not only those of religion and art – there is a kind of inherent diversity and implicit pluralism that manifests itself in at least two ways: as tensions and differences in and among classic works themselves and as tensions and differences in and among various communal and individual responses to classic works. In the next section we will explicitly treat social and communal factors as we discuss the counter-classic and the non-classic in relation to the classic 'proper' (which, properly speaking, is nothing perfectly fixed and eternal). Here we will focus on the plurality of the norms and expectations which necessarily derive simply from the different traits of the classics themselves. This we can best do by contrasting the characteristic traits of classic works of Christian art with the traits of classic works of theology; for, of all the forms of Christian classics, these perhaps differ the most from each other and spawn the most divergent responses. Specifically, we will want to reflect on major contrasts between their respective 'languages'.

Although the 'languages' spoken by Christian art and theology are related to each other not only in what they say but also to some extent in how they say it, they nonetheless cannot be translated without remainder one into the other. This is clear from the norms by which they are to be evaluated, from the aims they can rightly be expected to fulfil, and finally from the manner in which they exercise their influence as classic religious works.

Theological discourse in its most typical classical mode strives to be logically consistent, coherent, comprehensive, conceptually precise, and propositional. To be sure, even theology of this kind is rooted in symbol and metaphor and must be responsive to the norms of prayer and practice. This is reflected in the maxim *lex orandi, lex credendi* (the law of praying [is] the law of believing). Moreover, theology as a mode of explanation and understanding that works with the pre-understandings of the tradition must guard against explaining away what the tradition affirms as inexplicable mystery. Yet for faith to seek the understanding that theology itself can provide is for faith to seek expression, in so far as possible, in rational and intellectual form.

Clearly the expectations and criteria for artistic success are very different from those for theology, in addition to differing in some measure from one kind of art to another. It is true that the arts involve certain kinds of rationality and that even non-verbal religious art can sometimes present a particular doctrine with theological precision. This might be said of Masaccio's painting of 1425 entitled *The Holy Trinity with the Virgin and St John* (Santa Maria Novella, Florence). It might also be said of the Trinitarian symbolism in Monteverdi's setting of the 'Gloria Patri' in the 'Magnificat' that concludes his *Vespers of the Blessed Virgin* (1610). But the special gift of art is not doctrinal precision, conceptual clarity, or the ability to 'think straight'. Art's gift, when not given over simply to a delight that is almost sheerly aesthetic, is rather to explore fictively, metaphorically, and experientially what formal theology cannot itself present or contain. When certain works of Rembrandt, for instance, make divine forgiveness and grace 'visible',[14] they are far more than theological illustrations, and their peculiar profundity cannot therefore simply be absorbed directly into theological discourse, although it may penetrate in ways that ultimately affect the theologian's own vision and reflection.

Precisely because the means and ends of art diverge in many respects from those of theology and indoctrination, it often happens that the effect and meaning of an artwork exist in some tension with theological norms as these inform normal religious and liturgical practice. In Mozart's great but unfinished Mass in C Minor (K. 427), the setting of the 'Et Incarnatus Est' for soprano, three wind instruments, and strings is extraordinarily florid and sensuous (Plate 4). (Not coincidentally, it may have been intended to be sung by Mozart's new bride Constanze.) Accordingly, this work has aptly been described as not only 'the quintessence of the art of sound' but also 'ravished music in ecstasy before God made man'.[15] It would not occur to a theologian to imagine the Incarnation in quite the mode one imagines here. And no one would want to claim that here one finds *the* meaning of the Incarnation. Yet this beauty is not that of sheer carnality; its sensuality is transfigured. The peculiar tension between the doctrine of Word made flesh and the experience of musical ravishment creates a religious as well as aesthetic wonder – a Christian classic that courts heterodoxy only thereby to enrich the tradition itself.

In view of such contrasts between the characteristic language of theology and the languages of art, the arts cannot but differ from theology in the ways in which they establish their classics. Because art does not 'speak' theology *per se*, the judgment as to whether some style or work of art is a classic Christian 'statement' cannot responsibly be left simply to the theologian *qua* theologian any more than it can be left to the art connoisseur alone. Credible judgments as to the classic or non-classic status of religious aesthetic works, like judgments regarding their possible liturgical function, can only arise out of repeated experience and dialogue among representatives of a cross-section of Christianity, including those specially trained in the making and criticism of art.

The differences between theological and aesthetic 'languages' likewise manifest themselves in a contrast between the ways in which artistic religious classics and the classics of doctrine or theology are realized and transmitted. One can fully take in, variously restate, and clearly retain for an indefinite period of time the content and import of Thomas Aquinas's five proofs for the existence of God. To the extent that one needs to return to the text, it is in order to refresh one's memory. When one returns, however, to Dante's poetic presentation of the beatific vision in the *Paradiso* one never supposes it is just to refresh the memory one has. In response to art, memory begins to fail from the very start; every experience of the work is in some important respect new.

This means that the classic work of art not only can survive repeated exposure but also requires it, if it is to become and remain active as a classic. It also means that the work must be directly experienced by a large number of people, or at least by individuals of notable influence. This is not always a simple matter. Even in the case of works in media that circulate with relative ease, such as literature, music, film, and graphic art, the cooperation of powers and systems of distribution cannot be assumed. Hence, many works that are potential classics of art do not actually *function* as classics except for a small number of people.

From this last observation, however, we should not jump to the conclusion that, for everyone but the fortunate few, whatever is artistic is likely to be a classic in name only. Historically speaking, the classics of art have existed and persisted through the invention and influence of *styles*. Thus in a sense the Gothic style itself is as much a classic as is Rheims or Chartres or York Minster; for these Gothic churches are far more similar than they are different in artistic and religious meaning and effect. Again, the Masses of Palestrina and Victoria and even Byrd, which sound very much alike to everyone but the highly trained musician, are valuable to the Christian tradition more for what they share stylistically than for their individuality.

This is less the case in the modern period, to be sure; here if anywhere originality and individuality become paramount concerns. But in fact the degree and significance of such originality has been exaggerated. Works by the same artist often produce rather similar effects. One need not see all of Edvard Munch or hear every Mahler symphony to grasp much of what each artist has to offer, and these works have affinities with the creations of other artists as well. Even the 'inimitable' compositions of Mahler share a stylistic world with Wagner, Richard Strauss, the early Schoenberg, and lesser figures like Zemlinsky. Although such works are hardly interchangeable, neither is each one entirely *sui generis*.

It should be noted, in any case, that even individual artworks can now exercise greater influence as classics than formerly was the case. In the modern era comparative ease of travel and sophisticated modes of production and reproduction, from conventional photography to the new digital technologies, have begun to permit easier access to specific works, both past and present. As a consequence, now, more than ever before, the Christian tradition (among others) has the capacity actively to claim particular classics of art from its worldwide community and from every era of its history.

Finally, we would note that in any religious or artistic tradition there are classics of repetition and perpetuation, whereby the tradition sustains the status quo; there are classics of recovery and restoration, whereby the tradition rediscovers its roots; and there also are classics of discovery and exploration, whereby the tradition seeks out new directions. Because of the ambiguity and creative polyvalence inherent in the languages of art, it may be that the frequently unorthodox religious artworks of our time can function in the third capacity, potentially exploring more freely than theology itself the terrain along and beyond the margins of a religion. In any case, because of the exploratory character of so many modern classics, both artistic and intellectual, it is entirely possible than some of the works now most valuable to the Christian tradition are not widely recognized as classics by the tradition as a whole, but only by its avant-garde. It also may be that many works valuable to the majority of religious people in any given place and time are not classics at all. These are possibilities we are now prepared to examine.

Classic, Counter-Classic, and Non-Classic

In the year 1835 Thomas Macaulay made the following assessment of Indian literature and culture:

I have no knowledge of either Sanskrit or Arabic. But I have done what I could to form a correct estimate of their value. I have read translations of the most celebrated Arabic and Sanskrit works. I have conversed, both here and at home, with men distinguished by their proficiency in the Eastern tongues. I am quite ready to take the oriental learning at the valuation of the orientalists themselves. I have never found one among them who could deny that a single shelf of a good European library was worth the whole native literature of India and Arabia.[16]

That the bias represented by such a judgment plainly is extreme does nothing to alter the fact that the criteria that are used to establish canons and to recognize classics – whether artistic, intellectual, or specifically religious – are never completely *un*-biased. These biases, moreover, are always in some measure political, reflecting the structures and machinations of power. The extensive literature now developing around issues of the politics of interpretation and judgment, especially as viewed from the standpoint of minorities, women, and underclass or 'Third World' populations, testifies persuasively to the key role of power and prejudice in canonization.[17]

Doubtless, then, the term 'classic' itself is to a considerable extent not only relative but also 'loaded', much as the term 'good taste' traditionally has been. Accordingly, our aim in this section is to reach a more balanced understanding of the category of the 'classic' by locating it in relation to two other categories, which we will term the 'counter-classic' and the 'non-classic'.

We begin with the now common but once heterodox observation that every classic is only a classic relative to individuals and groups situated and prepared in certain ways. This means that the traditional idea of the universal and timeless classic is, at best, highly idealized. Even in the case of Scripture it is demonstrable that the biblical books that Christians all acknowledge to be canonical and so to be in some way valid in every time and place are actually interpreted and used differently by different groups at different times, creating in practice different canons within the canon.

That non-scriptural classics exhibit even less stability becomes apparent if one considers in some detail the adventures and uncertain destiny of a work such as Sir Edward Elgar's *The Dream of Gerontius* – a 'classic' of Macaulay's own native England. Commissioned for the Birmingham Triennial Musical Festival of 1900,

Gerontius has been described by one commentator as 'one of the great spiritual adventures of Romantic art, an intensely personal work on a theme that is timeless and universal: an ordinary man on the point of death'.[18] Elgar himself thought at the time of its composition that of all his works this one was most likely to endure. He even ventured to append to the autograph copy of the score a quotation from Ruskin: 'This is the best of me. . . . This, if anything of mine, is worth your memory'.[19]

Yet the text Elgar had chosen to set was a religious poem by John Henry Newman, whose Catholicism (like that of Elgar himself) was something Elgar feared would be a liability in Protestant England, potentially offending performer, audience, and critic – which in fact it did. But this was not the only burden the work would have to bear. It transpired that Charles Swinnerton Heap, who was to conduct the work at the festival, expired before the choir ever began to rehearse, leaving the whole affair in the hands of an elderly and much less sympathetic or capable conductor. Rehearsals were further delayed by modifications in the score that were urged on Elgar by his friend and editor A. J. Jaeger of the publishing firm Novello. Following what turned out to be a disastrous premier, Novello (without Jaeger's consent) tried to renege on its royalty agreement with Elgar, arguing that the work was a commercial failure. Meanwhile Elgar had written to Jaeger:

> I have worked hard for forty years and at the last, Providence denies me a decent hearing of my work: so I submit – I always said God was against art and I still believe it. Anything obscene or trivial is blessed in this world, and has a reward. . . . I have allowed my heart to open once – it is now shut against every religious feeling and every soft gentle impulse *for ever*.[20]

This self-pitying outburst turned out to be false to Elgar's later sentiments and failed to anticipate the appreciation that soon would be forthcoming in his homeland. At the same time, it must be said that even today there are many musicians and music lovers across the Atlantic who have never even heard *of* this work, let alone actually *heard* it – or who, having heard it, do not admire it.

On the other hand, it also is true that the current revival of interest in late-Romantic idioms has brought this and other Elgar compositions to the attention of a trans-Atlantic public that formerly showed only scorn for anything so 'ripe' in sound. Moreover, a new recording by the young English conductor Simon Rattle, whose own stock is very much on the rise, bodes well for still wider recognition of this piece. Certainly the work is avidly being promoted as a classic by the company GKN, which helped underwrite the new recording project and which has supplied promotional material declaring the work to be 'one of the world's finest pieces of choral music'.[21]

None of this calls for much additional commentary here. What is important in this case is something quite conspicuous: the interplay of personal ambition, institutional politics, public taste, chance, religion, economics, and national pride in the creation and recognition of a 'first-class' work. Elgar thus was quite right about one thing he had said in his outburst to Jaeger: it is indeed impossible to predict with any certainty what Providence will reward, or for how long. Classics, it would appear, are not made in heaven but on earth, in a very unstable, complex environment that we sometimes call 'culture'.

In view of all that can imperil the status and meaning of any classic, and in view of the interplay of powers involved in the recognition of any work's 'lasting' value, it is no wonder that particular communities tend to cultivate their own canons and classics and their own canonical interpretations of the classics they share in common with others. In this process one witnesses the emergence not merely of supplementary classics but also of counter-classics: works that are made or 'canonized' in opposition to, or in place of, certain works deemed classic by others. So it is that when one of the standard histories of art – that of H. W. Janson – surveys the whole span of art history without so much as mentioning a single woman artist, there is a strong impetus not just to add figures like Kollwitz, Cassatt, Vigée-Le Brun, and Artemisia Gentileschi to the list of notables, but also to suspect the original criteria of selection. Accordingly, feminist art historians and critics may employ new criteria to criticize or downgrade certain artists held in high esteem by Janson or some other 'mainline' historian, perhaps judging the art in question to be marred by patriarchal and otherwise exploitive values.[22]

Clearly, then, the proposal and invention of counter-classics is not simply a luxury indulged in by an elite avant-garde, though of course the avant-garde in art has given particular kinds of counter-classics notoriety. What is more important and serious is that traditions and social classes that have long been oppressed and marginalized cannot in fact exercise any significant measure of self-determination or achieve a moderately independent identity without to some extent developing their own canons and classics and claiming to be the best interpreters of their own best works – including those of art and religion. Realizing this, the Black liberation theologian James Cone declares, for example, 'I am ... convinced that it is not possible to render an authentic interpretation of black music without having shared and participated in the experience that created it. Black music must be *lived* before it can be understood'.[23]

As we have noted, a counter-classic exists as such only because it stands in contrast or opposition to some other classic that has been accorded high status by those in a position of dominance and power. The classics of Indian music and Sanskrit literature are not *counter*-classics until they come in conflict with empire and with traditions made to be their rivals. One must ask, therefore: Given its typical position of subordination or marginality, how can a counter-tradition attempt to justify its own classics *as* classic, whether in its own eyes or potentially in the eyes of others?

One strategy is to refuse to play the game of evaluation and comparison at all, taking instead a radically egalitarian stance. In this case, the counter-tradition counters the whole traditional notion of the importance of critical appraisal. Within the works of the counter-tradition, therefore, emphasis may be placed on process over product and on community over individual accomplishment. For example, the old-fashioned American 'quilting bee', in which sewing is truly communal, has been taken by some feminist artists as a model for their own more sophisticated group artistry. Similarly, Judy Chicago's *Dinner Party* was constituted as a multipart work executed by a large group of women working cooperatively, though under the direct supervision of Chicago herself.

A radically egalitarian approach obviously tends, however, to undermine the possibility of establishing the existence of genuine counter-*classics*, because it abolishes criteria for judging a work to be first-class. Eventually, therefore, almost all counter-traditions celebrate and argue for the special merits of some of their products. They begin in fact to use the same kinds of argument to legitimize their own classics that 'mainline' traditions use, only in support of different works.

In particular, as counter-traditions defend their favored works against critique or neglect on the part of 'mainline' traditions, they come to resemble the latter traditions to the extent of putting forward one or the other of two different and not entirely compatible claims. The first claim is that no work can be judged adequately from a standpoint outside that of the tradition that produced it and that maintains modes of interpretation suitable to it. The second is that the works of a particular tradition (one's own) are simply superior – in short, the truly classic classics – and can be judged so by those who are sufficiently enlightened or experienced, or in some way 'converted'.

It is in the interest of our pursuit of a critical pluralism – both in religion and art – to be able to demonstrate that each of these two claims, figuring as they do in the operations of traditional as well as counter-traditional norms, has something to commend it and that the two claims, properly modified, can in fact be reconciled. This we can commence to do by way of a close analogy drawn from the sphere of classical music.

In concert in Paris the choir of Christ Church Cathedral, Oxford, sings Byrd, Tallis, and Britten in an assured and exquisite manner that no group outside England can match. The same choir, however, quite misses the essential tone and piquancy of Poulenc's very French Mass in G, although the notes are right and the intonation perfect. It seems obvious that the English classics are 'in their bones', whereas the Poulenc is in a real sense foreign. Applied to the issue of appraisal as opposed to performance, this would appear to support the thesis that only those inside a tradition are fully qualified to judge, to interpret, and indeed to determine its classics.

Nevertheless, this estimate of the varying success of the choir in coping with such contrasting classics was made by an American, whose traditions are different still. Thus, if this appraisal has validity, it must be possible to transcend traditions enough to make comparative judgments. If so, could not one proceed with comparisons in such a way as to arrive finally at the judgment that the supreme classics of a particular tradition (usually one's own) really are superior to those of any other tradition?

Notice that one cannot have it both ways. That is, one cannot claim that a given tradition is the best judge of its own classics and at the time claim that one tradition's classics are superior to those of other traditions; for the latter claim infringes on the rights of other traditions to be their own best judges. As we have indicated, however, it may be that the valid features of each of these claims can be reconciled and synthesized. To begin with, it seems that no one today could reasonably deny that representatives of a particular tradition are in general best equipped to judge its works. To take an instance from what is in some respects a counter-tradition, we surely can say that Ravi Shankar is in a much better position to make reliable judgments on Indian music than Thomas Macaulay could ever have been, and that he might be more reliable still when it comes to evaluating classical Indian music for sitar.

Even so, as we have implied, Ravi Shankar's judgments must be regarded as in principle corrigible or at least as fruitfully debatable – first of all by his own community of Indian musicians and then by those outside. To admit this, however, is to open up the possibility that critical appraisals can in some measure cross boundaries between traditions. In short, it is to make room for a *critical pluralism* which invites exchange and challenge among traditions without presuming that the final outcome will be a collection of eternal and universal classics, whether traditional or counter-traditional.

To acknowledge the legitimacy and importance of critical dialogue between different and even rival traditions does nothing to diminish the integrity of a counter-tradition or, for that matter, of a 'mainline' tradition either. For it is only as a tradition engages in such dialogue and potentially appreciative exchange with other traditions that it can fully recognize the character of its own classics or can make any sort of public claim to be in possession of works worthy of wider attention. That Duke Ellington's jazz compositions from the Cotton Club days are now a part of international culture, having endured and surmounted a degree of belittlement and begrudging esteem, has in the long run buoyed the confidence of the Black jazz community in its own counter-classical products.

This still leaves unexamined, however, the question of the value of artworks (religious or secular) that are not regarded as classics. As we will see, even a brief overview of the 'non-classics' reveals that, whatever their value, they are not to be regarded simply as watered down versions of the classics proper. On the contrary, although the non-classic normally differs from the classic not only in status and in influence but also often in profundity, its aesthetic and religious qualities can be unique and valuable in their own right.

Sheerly incompetent art, to be sure, is unlikely to be of any intrinsic aesthetic or religious interest, though unsuccessful attempts at art-making may have value apart from the worth of the product. Other non-classics of art, some of them religious, are intended to be nothing more than minor amusements, or else commercial attractions. One thinks, for instance, of a number of the songs sung at religious youth camps or, in the other instance, of any number of advertisements. Still other non-classics are well made and exhibit genuine artistry, but simply do not aim high. Thus almost everyone would agree that the song 'Do Re Mi' from *The Sound of Music* is at most a minor classic, and arguably a lesser work than 'Summertime' from *Porgy and Bess*. In quite another class is the work that in popular terms is a 'classic' but that few people highly trained in its art would find first-class. A religious song like 'How Great Thou Art' falls into this category. Such a song *functions* as a religious and artistic classic for a large number of people. Yet the more deeply someone – almost anyone – is engaged in either music or theology, the less satisfying this kind of song is likely to be.

The category 'non-classic' also includes, however, works that might be tomorrow's classics, depending on chance and on the way the critical winds are blowing. It includes works that are counter-classics and hence seen as non-classic by the dominant traditions. And it includes works that share various of the stylistic features and qualities of acknowledged classics. Lastly there are numerous non-classic works of the kind produced by the talented amateur, such as the 'Sunday painter'. While no one imagines these works to be either major or minor classics, they may have individual qualities of literally incomparable worth, much as the individual person who is by no means 'great' may exhibit qualities to be cherished beyond measure.

If nothing else, this brief overview of the non-classic should raise serious doubts about the contrast that long has been made between the so-called 'great tradition' and the 'little tradition'. In describing this contrast the anthropologist Robert Redfield writes: 'In a civilization there is a great tradition of the reflective few, and there is a little tradition of the largely unreflective many. The great tradition is cultivated in schools or temples; the little tradition works itself out ... in the lives of the unlettered' dwelling in villages into which 'culture' flows from distant 'teachers and exemplars'.[24]

Redfield's analysis may apply reasonably well to peasant society, which is his main concern. Yet he states that in some ways the contrast between 'little tradition' and 'great tradition' corresponds to what frequently is described as a contrast between 'low' or 'popular' culture and 'high' or 'learned' culture. When thus applied, the terms 'great' and 'little' are misleading, and should perhaps be avoided in any case. Is the tradition of the many in every respect 'little'? And is the tradition of the few actually 'great' in every way? Doubtless there is a kind of greatness that can only be achieved through learning, discipline, and refinement of the sort found in 'elite' arts and 'great' traditions. Yet many works associated with the 'great' tradition make at most a minor contribution to culture. This could be said, for instance, of a number of the nineteenth-century sculptures on exhibit at the Musée d'Orsay in Paris. By contrast the folk songs collected passionately by such composers as Bartók and Vaughan Williams, and a good many traditional spiritual songs published in collections like *Southern Harmony*, have qualities greatly to be valued. Such music, moreover, is minimally indebted to the classics of the 'great' tradition.

This brings us to our last observation regarding non-classics, which is that at a popular level they are appreciated for reasons that never have conformed with the purist aesthetics stemming from Kant. Thus they often naturally and immediately have commerce with moral and religious values, as well as with the values of outright entertainment. Sallman's painting of Jesus as the Good Shepherd, which highly educated people usually dismiss as sentimental, is often reproduced in church school literature and widely admired. Yet its admirers rarely respond to it in terms of its sheerly formal properties or enjoy its beauty 'for its own sake'. Instead they notice that the pastoral scene looks peaceful, that the little sheep in Jesus' arms looks cuddly, and that Jesus himself appears kind and caring.

Pierre Bourdieu, who documents in great detail the prevalence of these non-Kantian features of popular taste, hesitates to speak of a popular aesthetic at all, preferring to speak instead of a popular 'ethos'. From a neo-aesthetic standpoint, however, we are free to say that the taste characteristic of such an ethos is aesthetic. It merely inclines toward the pole of aesthetic impurity, while the taste of the educated 'elite' inclines toward that of aesthetic purity. Whereas the danger of the cultivated, 'elite' mode of appreciation is an aestheticism oblivious of the moral and religious values intrinsic to much art and beauty, the danger of the popular mode is a moralism, didacticism, or sentimentality heedless of those qualities unique to aesthetic form and expression; thus, in Bourdieu's words, popular taste may perform 'a systematic reduction of the things of art to the things of life'.[25]

Again, however, we would stress that, contrary to what Bourdieu supposes, popular taste normally does not in fact exclude aesthetic awareness. The style and beauty of the Sallman painting is not ignored, after all, by the sensitive yet untrained eye; it is simply assimilated to the whole effect, without being sharply distinguished. That this natural deviation from dogmatic purism hardly indicates a defect in aesthetic sensibility is something we have tried to show all along. In this respect it is the sophisticated modernist devoted to the classics as pure aesthetica who is in need of aesthetic re-education.

We have described a very considerable diversity within religious (and other) artistic expression – classic, counter-classic, and non-classic – and likewise considerable diversity within the norms by which such works are appraised and appreciated. One may well wonder at this point whether any attempt on the part of a single religion to accommodate such diversity would not in the end compromise the integrity of that religion, threatening its very identity. It is this question regarding the limits and possibilities of religious pluralism that we will take up in conclusion, exploring it with the help of an image drawn from the arts – namely, the image of performance.

Performing the Tradition: The Makings of Religious Pluralism

'Beethoven's five piano concertos are as central to that repertoire as the four gospels are to the New Testament. . . . They belong to that select, canonized group of works performed and recorded regularly as a cycle'.[26] So writes Robert S. Winter in notes to a recent recording of this concerto cycle – a recording using the latest digital technology yet also featuring replicas of instruments from Beethoven's own time, including various 'period' fortepianos sounding markedly different from any modern concert grand.

Winter's allusion to the New Testament canon reminds one of the common assertion that the forty-eight preludes and fugues of Bach's *Well-Tempered Clavier* and the thirty-two Beethoven piano sonatas constitute, respectively, the Old Testament and the New Testament of the piano repertoire. Again, however, neither set of compositions was written for the modern piano or conceived stylistically along the lines of many a modern performance.

Pondering such things, we quickly could start to sink into the quicksand of those fine and endless debates about whether a classic work is better served by the studiously authentic performance or by the one that is inspired and freely recreative – debates, in effect, about the norms and aims of performance as science and art. Instead, let us accept as at least plausible what by now is the consensus view that there is no one right way to perform either classics or non-classics; that some very different performances of a work nonetheless are deeply satisfying and do it justice, whereas others (even some that adhere slavishly to the score) are inadequate; and, last, that the relative merits of any performance can meaningfully be debated, though never decided once and for all.

One may well wonder what all this has to do with religion and religious pluralism. Granted that references to a musical 'testament' and 'canon' suggest a comparison between the artistic and the religious classic, what does the musical performance of 'canonical' works have to do with actual religious practice and norms? This is what we now hope to spell out.

We usually, and justifiably, think of a religion as something that asks to be believed, believed in, and lived by. It is easy to forget that, to the extent that one can legitimately speak of 'a religion', one is referring not to an entity that is just simply there, to be accepted or rejected, taken or left, but rather to a tradition that must continually be recreated. A religion must be presented to and by the believer and devotee. Hence it must be *performed*, as it were, if it is to be perceived, received, or realized. The ongoing performance of a religion takes place in classic works and acts, as well as in non-classic modes; yet in a sense it is the religion itself that is the primary normative classic mediated in performance. And that which the religion as a classic discloses through performance is, from a Christian perspective, the transcendent reality to which the individual person and group is called to be responsive and responsible in faith and deed. Different Christian groups constitute, then, different performing ensembles and performance traditions, each with its own ways of rendering the classic which provides the group's identity and shapes its sense of what is ultimately important.

Where is one to locate the 'classic' – the religion – that must be performed? Like a work of music, a religion such as Christianity

can be said to exist for a community or individual in four ways: as
(1) a historically conditioned yet relatively abstract ideal, vaguely
imaginable apart from any particular realization; (2) the set of
primary artifacts, texts, and normative practices that serve as
the equivalent of a basic but sketchy musical score and that give
rise to definite but sometimes mutually incompatible interpretive
schemes; (3) what is actually practised and 'performed' in a given
time and setting; and (4) that which is realized in a particular
respondent's and participant's own 'hearing' and experience.

Clearly each Christian group or denomination in its role as a
performing ensemble representing a particular tradition of interpretation must reckon with these different levels on which its own
religion exists. Each one must imagine, reflect on, edit, fill out, and
orchestrate or score the classic that it then performs and faithfully
listens to – the majority of the audience in religion being in fact part
of the performing group, serving as the tradition's instrumental-
ists, so to speak.

No tradition, whether Catholic or Protestant, Anglican or Pentecostal, undertakes this task from scratch; it always does so in a
manner that draws on previous 'editions' and performance practices, some of which have become more or less canonical themselves. Yet every tradition seeks, at the same time, to realize the
work's potential in ever changing situations and so in ways
responsive to the creative movement of the 'spirit'.

In view of all the variables involved in religious 'performance',
the diversity of traditions is hardly surprising. Indeed, we can say
that a degree of pluralism is unavoidable within any religion that is
much extended geographically and historically. Some of Christianity's 'performance traditions' would argue, however, that such
pluralism must pertain only to the externals of religion. Everything
essential to Christianity, they would say, is indicated by features of
its 'score' which are relatively invariable and are there for all to see,
especially in Scripture and creed, or in authorized versions that
early entered the practice of the church. Unless one's 'performance' includes obligatory features such as certain basic scriptural
doctrines and authorized practices (both ritual and ethical), it
cannot be considered a 'performance' of Christianity at all. This
principle, they would claim, ensures both the continuity and
authenticity of one's tradition. As for other features of the 'performance', such as those having to do with religious art and the
aesthetic aspects of worship, these are optional elements that have

no major effect on the actual content of Christian teaching and practice. In this way the plurality of the tradition is limited, and its pluralism tightly circumscribed.

This line of argument, which in substance is by no means unusual, nevertheless is flawed. We can grant that such things as basic doctrines, creeds, and practices are indeed specified in almost every 'edition' of the score of Christianity, and need to be. Still, the fact that they are present wherever Christianity is 'performed' does not guarantee that their meaning will be the same – that they will have the same 'sound'. Every element of music is conditioned by every other, and the actual meaning and significance of doctrines, ritual practices, and ethical norms is likewise conditioned by the modes in which they are aesthetically embodied, including story, image, metaphor, and gesture. The 'music' of a religious tradition emerges from the interplay of all these elements. Its authenticity is guaranteed by none of them individually. Thus, while it is in some sense the same religion as 'classic' that is variously performed, even its doctrines and key ritual practices vary in import (if not in form or formulation), depending on many factors – social, historical, psychological, and aesthetic as well as theological.

Although the pluralism inherent in the theory just espoused is perhaps more neo-liberal than orthodox, its basic principles nonetheless could be expressed in language more familiar to mainstream Christianity than is talk about performance. Thus, if one were to employ the language of Christian theology, one might say: For the Christian, faithfulness primarily means being faithful not to specific works, or even to established Christian traditions and classics, but to the God known to, and made known in, Jesus – though surely not known to and in him alone. Simultaneously it means being faithful to what this God calls humanity to be, as imaged and dramatized in the story (or stories) of Jesus the Christ. This God, this Christ, and this human calling become real in the consciousness of a culture and community by means of mediations: classic and non-classic texts, ideas, symbols, practices, and so forth. But no form of mediation, even biblical, can or need be elevated beyond all criticism and change. It is up to God to be God. If God is the God of the future as well as of the past, and if Christ is Omega as well as Alpha – and finally if human beings individually and collectively are called through the Holy Spirit to be transformed participants in the New Creation that is both now and not yet – then it can be neither surprising nor regrettable that the

classics of the tradition undergo continual re-evaluation and modification as new possibilities and realities unfold. Christian classics
rightly speak with different voices; and the canon of classic
Christian expressions of the Christian gospel is rightly (if sometimes unintentionally) open to additions and adjustments.

Far from placing utmost reliance on human creativity and
norms, the theological position just outlined relativizes everything
human on the presumption that no such thing can be either divine
itself or a perfect replica of any truth or perception within the mind
of God. This stance does not sink into total relativism, however,
because it presumes the elusive but genuine realities of God and
world and human nature. These realities, which transcend all
definite imagining, continuously exert pressure on human beings
to be responsive and responsible to that which is beyond their own
immediate desire or invention – failing which they suffer as having
violated something fundamental to themselves, and to what reality
at its depths must be. Nor does this position end in some sort of
authoritarianism, since it denies that any human being or institution has direct access to a God's-eye view of the world.

That the sort of critical theological pluralism proposed here has
practical implications should be clear if we return to the performance analogy with which we began. In particular, we should now
be able to see more clearly in what way Christianity and its
sub-traditions can and should be in some sense exclusive and at
the same time, and in a more profound sense, broadly inclusive.

First, the performance analogy strongly implies that every major
church or denomination, as a tradition of Christian 'performance',
is necessarily in some measure exclusive. To perform Christianity
in one way is necessarily to choose not to perform it in another.
Even a rampant eclecticism is a style that excludes others. No
apology need be made for this kind and level of exclusivity.
Indeed, with respect to its aesthetic component, it is entirely
consistent with the fact that, as we saw in Chapter 5, particular
Christian ways of being religious seem to call for particular kinds of
aesthetica.

Having said that, however, we must recall three things. First,
people of different genders and of varying social classes, educa-
tional backgrounds, personal dispositions, and aptitudes often
respond differently to different aesthetic styles. They also, therefore, respond differently to what we now are calling a religion's

'performance practices' in so far as these are aesthetically conditioned.

Second, these different individuals and classes of people also
respond with differing levels of religious intensity and acuity to the
various aspects of a religion overall. The faith of some is more
attuned to doctrine and theology; the faith of others is more
attuned to moral practice, liturgy, or the arts.

Third, while even the most exclusive forms of Christianity
include some variety within their aesthetic modes of expression,
and while their 'performance' of Christianity includes in some
fashion most major elements of the Christian 'classic', it is not
uncommon for such a 'performance tradition' to define its religious
identity chiefly in terms of one religious element or another –
doctrine rather than liturgy, for instance, or the ethical rather than
the aesthetic; and within the aesthetic *per se* the range of acceptable
modes and styles of religious expression can be narrow indeed,
often confined to one art (typically music) and to one style within
that art.

The consequences of this for the religious 'audience' and for the
religion itself are scarcely negligible. Indeed, they are dire in a
context in which one 'performance tradition' is the only or primary
available form of religion, or advertises itself as such. For then
those in the actual or potential 'audience' who happen not to be
attuned to the particular priorities and modes of that tradition will
virtually be forced to identify themselves, and be identified by
others, as basically irreligious.

From all this it clearly follows that, for a religion that sees itself as
exemplifying a way that is open to all, the pluralistic concern to
allow a measure of distinctiveness and exclusivity for each religious sub-tradition must not become totally dominant. It needs to
be balanced by an equally pluralistic and theologically weighty
concern to be inclusive: to be diverse enough to include, potentially, the full range of humanity within the central practices and
modes of religious performance made available by this religion's
principal performing traditions in all their dimensions – theological, moral, liturgical, pastoral, social, aesthetic.

As a leading theologian recently has reaffirmed, Christianity has
from the very beginning believed that in crucial respects it is
possible to express 'the same faith, the same teaching, and the
same doctrine in diverse ways'.[27] What theological neo-aesthetics

prompts us to emphasize is that such diversity is not so much an option as a necessity, that there are theological grounds for incorporating considerable diversity within every major Christian group or denomination, and that an important dimension of the diversity of Christian 'performance' is aesthetic.

Fortunately, it is not just the theologian as aesthetician who has begun to insist upon these points. Indeed, the liturgist R. C. D. Jasper has made related claims in commenting on worship practices of the Church of England: 'Strict uniformity is no longer recognized as tenable: a church as comprehensive as the Church of England must make provision for differing attitudes – the sacramental and the prophetic, the corporate and the individual, simple austerity and rich splendour, the other-worldly and the this-worldly'.[28]

Finally, however, it must be acknowledged that no one 'performance tradition' of Christianity can be heard equally well in every setting and by every person, class, or culture. Indeed, such a statement still says too little and has us think too narrowly. For at least at this point in history there is no religion whatever that can or should expect actually to be normative and 'classic' for all the world. A given religion, as a 'classic' among the world's canonical traditions, can rightly claim uniqueness, and it can claim to be in general the best (though not infallible) judge of its own practices and classic works. Likewise, a particular religion can put forward more general claims regarding human life wherever it be lived. But any claim to universality and hence, implicitly, to superiority must be subject to numerous qualifications and open to critical challenge and dialogue if it is to be responsible, let alone credible.

Such inter-religious dialogue must be open not only to religionists and scholars of the usual sorts but also specifically to those with aesthetic acumen, who see that religion often is 'performed' as much through its more markedly aesthetic expressions as through its more practical or reflective features. For in the end these varied aspects of religion form a genuine if heterogeneous whole. That is to say, they all are in evidence whenever a religion is envisioned or 'heard' in its full diversity and depth – in its classic and non-classic works and styles and in the different lives and living expressions of those by whom it is mutually shared.

8

Conclusion:
Aesthetics from the
Standpoint of Theology

Standpoints of Aesthetic Understanding

Matters of concern to aesthetics and to religion include things that people are fond of calling imponderables: ineffable beauty and profound tragedy, or holiness and 'the meaning of life'. Nevertheless people do ponder and try to understand such things, if seldom in the abstract. One of the main purposes of this study has been to urge that matters of aesthetic and religious concern more frequently be pondered *in conjunction* – and not just by philosophers but also by religious thinkers and theologians.

As we also have observed, however, all understanding or 'pondering' takes place within a context, and hence from a particular standpoint distinguished by its own presuppositions and expectations. It is highly unlikely, therefore, that the philosopher working totally independently of religious traditions will view aesthetic makings and meanings in exactly the same way that someone immersed in the study of religion might understand them. Similarly, someone studying religion as a scholar consciously 'bracketing' any personal religious judgments or commitments will have a different perspective on aesthetics from that of the person engaged in systematic or practical theology.

Our main goal in this final chapter is to reflect briefly on the nature of these differences, and particularly to do so in such a way as to justify the standpoint for aesthetics that to the philosopher and academic religion scholar might seem least tenable: the explicitly theological. In providing a justification for theological aesthetics *per se*, and hence for aesthetics undertaken from a theistic and specifically Christian standpoint, we will in effect be arguing for the right of any religion (theistic or not) to employ criteria in some ways distinct from those of the philosopher or

185

pure academician and accordingly to formulate certain aesthetic theories especially appropriate to its own religious understandings. Before we turn to this task, however, it will be helpful to recall the standpoint from which this reflection itself is being (and has been) undertaken. This will remind us of where this study has stood all along and so will recall what it has hoped to accomplish.

Aesthetics from the Present Standpoint

If we want to clarify the relations between aesthetics as a form of philosophy, aesthetics as a form of the academic study of religion, and aesthetics as a form of theology – meaning, in effect, any form of religious reflection engaged in the service of a particular tradition – we are under some obligation to be clear about the standpoint from which this attempt at clarification is being made. Ours has been a study of aesthetics that has stood not entirely within any one of the three areas of aesthetics we have mentioned, but on their borders. From its marginal position this study has moved sometimes farther into one region, sometimes farther into another.

Where we have ventured farthest into the terrain of philosophy proper has been in our attempt to understand the nature of aesthetic phenomena: first to reconceive in integralist, neo-aesthetic terms the relation between the aesthetic and the non-aesthetic; and second to define and redescribe art, its makings, and its meanings. Where we have gone farthest into the realm of strictly academic religious study has been in our efforts to formulate an integralist understanding of religion itself – an understanding that would enable us to see certain kinds of aesthetic experience and objects as fully a part of religious traditions and as constituting different modes of religious experience and expression. Finally, we have moved farthest into the field of theology *per se* when we have attempted to indicate how the self-understanding of one theistic tradition, the Christian, would be affected by incorporating aesthetics among the theological disciplines. To be sure, there is also a sense in which this study as a whole has been theological; for we have attempted at nearly every stage to enhance this tradition's understandings of the aesthetic dimensions of its own thought, worship, and practice, the nature of which is inherently theistic and therefore theological in ultimate reference. Nevertheless, we have stopped short of full-fledged theology, since we have not assumed or asserted the priority or truth of Christian norms.

Obviously our endeavours in each of the three areas of aesthetics we have mentioned could be – and in some respects have been – pursued further and rather differently in more specialized studies. The philosopher is likely to be especially concerned, for instance, to refine what here are rather broadly delineated theories of artistic expression, representation, truth, imagination, and meaning. The academic student of religion, in addition to sharing some of the philosopher's concerns, will want to reflect more fully than we have been able to on the aesthetic religious dimensions of life as a whole and on the uses and understandings of aesthetics that seem especially appropriate to particular world and regional religions. Finally the theologian – the affiliated and 'engaged' religious thinker – will want to examine more carefully existing theologies of art and beauty and to provide more substantial exposition of theology's own possible aesthetic views by drawing out implications of the tradition's classic texts, formal doctrines, worship practices, and ethical goals and actions. At the same time, the theologian will have an interest in linking aesthetic principles developed here with principles already worked out in such areas of proven theological import as hermeneutics, narrative theory, and ritual studies – all of which naturally converge with aesthetics at many points.

What we can claim (and hope) to have provided is new and ampler justification for these various undertakings, and hence for integrating aesthetics into the mainstream of religious, theological, and even philosophical reflection. We still must address more directly, however, the question we have proposed to ponder in conclusion: In what ways can aesthetics be expected to be different when undertaken from these different standpoints?

Aesthetics: Philosophical, Religious, Theological

In the simplest terms we can say that philosophical aesthetics entails reflection on basic questions regarding art and beauty or, more broadly, on what we have termed aesthetica. It ponders what is made in the arts in particular, seeking to define and describe artistic acts and products in such a way as to show what they are, what they are good for, how they are to be evaluated, and how their effects and meanings are related to matters of truth and morality. Ordinarily the philosopher's approach has been seen as one that relies entirely on the powers of rational analysis and understanding. Taking nothing on the basis of authority or tradition, such an approach engages in free and critical inquiry.

One consequently might assume that, of all the possible standpoints for understanding aesthetica, the philosopher's would be the most reasonable and reliable, resisting as it does the impulse to place certain 'truths' above criticism and beyond the reach of the free and reasonable inquirer. It has become increasingly clear, however, that philosophers and even scientists are not utterly free in their thoughts. Rationality itself has no one and eternal foundation. And philosophical thinking, like all other kinds, is carried out in connection with particular traditions and assumptions. Consequently not every reasonable hypothesis, question, or deduction is even potentially available at any given moment to the philosopher who is thinking clearly and well. There always will be an indefinite number of rational possibilities that the philosopher's own tradition and context will have screened out.

That this is the case in aesthetics *per se* is suggested by the very condition of philosophical aesthetics; for modern philosophy's preoccupations and presuppositions have been such as almost to guarantee that aesthetics would remain relatively undeveloped from the time it became a self-conscious field of study.[1] Certainly had Western philosophy been exposed in any degree to the arts and theories of worldwide religious traditions, it long ago might have found modern European purist concepts to be provincial in the extreme.

Strange to say, then, it may be valuable even for the philosopher *qua* philosopher to take into consideration various religious approaches to things artistic, expressive, or beautiful – whether Hindu or Buddhist, Jewish or Muslim, non-literate or 'ethnic'.[2] This is not to ask the philosopher to stop being a philosopher. It is not to say that the philosopher is obligated to accept Tibetan (Tantric) Buddhist views on the powers of music as a means of exorcism or Hindu theories of music-making as a mode of meditation. Nor, for that matter, is it to claim for religious traditions in general a level of sophistication in aesthetics *per se* that we began our study by denying. It is rather to point out that philosophy in dialogue with religion might arrive at a broader or at least different understanding of the purposes and powers of things artistic and aesthetic. For religious ideas or assumptions about the arts normally provide alternatives to the philosophical orthodoxy of any given moment. Of course where the distinction between philosophical and religious reflection is minimal or non-existent, as is the case in some phases of Oriental thought, the philosophical and the religious modes of aesthetics are more or less identical. In the modern West, however, they continually coexist in some degree of tension, from which it appears both can profit.

The religion scholar, as historian and interpreter of religious traditions, naturally can perform a valuable service for the philosopher interested in gaining access to religious notions of the arts and aesthetica. But the role of the religion scholar as aesthetician extends beyond that of supplying the philosopher with broader knowledge of alternative traditions. This is evident from two varieties of academic religious aesthetics implicit in the work of the late and renowned historian of religions Mircea Eliade – a scholar who, though seldom if ever using the term 'religious aesthetics', was deeply involved in understanding the nature and role of the arts in religion.[3]

What we are terming Eliade's implicit religious aesthetics is, at one level, not intended to be his at all. In his role as historian and phenomenologist (in the non-technical sense), Eliade tries to describe the religious purpose and meaning of artistic and typically ritualistic acts and objects in terms that are true to the perceptions of whatever tradition he happens to be studying. He explains, for example, how certain acts and artifacts that we would call artistic or aesthetic can function as hierophanies, as integral parts of ceremonies sacralizing time and space, as means of meditation, or as tools of mystic and shamanistic vision.

This descriptive and interpretive sort of aesthetics is not part of any direct attempt to help religious traditions clarify or reshape their own thinking, as someone acting as theologian for a given tradition might do. Yet it differs as well from the endeavors of the philosopher; for Eliade is neither striving to arrive at Husserlian essences of phenomena nor attempting to make independent and rational appraisals of the validity of any religion's own aesthetic/religious understandings. Instead, Eliade's intention at this level of his work is simply to illuminate for everyone the artistic or symbolic ideas and practices characteristic of various or perhaps all religions.

There is, however, another level at which Eliade engages in religious aesthetics as an academic student of religions. While Eliade stands outside the traditions he describes, he regards these traditions as offering something that he takes to be genuine wisdom and that he chooses to reinterpret and make his own. Thus, taking a cue from religions themselves, Eliade interprets such things as ancient megaliths, Mesopotamian temples, mosaics of Christ as Pantocrator, Romanian folk dances, and Brancusi sculptures as creations that often can open up a higher or deeper kind of consciousness even now. According to Eliade, this mode of consciousness and being, which in the modern secular age may be glimpsed in dreams as well as in art, is one whereby the individual or group participates in sacred time and space and in this way discovers transcendent, timeless meaning.

Eliade's religious aesthetic theory is at this level separable in principle from his comparative and historical research, though it leans on such research for support. In fact it can yield quite general (and highly debatable) claims about art, religion, and imagination. This is evident when Eliade asserts, for instance, that 'understanding the universal and exemplary significations of literary creations is tantamount to recovering the meaning of religious phenomena'. It also is evident when he affirms the 'objectivity and intellectual value of the *mundus imaginalis*, of the imaginary universe created or discovered by any significant author' – a universe which Eliade believes exists in continuity with the realities of religious myth.[4] Theoretical statements of this sort represent something other than what any particular religious tradition might recognize as true to its own perceptions.

Even on this second level of religious aesthetics, however, the ground on which Eliade stands is different from the philosopher's.[5] For one thing, Eliade's fascination with dreams, with the unconscious, with archetypical patterns, and with revelatory 'imaginary universes' indicates that his thinking may have more affinities with Jungian psychology and with the spirit of Romanticism in general then it has with most formal philosophies of art. Yet his aesthetic remains fundamentally religious, because it is the sacred dimension of these things that occupies the center of Eliade's theorizing. If Eliade's exposition of the relation of the arts to the sacred falls short of philosophical standards of rigor, what it claims about religious possibilities of artistry is nonetheless suggestive as the product of a penetrating religious thinker and scholar who is neither a philosopher nor (in our sense) a theologian.

What we have seen in this chapter so far is that aesthetics can legitimately be undertaken from more than one point of view. It can be engaged in from the standpoint of the philosopher, who may or may not be informed by non-philosophical traditions such as those of religion. And it can be expounded and developed by the religion scholar who is writing descriptively or even constructively, yet in either case from an academic standpoint that serves the interests of human understanding in general rather than mainly the interests of a particular religion.

That aesthetics also can be undertaken from the standpoint of the theologian accountable to a particular religion is in some respects no more difficult to demonstrate. Indeed, by this point in our study it should be quite plain. For we have gone to some trouble to show that, if the premises of neo-aesthetics are sound, then there is a significant aesthetic dimension to most primary religious experience and expression. And this in itself warrants theological aesthetics of some sort; because it means that the theologian who fails to recognize or understand the interrelation of the aesthetic and the religious will misunderstand much of what grounds and motivates a particular tradition's thought, imagination, and action. It is hardly deniable, therefore, that the theologian should in some fashion undertake to engage in aesthetics.

It also is undeniable that some theologians and religious thinkers are so engaged, and are in fact engaged in aesthetics in a manner that is in some measure independent of both academic religious scholarship and of secular philosophy. For instance, in his book on Islamic art and spirituality, Seyyed Hossein Nasr writes that his work seeks to examine 'certain aspects of Islamic art from the point of view of Islamic spirituality and in relation to the principles of the Islamic revelation'.[6] Although Nasr speaks of these principles as providing what one might call an Islamic philosophy of art, it is clear that such a 'philosophy', being dependent on theistic revelation, is tantamount to what the West usually terms theology.

Again, a Christian theologian like von Balthasar believes that certain truths are revealed by God – truths higher or deeper than anything that human reason can discover or encompass – and that some of these have implications for aesthetics. At least in the eyes of the religious tradition itself, this appeal to revelation can provide credible justification for a relatively autonomous theological aesthetic. Indeed, even without embracing a view of revelation that sees it as a disclosure of absolutely true and perfectly unchanging ideas, the theologian can rely on what the tradition judges to be the highest or deepest insights disclosed by its sacred and classic works and can use these in order to develop aesthetic theories. The Christian theologian may argue on the basis of Genesis, for instance, that when human beings engage in aesthetically creative activity (and not only in the arts) they reflect that they are made in the image of God the Creator. Or the theologian might claim that human beings cannot responsibly exercise stewardship over the earth if they deface its beauty and destroy its God-given variety, which in itself is aesthetically good. Again, it could be argued on theological grounds that the ultimate human good as realized in the Kingdom of God (whether on earth or in heaven) must allow for aesthetic delight, and that beauty itself may rightly be seen as a manifestation or analogue of goodness or even divinity. Thus, all in all, the proper ordering of life and the hope of salvation might be interpreted theologically as entailing a sense of wholeness and harmony that is in part aesthetic.

None of these claims could be made on the basis of philosophy alone or from a religiously neutral academic standpoint. They could come only from the side of theology, which judges their relative adequacy on the basis of what it takes to be its most reliable norms, traditionally regarded as having been divinely revealed through human agents at special times.

But though it seems plain that theological aesthetics can employ criteria that differ from those of the philosopher or of the religion scholar in the secular academy, it is not at all plain that the claims of the theologian with regard to aesthetics can or will be seen by the academician as having any possible legitimacy. Or, more precisely, the philosopher and the purely academic religionist may both suppose that to the extent to which the theories employed within theological aesthetics have any validity, they are theories that can be judged valid only on the basis of philosophical or strictly scholarly criteria.

It is easy to see why the pure academician might say such a thing. Both the philosopher and the strictly academic religion scholar are more immediately concerned than the theologian typically is with making public sense, with pointing to publicly observable data, and with arguing in whatever are seen as entirely rational and logical ways. By contrast the theologian – except when engaging in certain modes of philosophical theology that overlap philosophy itself – is prone, as we have seen, to appeal at some point to an insight, truth, or reality that must be taken on faith or that is said to lie beyond ordinary experience or reason alone. Moreover, just at the crucial point in an argument, the theologian is likely to lapse into metaphor, analogy, or – worse yet – paradox. Thus it is the standpoint of the philosopher and 'detached' religion scholar that seems to have the more trustworthy criteria for judging whether a particular aesthetic theory is credible.

This is not the place for a full-scale defense of theology as such; in point of fact there are a number of kinds of theology that it would hardly be in the interests of this study to defend at all. Nevertheless, it is important to point out that these arguments against the credibility of theology show only that normally it is something other than a strictly academic and rational enterprise. They do not show – but only assume – that the only credible or fruitful modes of reflection and expression are strictly academic and rational.

The latter assumption, however, is one that much of the present study would call into question. After all, Kant's idea of the power of 'aesthetic ideas' and our own theory of aesthetic imagination both suggest that at the limits of rationality there is a kind of pondering and exploring that takes place chiefly by means of aesthetically rich 'languages' that are at once deeply meaningful and yet incapable of complete translation into intellectual propositions and concepts. Although this claim might be judged Romantic, it is more ancient than that. As long ago as Plato and his dialogue the *Phaedo*, philosophy itself recognized that the most penetrating thoughts often of necessity take figurative form – the form of myth or symbol or some other aesthetic fabrication.

The fact that the primary language of religion is markedly poetic, mythic, and otherwise aesthetic means that it is with such language that theology repeatedly begins and that it is to such language that theology must often return. Theological reflection, however abstract and internally consistent, thus is intimately connected with 'aesthetic ideas'. Yet this cannot be used to argue against the credibility of theological reflection, or specifically against the credibility of theological ideas *about* the aesthetic. It can only show that whatever credibility theological aesthetics has cannot be judged entirely on strictly philosophical grounds or only by the criteria of religious scholarship within the secular academy.

More positively, theological ideas, including those of explicitly theological aesthetics, might profitably be treated by the methodologically agnostic scholar (whether of philosophy or religion) as themselves potentially fruitful fictions, like those of art itself. In this way the theologian's exploration of 'imponderables', including those of art and beauty, and indeed of life and death, might be seen as exercises in imaginative construction: in entertaining earthly and unearthly possibilities that, eluding full comprehension, nonetheless engage us wholly and make for us a kind of meaning.

None of this is meant to imply that theological aesthetics, having been granted a measure of autonomy, can simply forget about the other forms of aesthetics, whether philosophical or religious. Our entire study would suggest that the theologian must engage in dialogue with the strictly academic scholar of religions and with the philosopher, since they provide the theologian with vital critical challenges, with a wide range of awareness, and with an extensive array of conceptual tools, all of which any reasonably adequate theology requires. In the end, however, it is the theologian as aesthetician – and the ongoing religious tradition which the theologian represents – that must judge the relative adequacy of any particular theological aesthetic. And it is theology itself that must discover the extent to which theological aesthetics can actually become a thriving and religiously fruitful enterprise.

Notes

PREFACE

1. Hans Urs von Balthasar, *The Glory of the Lord: A Theological Aesthetics*, 7 vols, various translators; vol. 1 (San Francisco: Ignatius; and New York: Crossroad, 1982); vols 2–3 (San Francisco: Ignatius, 1984–86); vols 4–7, trans. in progress. The range and depth of von Balthasar's treatment of various theological issues and figures relevant to matters of theological aesthetics makes his work a major resource for study in the field, and especially for historical understanding of a kind impossible to pursue here. His treatment of issues normally dealt with in aesthetics is nonetheless spotty and erratic; many of the theological and philosophical topics central to the present study are ones on which he barely touches. That is to say, von Balthasar's work is *sui generis*, standing outside the main arenas of both contemporary aesthetics and modern theology. For the most part I have had to be content to let him speak for himself.

2. Nicholas Wolterstorff, *Art in Action: Toward a Christian Aesthetic* (Grand Rapids, Mich.: Eerdmans, 1980).

3. Gerardus van der Leeuw, *Sacred and Profane Beauty: The Holy in Art*, trans. David E. Green (New York: Holt, Rinehart and Winston, 1963).

4. John Dillenberger, *A Theology of Artistic Sensibilities: The Visual Arts and the Church* (New York: Crossroad, 1986).

5. Thomas R. Martland, *Religion as Art* (Albany: State University of New York Press, 1981).

6. F. David Martin, *Art and the Religious Experience: The 'Language' of the Sacred* (Lewisburg, Penn.: Bucknell University Press, 1972).

7. Frank Burch Brown, *Transfiguration: Poetic Metaphor and the Languages of Religious Belief* (Chapel Hill and London: University of North Carolina Press, 1983).

CHAPTER 1: INTRODUCTION

1. Hal Foster, 'Postmodernism: A Preface', in *The Anti-Aesthetic: Essays on Postmodern Culture*, ed. Hal Foster (Port Townsend, Wash.: Bay Press, 1983).

2. David Carroll, *Paraesthetics* (London: Methuen, 1987) pp. xiv, xv. See also Christopher Norris, *Paul de Man: Deconstruction and the Critique of Aesthetic Ideology* (London: Routledge, 1988).

3. Janet Wolff, *Aesthetics and the Sociology of Art* (London: Allen & Unwin, 1983) p. 107.

4. See Jacques Derrida, 'Parergon', in *The Truth in Painting*, trans. Geoff Bennington and Ian McLeod (Chicago: University of Chicago Press, 1987).

5. Hans-Georg Gadamer, *Truth and Method*, 1960; trans. G. Barden and J. Cumming (New York: Continuum, 1975). Aesthetics naturally

merges with hermeneutics at the point of inquiring specifically into meaning and meaningfulness, or into truth and significance. Our divergence from Gadamer is partly a matter of emphasis.

6. See Martin Heidegger, 'The Origin of the Work of Art', in *Poetry, Language, Thought*, trans. Albert Hofstadter (New York: Harper & Row, 1971).

7. See Roland Barthes, *The Rustle of Language*, trans. Richard Howard (New York: Hill & Wang, 1986) pp. 76–7; Barthes, *Image, Music, Text*, trans. Stephen Heath (New York: Hill & Wang, 1977) pp. 179–89; and Julia Kristeva, *Desire in Language: A Semiotic Approach to Literature and Art*, ed. Leon Roudiez (New York: Columbia University Press, 1980) p. 133.

8. Both of these kinds of concern are expressed, for example, by Sallie McFague in *Models of God: Theology for an Ecological, Nuclear Age* (Philadelphia: Fortress, 1987).

9. Cf. Giles Gunn, *The Culture of Criticism and the Criticism of Culture* (Oxford: Oxford University Press, 1987).

CHAPTER 2: CAN AESTHETICS BE CHRISTIAN?

1. See Stanley Hauerwas, *The Peaceable Kingdom: A Primer in Christian Ethics* (Notre Dame, Ind.: University of Notre Dame Press, 1983) pp. 50–4.

2. James M. Gustafson, *Can Ethics Be Christian?* (Chicago: University of Chicago Press, 1975).

3. See Oliver O'Donovan, *Resurrection and Moral Order: An Outline for an Evangelical Ethics* (Grand Rapids, Mich.: Eerdmans, 1987).

4. Hans Urs von Balthasar, *The Glory of the Lord: A Theological Aesthetics*, 7 vols; vol. 1 (San Francisco: Ignatius; and New York: Crossroad, 1982); vols 2–3 (San Francisco: Ignatius, 1984–6) vols 4–7, trans. in progress.

5. For documentation on the theological study of the arts and aesthetics in North America, see Wilson Yates, *The Arts in Theological Education* (Atlanta: Scholars Press, 1987).

6. Dorothy L. Sayers, 'Towards a Christian Aesthetic', 1944; reprinted in Nathan A. Scott, Jr, ed., *The New Orpheus: Essays Toward a Christian Poetic* (New York: Sheed & Ward, 1964) pp. 3–20; quotation from p. 4.

7. von Balthasar, *Glory* i, 117.

8. For a discussion of writings sharply critical of aesthetics, see Mary Mothersill, *Beauty Restored* (London: Oxford University Press-Clarendon, 1984) pp. 1–73.

9. Ludwig Wittgenstein, *Lectures and Conversations: On Aesthetics, Psychology and Religious Belief*, ed. Cyril Barrett (Berkeley: University of California Press, 1967) p. 1.

10. Alexander Gottlieb Baumgarten, *Aesthetica*, 2 vols, 1750–8; reprint edn (Hildesheim: G. Olms, 1961). See also Ted Cohen and Paul Guyer, eds, *Essays in Kant's Aesthetics* (Chicago: University of Chicago Press, 1982) p. 1n.

11. William Blake, 'Aphorisms on the Laocoon Group', in *Selected Poetry and Prose of Blake*, ed. Northrop Frye (New York: Random House – Modern Library, 1953) pp. 330, 328.

12. See R. G. Collingwood, *The Principles of Art* (New York: Oxford University Press-Galaxy, 1958); and Benedetto Croce, 'Aesthetics', in the *Encyclopedia Britannica*, 14th edn; reprinted in *Philosophies of Art and Beauty*, ed. Albert Hofstadter and Richard Kuhns (Chicago: Univerity of Chicago Press-Phoenix, 1976) pp. 556–76. Collingwood, in particular, is inconsistent, finally deciding that there is no good writing that is not art. See ibid., pp. 298–9.

13. See, for example, Monroe C. Beardsley, 'The Aesthetic Point of View', in *Philosophy Looks at the Arts*, rev. edn, Joseph Margolis, ed. (Philadelphia: Temple University Press, 1978) pp. 6–24.

14. Harold Osborne, 'Aesthetic Relevance', *British Journal of Aesthetics* 17 (1977): 294.

15. Jerome Stolnitz, *Aesthetics and Philosophy of Art Criticism* (Boston, Houghton Mifflin 1960) p. 36.

16. Virgil Aldrich, *Philosophy of Art* (Englewood Cliffs, NJ: Prentice-Hall, 1963) p. 20. Stolnitz and Aldrich are criticized by George Dickie in his *Art and the Aesthetic: An Institutional Analysis* (Ithaca, NY: Cornell University Press, 1974) pp. 113–46.

17. See Ernst Cassirer, *The Philosophy of Symbolic Forms*, trans. Ralph Manheim, 3 vols. (New Haven, Conn.: Yale University Press, 1953); and Nelson Goodman, *Ways of Worldmaking* (Indianapolis: Hackett, 1978).

18. See Martin Heidegger, 'The Origin of the Work of Art' and 'What Are Poets For?', in *Poetry, Language, Thought*, trans. Albert Hofstadter (New York: Harper & Row, 1971).

19. See Etienne Gilson, *The Arts of the Beautiful*, 1965; reprint edn (Westport, Conn.: Greenwood, 1976); *Painting and Reality*, 1957; reprint edn (Cleveland: World-Meridian, 1959); and Jacques Maritain, *Creative Intuition in Art and Poetry*, 1953; reprint edn (New York: Meridian, 1955). Of the two thinkers Maritain is less purist in inclination, writing that 'poetry [in the very broadest sense] is the fruit neither of the intellect alone, nor of imagination alone. Nay more, it proceeds from the totality of man, sense, imagination, intellect, love, desire, instinct, blood and spirit together' (p. 80). Yet even Maritain is hemmed in by Aristotelian categories. In restricting art to the productive intellect, he cannot reckon adequately with the ways in which theoretical reason and moral deliberation may interact with poiesis and aesthesis, or vice versa.

20. See Susanne K. Langer, *Feeling and Form* (New York: Scribner's, 1953); and Mikel Dufrenne, *The Phenomenology of Aesthetic Experience*, trans. Edward S. Casey et al (Evanston, Ill.: Northwestern University Press, 1973), esp. p. 551.

21. See John Dewey, *Art as Experience*, 1934; reprint edn (New York: G. P. Putnam's Sons-Capricorn, 1958). Dewey would be the last person to want to separate art from the everyday interests and experiences of life, having fought vigorously against what he terms

the 'compartmental conception of fine art' (p. 8). Yet he is better at describing formal 'rhythms' of art and everyday aesthetic experience than in seeing how they actually qualify thoughts, moral judgments, intellectual systems, and religious valuations.

22. Sir Thomas Browne, *Religio Medici*, in *Selected Writings*, ed. Sir Geoffrey Keynes (London: Faber & Faber, 1968), p. 80.

23. Igor Stravinsky, *Poetics of Music*, trans. Arthur Knodel and Ingolf Dahl, 1942; reprint edn (New York: Random House-Vintage, 1947) p. 146.

24. Karl Barth, *Wolfgang Amadeus Mozart*, trans. Clarence K. Pott (Grand Rapids, Mich.: Eerdmans, 1986) pp. 16, 20, 33–40, 55–7.

25. Clive Bell, *Art*, 1913; reprint edn (New York: G. P. Putnam's Sons-Capricorn, 1958) p. 54.

26. Lynn Poland well documents this feature of the New Criticism in her book *Literary Criticism and Biblical Hermeneutics: A Critique of Formalist Approaches* (Chico, Calif.: Scholars Press, American Academy of Religion Academy Series, no. 48, 1985).

27. Hans-Georg Gadamer explicitly constructs an analogy between, on the one hand, a Lutheran or Catholic conception of the sacramental bread and wine as the flesh and blood of Christ and, on the other hand, the way in which the work of art, rather than referring to something outside itself, constitutes and signifies in itself 'an increase in being'. See Gadamer, *The Relevance of the Beautiful and Other Essays*, trans. Nicholas Walker, ed. Robert Bernasconi (Cambridge: Cambridge University Press, 1986) p. 35. Cf. Erich Heller, *The Disinherited Mind: Essays in Modern German Literature and Thought*, 1952; reprint edn (Cleveland: World-Meridian, 1959) pp. 261–4.

28. Mark C. Taylor, *Erring: A Postmodern A/theology* (Chicago: University of Chicago Press, 1984) pp. 146–69.

29. von Balthasar, I, 117, 118.

30. John Henry Newman, 'Poetry, with Reference to Aristotle's Poetics', in *Essays and Sketches*, ed. Charles Frederick Harrold. 3 vols (London: Longmans, Green, 1948) vol. I, p. 76.

31. Søren Kierkegaard, *On Authority and Revelation: The Book on Adler, or a Cycle of Ethico-Religious Essays*, trans. Walter Lowrie (Princeton, NJ: Princeton University Press, 1955) pp. 104–5. Kierkegaard tends to use the term 'aesthetic' to refer to a way of life devoted to the immediate and often to the sensual: but his usage also overlaps the more customary sense, denoting that which pertains to art and beauty.

32. W. H. Auden, 'Postscript: Christianity and Art', from *The Dyer's Hand* (New York: Random House, 1962); reprinted in Scott, ed., *New Orpheus*, pp. 74–9; quotation from p. 74.

33. Reported in *Christian Century*, 9 Dec. 1987, 1112.

34. See Edward Farley, *Theologia: The Fragmentation and Unity of Theological Education* (Philadelphia: Fortress, 1983). See also Theodore W. Jennings, Jr, ed., *The Vocation of the Theologian* (Philadelphia: Fortress, 1985).

35. Jaroslav Pelikan, *Jesus Through the Centuries: His Place in the History of*

Culture (New Haven, Conn.: Yale University Press, 1985).

36. Matthew Arnold, 'The Study of Poetry' (1880); reprinted in *Essays in Criticism, Second Series* (London: Macmillan, 1896) pp. 1–3.

37. Ibid.

38. The aspect of this dialectic in which symbolic or aesthetic expression gives rise to thought – the aspect emphasized by Karl Jaspers and Paul Ricoeur, for instance – is pondered with evident fascination and perplexity by Kant in *The Critique of Judgment*, Section 49. Both sides of this dialectical process are explored in some detail in Frank Burch Brown, *Transfiguration: Poetic Metaphor and the Languages of Religious Belief* (Chapel Hill, NC: University of North Carolinia Press, 1983) pp. 148–81.

39. The use of Christian doctrines to interpret the arts is discussed in David Baily Harned, *Theology and the Arts* (Philadelphia: Westminster, 1966). For such a use of the doctrine of the Incarnation, see Aidan Nichols, *The Art of God Incarnate* (New York: Paulist, 1980).

40. George A. Lindbeck, *The Nature of Doctrine: Religion and Theology in a Postliberal Age* (Philadelphia: Westminster, 1984) p. 84. With respect to the visual arts, for instance, this point is made emphatically in Margaret R. Miles, *Image as Insight: Visual Understanding in Western Christianity and Secular Culture* (Boston: Beacon, 1985).

41. David Tracy, *The Analogical Imagination: Christian Theology and the Culture of Pluralism* (New York: Crossroad, 1981).

CHAPTER 3: ART, RELIGION, AND THE AESTHETIC MILIEU

1. See Hal Foster, ed., *The Anti-Aesthetic: Essays on Postmodern Culture* (Port Townsend, Wash.: Bay Press, 1983); and Jacques Derrida, 'Economimesis', *Diacritics* 11 (1981): 3–25.

2. See Gregory L. Ulmer, 'The Object of Post-Criticism', in Foster, ed., *The Anti-Aesthetic*, pp. 83–110.

3. As Eva Schaper points out, Kant thinks our pleasures are 'disinterested' not because their object is uninteresting but because 'we have found the "why" of them to be independent of gratified or anticipated desire on the one hand, and of moral or prudential satisfaction on the other'. 'The Pleasures of Taste', in *Pleasure, Preference and Value: Studies in Philosophical Aesthetics*, ed. Eva Schaper (Cambridge: Cambridge University Press, 1983) p. 50. Cf. George Santayana's rather different thesis that beauty is objectified self-enjoyment, in *The Sense of Beauty*, 1896; reprint edn (New York: Dover, 1955) pp. 11–33.

4. Francis Sparshott charts numerous kinds of aesthetic theory, one of which he calls the 'purist line'. But this line is different from purism in our sense, which is in fact an important feature of most of the lines he discusses. See *The Theory of the Arts* (Princeton, NJ: Princeton University Press, 1982).

5. For the classic identification of religion with feeling of a certain kind see Friedrich Schleiermacher, *On Religion: Speeches to its Cultured Despisers*, first published in German in 1799; English trans., John

Oman (New York: Harper & Row, 1958). Cf. Geddes MacGregor, *Aesthetic Experience in Religion* (London: Macmillan, 1947), esp. pp. 118–19, 200, 227.

6. See Wayne Proudfoot, *Religious Experience* (Berkeley: University of California Press, 1985).

7. Cf. Kendall L. Walton, 'Categories of Art', 1970; reprinted in Joseph Margolis, ed., *Philosophy Looks at the Arts*, 2nd edn rev. (Philadelphia: Temple University Press, 1978). See also Denis Dutton, 'Why Intentionalism Won't Go Away', in *Literature and the Question of Philosophy*, ed. Anthony J. Cascardi (Baltimore: Johns Hopkins University Press, 1987) pp. 194–209.

8. See Joseph Margolis, 'Works of Art as Physically Embodied and Culturally Emergent Entities', *British Journal of Aesthetics* 14 (Summer 1974): 187–96; see also Margolis, *Art and Philosophy: Conceptual Issues in Aesthetics* (Atlantic Highlands, NJ: Humanities, 1980) pp. 27–49.

9. See Roman Ingarden, 'Artistic and Aesthetic Values', in his *Selected Papers in Aesthetics*, ed. Peter J. McCormick (Munich: Philosophia Verlag; Washington, D.C.: Catholic University of America Press, 1985) pp. 91–106; and *The Cognition of the Literary Work of Art*, trans. Ruth Ann Crowley and Kenneth R. Olson (Evanston, Ill.: Northwestern University Press, 1973) pp. 175–218. Ingarden himself does sometimes refer to the work of art as the aesthetic object, but the above essay makes this seem an inconsistency.

10. Emile Zola, from 'Mon Salon', in *A Documentary History of Art, vol. III: From the Classicists to the Impressionists – Art and Architecture of the 19th Century*, ed. Elizabeth Gilmore Holt (Garden City, NY: Doubleday-Anchor, 1966) p. 383.

11. Claude Debussy, 'Monsieur Croche the Dilettante Hater', in *Three Classics in the Aesthetic of Music*, ed. anon. (New York: Dover, 1962) p. 49.

12. The whole idea of an aesthetic attitude is rejected in George Dickie, *Art and the Aesthetic: An Institutional Analysis* (Ithaca, NY: Cornell University Press, 1974).

13. See Michael Polanyi, *The Tacit Dimension*, 1966; reprint edn (Garden City, NY: Doubleday-Anchor, 1967); and *Meaning* (Chicago: University of Chicago Press, 1975).

14. See Ingarden, *Cognition*; and Wolfgang Iser, *The Act of Reading: A Theory of Aesthetic Response* (Baltimore: Johns Hopkins University Press, 1978) pp. 20–2.

15. See Otto von Simson, *The Gothic Cathedral*, 3rd edn (Princeton, NJ: Princeton University Press, 1987) p. 129.

16. Quoted in Erwin Panofsky, 'Abbot Suger of St.-Denis', in *Meaning in the Visual Arts* (Garden City, NY: Doubleday-Anchor, 1955) p. 129. Suger is thinking here particularly of the beauty of the precious stones of the main altar, but he writes in a similar vein about other beautiful features of the church.

17. All information regarding the proposed space art comes from an article reprinted in the *Roanoke Times and World News*, 27 May 1987, Extra Section.

18. J. O. Urmson, 'What Makes a Situation Aesthetic?', 1957; reprinted in Joseph Margolis, ed., *Philosophy Looks at the Arts*, 1st edn (New York: Scribner's, 1962) pp. 13–27.
19. Etienne Gilson, *The Arts of the Beautiful*, 1965; reprint edn (Westport, Conn.: Greenwood, 1976) pp. 160–82, 173.
20. Ibid., p. 182.
21. René Wellek, Foreword to Immanuel Kant, *Philosophical Writings*, The German Library: vol. 13, ed. Ernst Behler; gen. ed. Volkmar Sander (New York: Continuum, 1986) pp. xi–xii.
22. For other (and somewhat different) interpretations of Kant on free and dependent beauty see Hans-Georg Gadamer, *Truth and Method*, trans. G. Barden and J. Cumming (New York: Continuum, 1975) pp. 42–51; Francis X. J. Coleman, *The Harmony of Reason: A Study in Kant's Aesthetics* (Pittsburgh: University of Pittsburgh Press, 1974); Donald W. Crawford, *Kant's Aesthetic Theory* (Madison, Wis.: University of Wisconsin Press, 1974); Paul Guyer, *Kant and the Claims of Taste* (Cambridge, Mass.: Harvard University Press, 1979); Salim Kemal, *Kant and Fine Art: An Essay on Kant and the Philosophy of Fine Art and Culture* (Oxford: Clarendon Press, 1986); and Jacques Derrida, 'Parergon', in *The Truth in Painting*, trans. Geoff Bennington and Ian McLeod (Chicago: University of Chicago Press, 1987).
23. Section 16. References are to the J. H. Bernard trans., Hafner Library of Classics (New York, 1951). See also the most recent English translation, by Werner S. Pluhar (Indianapolis: Hackett, 1987).
24. Section 16, p. 67.
25. Ibid.
26. Section 26, p. 94.
27. Sections 28, 29.
28. Section 29, pp. 110–11.
29. Section 29, pp. 104, 105.
30. Section 25, pp. 90–1.
31. Section 41, p. 140.
32. Section 42, pp. 140–5. Quoted passages on p. 143.
33. Section 48.
34. Section 49, p. 157.
35. Ibid. Quoted passages on pp. 157, 157–8.
36. One must keep in mind that for Kant understanding – *Verstand* – has to do with *a priori* categories of thought that make knowledge possible; practical reason – *Vernunft* – has to do with morality and its conditions of possibility.
37. Section 51, pp. 165, 166.
38. Section 53, p. 174; cf. p. 175.
39. The theoretical point being made here requires only the vaguest of ideas about how *Arsat* might actually appear.
40. Such conditioning characterizes almost all aesthetic response to natural phenomena. Even a flower arrangement that at first glance looks exquisite can look gaudy and tasteless once one recognizes that it is artificial.
41. For further support of this thesis see the arguments and examples in

Arthur C. Danto, *The Transfiguration of the Commonplace: A Philosophy of Art* (Cambridge, Mass.: Harvard University Press, 1981). Cf. Kant, Section 45.

CHAPTER 4: ARTISTIC MAKINGS AND RELIGIOUS MEANINGS

1. Cf. John Dewey, *Art as Experience*, 1934; reprint edn (New York: Putnam's-Capricorn, 1958), where the integral quality of the aesthetic is discussed – with perhaps too much emphasis, however, on its unity.

2. See, for example, Wolfgang Iser, *The Act of Reading: A Theory of Aesthetic Response* (Baltimore: Johns Hopkins University Press, 1978); Mikel Dufrenne, *The Phenomenology of Aesthetic Experience*, trans. Edward S. Casey et al (Evanston, Ill.: Northwestern University Press, 1973); and Hans Robert Jauss, 'Sketch of a Theory and History of Aesthetic Experience', in *Aesthetic Experience and Literary Hermeneutics*, trans. Michael Shaw (Minneapolis: University of Minnesota Press, 1982) pp. 3–151.

3. Monroe C. Beardsley, 'An Aesthetic Definition of Art', in Hugh Curtler, ed., *What is Art?* (New York: Haven, 1983) p. 21.

4. Nikolaus Pevsner, *An Outline of European Architecture*, 7th edn (Harmondsworth, Middlesex: Penguin, 1963) p. 15.

5. See Paul Kristeller, 'The Modern System of the Arts', *Renaissance Thought II: Papers on Humanism and the Arts* (New York: Harper & Row-Torchbook, 1965); and Wladyslaw Tatarkiewicz, *A History of Six Ideas: An Essay in Aesthetics* (The Hague: Martinus Nijhoff, 1980).

6. André Malraux, *Museum without Walls*, revised and expanded from *The Voices of Silence*, vol. 1, trans. Stuart Gilbert and Francis Price (Garden City, NY: Doubleday, 1967). For a critique of Malraux that intersects the one presented here, see Nicholas Wolterstorff, *Art in Action: Toward a Christian Aesthetic* (Grand Rapids, Mich.: Eerdmans, 1980) pp. 203–13.

7. See Clifford Geertz, 'Art as a Cultural System', in *Local Knowledge: Further Essays in Interpretive Anthropology* (New York: Basic Books, 1983) pp. 94–120.

8. See Julius Moravcsik, 'Noetic Aspiration and Artistic Inspiration', in *Plato: On Beauty, Wisdom, and the Arts*, ed. Julius Moravcsik and Philip Temko (Totowa, NJ: Rowman & Littlefield, 1982).

9. Aristotle, *Nicomachean Ethics*, trans. Martin Ostwald (Indianapolis: Bobbs-Merrill, Library of the Liberal Arts, 1962), VI (4) 1140a, p. 151.

10. Tillich's inclination to relate all meaning to ultimate meaning and all concern to ultimate concern leads him to make such claims as that 'ultimately no irreligious art is possible'. Presumably Tillich thinks that this coincides with his notion that there finally are no irreligious people – people devoid of any 'ultimate concern' – but only people whose religiosity is distorted, undeveloped, or demonic. But even if the latter were true, it does not follow that every act of a religious person is a religious act. That Tillich himself talks about art that lacks religious meaning shows that his theorizing on this point is con-

fused. See, for example, 'Theology and Architecture', in Paul Tillich, *On Art and Architecture*, ed. John Dillenberger and Jane Dillenberger (New York: Crossroad, 1987). For telling criticisms of Tillich on these points see Michael F. Palmer, *Paul Tillich's Philosophy of Art* (New York: Walter de Gruyter, 1984).

11. See Karl Rahner, 'Priest and Poet', in *Theological Investigations*, vol. III, trans. Karl-H. and Boniface Kruger (London: Darton, Longman & Todd, 1967) pp. 295–317.

12. Hans Küng, *Art and the Question of Meaning*, trans. Edward Quinn (New York: Crossroad, 1981), quotation on p. 52.

13. See Morris Weitz, 'The Role of Theory in Aesthetics', *Journal of Aesthetics and Art Criticism* 15 (1956): 27–35. See also critiques of such thinking in Maurice Mandelbaum, 'Family Resemblances and Generalization Concerning the Arts', in George Dickie and R. J. Sclafani, ed. *Aesthetics* (New York: St. Martin's Press, 1977) pp. 500–15; and Mary Mothersill, *Beauty Restored* (London: Oxford University Press, 1985) pp. 33–73.

14. See Arnold Hauser, *The Sociology of Art*, trans. Kenneth Northcott (Chicago: University of Chicago Press, 1982) pp. 702, 704.

15. Gordon Kaufman, *The Theological Imagination: Constructing the Concept of God* (Philadelphia: Westminster, 1981) p. 276.

16. In this definition an implicitly 'institutional' requirement is entailed in the notion of a public; and in fact judgments regarding know-how and appreciability are always in part socially and institutionally mediated. Although this definition bears some resemblance to the one earlier cited from Monroe Beardsley, it is different in several notable respects. It is part of a larger theory that assumes a broader notion of the meaning of 'aesthetic'; it insists that aesthetic qualities must in some measure be recognizable and not merely intended by the artist; and it allows that, although the work must have been intentionally made, it need not have been made with the idea of satisfying specifically aesthetic interests, which may not even have been identified as such.

    The term 'expressive' as used in our definition of the work of art should not simply be equated with self-expression; for a composer can easily make up a tune expressive of happiness, for instance, while in a fundamentally morose state of mind. It is then the tune itself that expresses the happiness. For provocative and penetrating analyses of artistic expression, see, for example, Guy Sircello, *Mind and Art: An Essay on the Varieties of Expression* (Princeton, NJ: Princeton University Press, 1972); and Peter Kivy, *The Corded Shell: Reflections on Musical Expression* (Princeton, NJ: Princeton University Press, 1980).

17. Joseph A. Jungmann, *The Mass of the Roman Rite: Its Origins and Development*, 2 vols, trans. Francis A. Brunner, 1951; reprint edn (Westminster, Md: Christian Classics, 1986) vol. I, pp. 3–4.

18. Bard Thompson, ed., *Liturgies of the Western Church* (Cleveland: Collins, 1962) p. 146.

19. See John Dominic Crossan, *In Parables: The Challenge of the Historical*

Jesus (New York: Harper & Row, 1973); Robert Alter, *The Art of Biblical Narrative* (New York: Basic Books, 1981); Meir Sternberg, *The Poetics of Biblical Narrative: Ideological Literature and the Drama of Reading* (Bloomington, Ind.: Indiana University Press, 1985); Stephen Prickett, *Words and* The Word: *Language, Poetics and Biblical Interpretation* (Cambridge: Cambridge University Press, 1986); David Jasper, *The New Testament and the Literary Imagination* (Atlantic Highlands, NJ: Humanities, 1986); and Robert Alter and Frank Kermode, eds, *The Literary Guide to the Bible* (Cambridge, Mass.: Harvard University Press, 1987).

20. See Roman Jakobson, 'Linguistics and Poetics', in *Language in Literature* (Cambridge, Mass.: Harvard University Press–Belknap, 1987). Jakobson is quite clear that the 'aesthetic function' is only one among several even in a work of literature; but his analysis does not allow for the possibility that some aesthetic effects could, for instance, be influenced or mediated by referential implications.

21. See Linda Waugh, 'The Poetic Function and the Nature of Language', in Roman Jakobson, *Verbal Art, Verbal Sign, Verbal Time*, ed. Krystyna Pomorska and Stephen Rudy (Minneapolis: University of Minnesota Press, 1985) pp. 143–68.

22. This means that, contrary to what critics like Northrop Frye suppose, what keeps the Bible from being *thoroughly* a work of literature has nothing to do with its very real concern for truth, description, and assertion: with its being 'centrifugal' in meaning as well as 'centripetal'. The Bible would not necessarily be more literary if Frye were correct in his dubious claim that 'the two testaments form a double mirror, each reflecting the other but neither the world outside' – a claim that is heedless of the Jewish and Christian belief that the God of the Bible is known through historical events beyond sheer textuality. See Northrop Frye, *The Great Code: The Bible and Literature* (New York: Harcourt Brace Jovanovich, 1982) pp. 29, 60–1, 78.

23. Cf. Timothy Binkley, 'Piece: Contra Aesthetics', *Journal of Aesthetics and Art Criticism* 35 (1977): 265–77.

24. Paul Tillich, 'Address on the Occasion of the Opening of the New Galleries and Sculpture Garden of The Museum of Modern Art', 1964; reprinted in Paul Tillich, *On Art*, ed. Dillenbergers, p. 247.

25. Paul Tillich, 'One Moment of Beauty', 1955; reprinted in ibid., p. 235.

26. Jacques Barzun, *The Use of Abuse of Art*, Bollingen Series vol. 35 (Princeton, NJ: Princeton University Press, 1975) pp. 92, 74.

27. See Paul Ricoeur, *Interpretation Theory: Discourse and the Surplus of Meaning* (Fort Worth: Texas Christian University Press, 1976).

28. For some religious connotations of this 'more', see William James, *Varieties of Religious Experience*, 1902; reprint edn (London: Collier-Macmillan) pp. 393 ff.

29. Theodor Adorno, *Aesthetic Theory*, trans. C. Lenhardt (London: Routledge & Kegan Paul, 1984) p. 21.

30. See Rudolf Arnheim, *Toward a Psychology of Art* (Berkeley: University of California Press, 1966), and *Visual Thinking* (Berkeley: University

of California Press, 1969); and Wassily Kandinsky, *On the Spiritual in Art* (1912), trans. Michael Sadleir, Francis Golffing, et al. (New York: Wittenborn, 1947).

31. See Alfred North Whitehead, *Modes of Thought*, 1938; reprint edn (New York: Macmillan-Free Press, 1968) pp. 114–16; and Maurice Merleau-Ponty, *Phenomenology of Perception*, trans. Colin Smith (London: Routledge & Kegan Paul, 1962) pp. 3–12.

32. Oliver Sacks, *The Man Who Mistook His Wife for a Hat* (New York: Harper & Row-Perennial Library, 1987) pp. 43–54.

33. Iser, *Act of Reading*, p. 22.

34. Mark Johnson, *The Body in the Mind: The Bodily Basis of Meaning, Imagination, and Reason* (Chicago: University of Chicago Press, 1987).

35. Ibid., p. 24.

36. Ibid., pp. 103, 65–100.

37. Ibid., pp. 102, 176; italics in original.

38. Mary Warnock, 'Religious Imagination', in *Religious Imagination*, ed. James P. Mackey (Edinburgh: Edinburgh University Press, 1986) pp. 142–57; quotation from p. 142.

39. Mary Warnock, *Imagination* (London: Faber & Faber, 1976) p. 196.

40. T. S. Eliot, 'Religion and Literature', in *Selected Essays*, 3rd edn (London: Faber & Faber, 1951) p. 394.

41. Some of the technicalities and intricacies of modern theories of meaning are sorted out expertly in Thomas E. Hill, *The Concept of Meaning* (New York: Humanities, 1971); in Edgar V. McKnight, *Meaning in Texts: The Historical Shaping of a Narrative Hermeneutics* (Philadelphia: Fortress, 1978); and in Johnson, *Body in Mind*.

42. For such an argument see Wolterstorff, *Art in Action*, p. 169.

43. See Küng, *Art and Meaning*; and Karl Barth, *Wolfgang Amadeus Mozart* (Grand Rapids, Mich.: Eerdmans, 1986).

44. This is not meant to defend a literally aesthetic solution to the problem of evil, which would say (as Augustine did) that evil becomes in the end simply a dark part of an ultimately and totally beautiful mosaic.

45. See, for example, Thomas G. Pavel, *Fictional Worlds* (Cambridge, Mass.: Harvard University Press, 1986); Nicholas Wolterstorff, *Works and Worlds of Art* (Oxford: Oxford University Press, 1980); and John Gilmour, *Picturing the World* (Albany: State University Press of New York, 1986).

46. Quoted in Ronald Kinloch Anderson, notes to *Yehudi Menuhin Plays Bach: The Unaccompanied Violin Sonatas and Partitas* (BWV 1001–6), LP recording, EMI/Angel RLC–3203.

CHAPTER 5: VARIETIES OF RELIGIOUS AESTHETIC EXPERIENCE

1. Jonathan Z. Smith, *Imagining Religion* (Chicago: University of Chicago Press, 1982) pp. xi, 104.

2. See Wilfred Cantwell Smith, *The Meaning and End of Religion* (New York: New American Library, 1962). See also David Tracy and Mircea Eliade, eds, *What Is Religion?: An Inquiry for Christian*

Theology (Edinburgh: T & T Clark); *Concilium* 136 (June 1980).
3. Cf. Joachim Wach, *Types of Religious Experience: Christian and Non-Christian* (Chicago: University of Chicago Press, 1951) pp. 32–3.
4. Clifford Geertz, 'Religion As a Cultural System', in *The Interpretation of Cultures* (New York: Basic Books, 1973) p. 90.
5. On this interpretation, Marxism should be classified as a secular counterpart to religion rather than as a religion proper, whereas even the ethically centered system of Confucianism and the basically non-theistic way of Theravada Buddhism can be considered full-fledged religions; for they orient one toward a cosmos whose realities and laws ultimately are different from what can be described in sheerly naturalistic or narrowly humanistic ter-is.
6. See Donna Marie Wulff, 'On Practicing Religiously: Music as Sacred in India', in Joyce Irwin, ed., *Sacred Sound: Music in Religious Thought and Practice*, JAAR Thematic Studies 50:1 (Chico, Calif.: Scholars Press, 1983).
7. See Diana L. Eck, *Darsan: Seeing the Divine Image in India* (Chambersburg, Penn.: Anima, 1981).
8. Samuel Laeuchli, *Religion and Art in Conflict* (Philadelphia: Fortress, 1980) p. 7.
9. In view of such variety, we should be leery of speaking as one scholar does of 'art and *the* religious experience' or of following writers who restrict the religiosity of art to some one mode. See F. David Martin's otherwise valuable study *Art and the Religious Experience: The 'Language' of the Sacred* (Lewisburg, Penn.: Bucknell University Press, 1972). An analogous weakness mars Geddes MacGregor's book *Aesthetic Experience in Religion* (London: Macmillan, 1947), where preconceptual 'aesthetic intuition' is treated as invariably the core of aesthetic experience, which then is regarded as the *terminus ad quo* of religion, whose *terminus ad quem* is regarded as inevitably union with God.
10. Théophile Gautier, 'Fanny Elssler' in "La Tempete"', in Roger Copeland and Marshall Cohen, eds, *What is Dance?: Readings in Theory and Criticism* (Oxford: Oxford University Press, 1983) p. 431.
11. From John of Salisbury, *Policratus* (1159), quoted in Piero Weiss and Richard Taruskin, eds, *Music in the Western World: A History in Documents* (New York: Schirmer, 1984) p. 62. Cf. documents from the Council of Trent (1545–1563), in Robert F. Hayburn, *Papal Legislation on Sacred Music* (Collegeville, Minn.: Liturgical Press, 1979).
12. Matthew Fox, *Breakthrough: Meister Eckhart's Creation Spirituality in New Translation* (Garden City, NY: Doubleday-Image, 1980) p. 169.
13. See Mark C. Taylor, *Erring: A Postmodern A/theology* (Chicago: University of Chicago Press, 1984); and Charles E. Winquist, *Epiphanies of Darkness: Deconstruction in Theology* (Philadelphia: Fortress, 1986).
14. See John Dominic Crossan, *Cliffs of Fall: Paradox and Polyvalence in the Parables of Jesus* (New York: Crossroad-Seabury, 1980).
15. See Barbara Kiefer Lewalski, *Protestant Poetics and the Seventeenth-*

Century Religious Lyric (Princeton, NJ: Princeton University Press, 1979). Quotation from Donne on p. 85.

16. See ibid.; and Terrence Erdt, *Jonathan Edwards: Art and the Sense of the Heart* (Amherst: University of Massachusetts Press, 1980) pp. 63–77.

17. See Stanley E. Fish, *Self-Consuming Artifacts: The Experience of Seventeenth-Century Literature* (Berkeley: University of California Press, 1972). Fish makes it plain that artifacts that self-consume are not all of one religious persuasion – Anglican or Puritan, for instance. Many are indeed Calvinist, however.

18. Quoted in C. John Sommerville, 'The Religious Music of the Twentieth and Twenty-First Centuries', *Religion* (July 1984) 14: 245–67.

19. Quoted in Friedrich Blume, ed., *Protestant Church Music* (New York: Norton, 1975) p. 10.

20. Quoted in Jaroslav Pelikan, *The Christian Tradition*, vol. 2: *The Spirit of Eastern Christendom (600–1700)* (Chicago: University of Chicago Press, 1974) p. 122.

21. On the principle of sacramentality see Richard P. McBrien, *Catholicism* (Minneapolis: Winston, 1981).

22. See Otto G. von Simson, *Sacred Fortress: Byzantine Art and Statecraft in Ravenna*, 1948; reprint edn (Princeton, NJ: Princeton University Press, 1987); and Pelikan, *Eastern Christendom*, pp. 91–145.

23. See Wyatt Tee Walker, *'Somebody's Calling My Name': Black Sacred Music and Social Change* (Valley Forge, Penn.: Judson, 1979) p. 23.

24. See James H. Cone, *The Spirituals and the Blues* (New York: Seabury, 1972) pp. 40–1.

25. Quoted in Heinrich Bornkamm, *Luther's World of Thought*, trans. Martin H. Bertram (Saint Louis: Concordia, 1958) p. 189.

26. The works of Alfred North Whitehead, Charles Hartshorne, and John Cobb exemplify this understanding of the relation between God and world. Teilhard de Chardin develops a more mystical form of this kind of vision.

27. Quoted in W. H. Gardner, *Gerard Manley Hopkins*, vol. 2 (London: Secker & Warburg, 1949) p. 230.

28. Edward W. Said, *The World, the Text, and the Critic* (Cambridge, Mass.: Harvard University Press, 1983) p. 290.

29. Thomas R. Martland, *Religion As Art: An Interpretation* (Albany: State University of New York Press, 1981) pp. 162, 124, 123. Martland's stimulating book does take some account of the 'conservative' function of art and religion, but is very much weighted toward the creative.

30. See several interpretations of spirituals cited, and judged to be one-sided, in Cone, *Spirituals*, pp. 8–19.

CHAPTER 6: SIN AND BAD TASTE

1. See H. A. Needham, ed., *Taste and Criticism in the Eighteenth Century* (London: Harrap, 1952) p. 224.

2. See Paul Kristeller, 'The Modern System of the Arts', *Renaissance*

Thought II: Papers on Humanism and the Arts (New York: Harper & Row-Torchbook, 1965).

3. For the precise wording and import of Kant's various definitions, see Immanuel Kant, *Critique of Judgment*, trans. J. H. Bernard, 1911; reprint edn (New York: Hafner, 1951) Sections 1, p. 37; 5, p. 44; 40, p. 138.

4. Frank Sibley, 'Aesthetic Concepts', 1959; reprinted in *Philosophy Looks at the Arts*, rev. edn ed. Joseph Margolis (Philadelphia: Temple University Press, 1978) pp. 64–87; quotation from p. 66.

5. Edmund Burke, *A Philosophical Enquiry into the Origin of our Ideas of the Sublime and Beautiful*, 2nd edn, 1759; facsimile edn (New York: Garland, 1971) pp. 30–1. Kant, of course, acknowledges that the faculty of taste brings into unity the faculties of imagination, understanding, and spirit. Yet in this unity they engage merely in 'free play'. Thus they are deprived of their usual functions. See Kant, *Judgment*, Section 50, note 1.

6. David Hume, *Of the Standard of Taste*, 1757; modern edition: *Of the Standard of Taste and Other Essays*, ed. with an Introduction, John W. Lenz (Indianapolis: Bobbs-Merrill Library of Liberal Arts, 1965) pp. 13, 18.

7. Roger Scruton, 'Architectural Taste', *British Journal of Aesthetics* 15 (1975): 294–328.

8. This is a close paraphrase of the definition given in *The Encyclopedia of Philosophy*, ed. Paul Edwards (1967), s.v. 'apperception'. More technical uses of the term are found in Leibnitz, Husserl, and others.

9. For one of the few published statements of the view that liking and valuing aesthetically are not identical, see John Fisher, 'Evaluation without Enjoyment', *Journal of Aesthetics and Art Criticism* 27 (1968): 135–9.

10. See Sibley, 'Aesthetic Concepts', p. 64.

11. See Paul Guyer, 'Pleasure and Society in Kant's Theory of Taste', in Ted Cohen and Paul Guyer, *Essays in Kant's Aesthetics* (Chicago: University of Chicago Press, 1982) pp. 21–54. As Guyer points out, there are inconsistencies in Kant's exposition of the relation of pleasure to judgments of taste. We assume here the basic validity of Guyer's reconstruction of Kant's main line of reasoning. See Kant, *Critique of Judgment*, Sections 7–9.

12. See Martin Luther, *The Freedom of a Christian*, trans. W. A. Lambert, rev. Harold J. Grimm, in *Three Treatises*, rev. edn (Philadelphia: Fortress, 1970) pp. 277–316.

13. 1 Corinthians 10:31 (RSV).

14. Alice Walker, *The Color Purple*, 1982; reprint edn (New York: Washington Square-Pocket, 1983), dedication page. Original emphasis.

15. Lionel Richie, *Can't Slow Down*. Motown 6059 ML.

16. Kant, *Critique of Judgment*, Section 59; see also Section 29, p. 108.

17. Scruton, 'Architectural Taste', p. 328.

18. Marcia Cavell, 'Taste and the Moral Sense', *Journal of Aesthetics and Art Criticism* 34 (1975): 30–3.

19. John Dewey, *Art as Experience*, 1934; reprint edn (New York: G. P. Putnam's Sons-Capricorn, 1958), p. 349.
20. See, for example, Stanley Hauerwas (with David Burrell), 'From System to Story' and 'Story and Theology', in Hauerwas, *Truthfulness and Tragedy: Further Investigations in Christian Ethics* (Notre Dame, Ind.: University of Notre Dame Press, 1977).
21. See James M. Gustafson, *Ethics from a Theocentric Perspective*, vol. 1: Theology and Ethics (Chicago: University of Chicago Press, 1981) pp. 116–17, 291.
22. See Kant, *Critique of Judgment*, Section 16.
23. Nicholas Wolterstorff, *Art in Action: Toward a Christian Aesthetic* (Grand Rapids, Mich.: Eerdmans, 1980) p. 169, emphasis added. Cf. pp. 78–83.
24. Dewey, p. 195.
25. See the translation of passages on beauty from Thomas Aquinas's *Exposition of Dionysius on the Divine Names*, in Vernon J. Bourke, ed., *The Pocket Aquinas* (New York: Simon & Schuster-Pocket, 1960). Cf. Armand A. Maurer, *About Beauty: A Thomistic Interpretation* (Houston: Center for Thomistic Studies, 1983).
26. See Jonathan Edwards, *Religious Affections*, ed. John E. Smith (New Haven, Conn.: Yale University Press, 1959) pp. 298–9. See also Terrence Erdt, *Jonathan Edwards: Art and the Sense of the Heart* (Amherst: University of Massachusetts Press, 1980) pp. 4, 58–9; and Roland Delattre, *Beauty and Sensibility in the Thought of Jonathan Edwards* (New Haven, Conn.: Yale University Press, 1968).
27. For two outstanding interpretations of the Romantic vision of the religiously aesthetic, see Barbara Novak, *Nature and Culture: American Landscape and Painting, 1825–1875* (New York: Oxford University Press, 1980); and M. H. Abrams, *Natural Supernaturalism: Tradition and Revolution in Romantic Literature* (New York: W. W. Norton, 1971).
28. See Hans Urs von Balthasar, *The Glory of the Lord: A Theological Aesthetics*, 7 vols ; vol. 1 (San Francisco: Ignatius and New York: Crossroad, 1982); vols 2–3 (San Francisco: Ignatius, 1984–6); vols 4–7, trans. in progress. Von Balthasar (and, for that matter, Edwards too) speaks of earthly beauties as only analogous to spiritual, but for him the Incarnation means that the physical is not divorced from or unworthy of the spiritual.
29. See Paul Tillich, *Theology of Culture*, ed. Robert C. Kimball (New York: Oxford University Press-Galaxy, 1964); and *The Protestant Era*, abridged edn (Chicago: University of Chicago Press-Phoenix, 1957).
30. Such are the views of Abbot Suger, who supervised the first Gothic church architecture. See Erwin Panofsky, 'Abbot Sugar of St.-Denis', in his *Meaning in the Visual Arts* (Garden City, NY: Doubleday-Anchor, 1955).
31. Perhaps the closest approximation to this conclusion is reached by Karl Rahner, who nonetheless clearly is troubled by its implications and backs away from pursuing in depth the relationship between aesthetic sensitivity, artistic sensibility, and what he terms 'sanctity'.

See *Thought* 57 (Special Issue on Faith and Imagination, March 1982); 17–29.

32. See Kant, *Critique of Judgment*, Section 59.
33. For more on commending instead of commanding, see Paul Guyer, 'Mary Mothersill's *Beauty Restored'*, *Journal of Aesthetics and Art Criticism* 44 (1986): 245–55. See also Mary Mothersill, *Beauty Restored* (London: Oxford University Press, 1985) pp. 311, 79, 224.
34. Gustafson, *Ethics from a Theocentric Perspective*, vol. 1, p. 294.
35. George Steiner, *In Bluebeard's Castle: Some Notes towards the Redefinition of Culture* (New Haven, Conn.: Yale University Press, 1971) p. 77.
36. Walker, *The Color Purple*, p. 178.
37. For a sophisticated and informative discussion of class, society, and the arts that nevertheless reflects the narrowness of Marxian presuppositions, see Arnold Hauser, *The Sociology of Art*, trans. Kenneth J. Northcott (Chicago: University of Chicago Press, 1982) pp. 547–653.
38. See Max Horkheimer, 'Art and Mass Culture', in his *Critical Theory*, trans. Matthew J. O'Connell and others (New York: Seabury Press-Continuum, n.d.) p. 283
39. For a critique of Marxian theories, see Patrick Brantlinger, *Bread and Circuses: Theories of Mass Culture as Social Decay* (Ithaca, NY: Cornell University Press, 1983). See also Pierre Bourdieu, *Distinction: A Social Critique of the Judgement of Taste*, trans. Richard Nice (Cambridge, Mass.: Harvard University Press, 1984); and Herbert J. Gans, *Popular Culture and High Culture: An Analysis and Evaluation of Taste* (New York: Basic Books, 1974).
40. Quoted in Hauser, *The Sociology of Art*, p. 316.
41. R. G. Saisselin, *Taste in Eighteenth Century France: Critical Reflections on the Origins of Aesthetics* (Syracuse, NY: Syracuse University Press, 1965) p. 65.
42. Paul Thek, quoted in Richard Flood, 'Paul Thek: Real Misunderstanding', *Artforum*, Oct. 1981, p. 53.
43. Flannery O'Connor, 'Revelation', in *The Complete Stories* (New York: Farrar, Straus and Giroux, 1971) p. 508.
44. Gustave Flaubert, 'A Simple Heart', in *Three Tales*, trans. Robert Baldick (Harmondsworth, Middlesex: Penguin, 1961) p. 56.

CHAPTER 7: QUESTIONING THE CLASSICS

1. Margaret R. Miles, *Image as Insight: Visual Understanding in Western Christianity and Secular Culture* (Boston: Beacon, 1985) pp. 95–125.
2. Augustine, *Confessions*, trans. R. S. Pine-Coffin (Harmondsworth, Middlesex: Penguin, 1961) Book X, Chapter 33, p. 239.
3. From Bernard of Clairvaux, *Apology*, unpublished trans. by David Burr; alternate trans. in Umberto Eco, *Art and Beauty in the Middle Ages*, trans. Hugh Bredin (New Haven Conn.: Yale University Press, 1986) p. 8.
4. See, for instance, James W. Fowler, *Stages of Faith: The Psychology of*

Human Development and the Quest for Meaning (San Francisco: Harper & Row, 1981).

5. David Tracy, *The Analogical Imagination: Christian Theology and the Culture of Pluralism* (New York: Crossroad, 1981) pp. 134, 163, 172, 174, 176–7, 200–1, 380.
6. See ibid., pp. 200–1; quotation from p. 201.
7. See ibid., p. 130.
8. Ibid., p. 200.
9. See ibid., p. 176.
10. Paul Tillich sometimes leaves the impression that he thinks this is the main, if not exclusive, function of art in relation to Christian theology. See *Systematic Theology*, 3 vols (Chicago: University of Chicago Press, 1951–63), I: 62–4.
11. See Nicholas Wolterstorff, *Art in Action: Toward a Christian Aesthetic* (Grand Rapids, Mich.: Eerdmans, 1980) p. 196.
12. Quotations from notes to Joseph Haydn, *Die Schöpfung*, La Petite Bande, Collegium Vocale, cond. Sigiswald Kuijken, CD recording, Accent, ACC 58228–9, 1983.
13. See Peter Jacobi, *The Messiah Book* (New York: St. Martin's, 1982) pp. 1, 99.
14. See William H. Halewood, *Six Subjects of Reformation Art: A Preface to Rembrandt* (Toronto: University of Toronto Press, 1982).
15. Carl de Nys, notes to Mozart, *Sacred Arias*, Barbara Hendricks, sop., ASMF, Neville Marriner, CD recording, EMI CDC–7492832.
16. Quoted in Edward Said, *The World, the Text, and the Critic* (Cambridge, Mass.: Harvard University Press, 1983) p. 12.
17. See, for example, Robert von Hallberg, ed., *Canons* (Chicago: University of Chicago Press, 1984); and Norma Broude and Mary D. Garrard, eds, *Feminism and Art History: Questioning the Litany* (New York: Harper & Row-Icon, 1982). Some features of the more recent attacks on canon and classic do not stand up well to close scrutiny. The claim of various neo-Marxians that 'aesthetic value arises from class conflict' is too crude to be accepted at face value; and there is equally little to commend the thoroughly pragmatic relativism of some theorists. See Richard Ohmann, 'The Shaping of a Canon: U.S. Fiction, 1960–1975', in von Hallberg, *Canons*; and Barbara Herrnstein Smith, 'Contingencies of Value', in ibid., pp. 5–39. For a critique of such positions, see Hazard Adams, 'Canons: Literary Criteria/Power Criteria', *Critical Inquiry* 14 (Summer 1988): 748–64.
18. Diana McVeagh, from Notes to *Elgar: Dream of Gerontius, Op. 38*, Scottish National Orchestra and Chorus, cond. Alexander Gibson, LP recording, CRD 1026/7, 1976.
19. Quoted in ibid.
20. Quoted in Notes to Sir Edward Elgar, *The Dream of Gerontius*, London Philharmonic Choir, John Alldis Choir, New Philharmonia Orchestra, cond. Sir Adrian Boult, tape recording, EMI/Angel TC–SAN 389–90.
21. See promotional statement in *Edward Elgar: The Dream of Gerontius, Op. 38*, City of Birmingham Symphony Orchestra and Chorus, cond.

Simon Rattle, CD recording, EMI-CDS 7 49549 2.
22. See H. W. Janson, *History of Art*, 2nd edn (Englewood Cliffs, NJ and New York: Prentice-Hall and Abrams, 1977); and Broude & Garrard, *Feminism and Art History*.
23. James H. Cone, *The Spirituals and the Blues* (New York: Seabury, 1972) p. 4.
24. Robert Redfield, *The Little Community* and *Peasant Society and Culture*, in one vol. (Chicago: University of Chicago Press-Phoenix, 1960); *Peasant Society*, pp. 41, 42.
25. Pierre Bourdieu, *Distinction: A Social Critique of the Judgement of Taste*, trans. Richard Nice (Cambridge, Mass.: Harvard University Press, 1984) p. 5.
26. Robert S. Winter, 'Beethoven and the Piano Concerto', in notes for *Beethoven: The Five Piano Concertos*, Steven Lubin, piano; Christopher Hogwood, cond.; Academy of Ancient Music, CD recording, Decca/ L'Oiseau-Lyre CD 421 408–2, 1988.
27. George A. Lindbeck, *The Nature of Doctrine: Religion and Theology in a Postliberal Age* (Philadelphia: Westminster, 1984) p. 92.
28. R. C. D. Jasper, 'Anglican Worship', in *The New Westminster Dictionary of Liturgy and Worship*, ed. J. G. Davies (Philadelphia: Westminster, 1986) p. 21.

CHAPTER 8: CONCLUSION

1. See Nicholas Wolterstorff, 'Philosophy of Art after Analysis and Romanticism', *Journal of Aesthetics and Art Criticism*, Special Issue on Analytic Aesthetics, 46: 151–67.
2. See Susan Bush and Christian Murck, eds, *Theories of the Arts in China* (Princeton, NJ: Princeton University Press, 1983); Seyyed Hossein Nasr, *Islamic Art and Spirituality* (Albany: State University of New York Press, 1987); Richard B. Pilgrim, *Buddhism and the Arts of Japan* (Chambersburg, Penn.: Anima, 1981); Robert Farris Thompson, *African Art in Motion: Icon and Act* (Los Angeles: University of California Press, 1979); Makoto Ueda, *Literary and Art Theories in Japan* (Cleveland: Press of Western Reserve University, 1967); and Gary Witherspoon, *Language and Art in the Navajo Universe* (Ann Arbor: University of Michigan Press, 1977).
3. For pertinent samplings from Eliade's voluminous writings, see Mircea Eliade, *Symbolism, the Sacred, and the Arts*, ed. Diane Apostolos-Cappadona (New York: Crossroad, 1985). Interestingly, Eliade lauds what he terms the 'theological' aesthetics of Gerardus van der Leeuw in a preface to the latter scholar's *Sacred and Profane Beauty: The Holy in Art*, trans. David E. Green (New York: Holt, Rinehart and Winston, 1963).
4. Eliade, *Symbolism*, p. 176; cf. p. 5.
5. Philosophy, to be sure, is itself multifaceted, and Eliade's constructive aesthetic proposals bear some resemblance to ideas that arise out of the philosophical and hermeneutical phenomenology of Paul Ricoeur, for instance. Yet the closest parallel to both the descriptive

and constructive religious aesthetics adumbrated by Eliade is probably to be found in certain sorts of aesthetics undertaken from the standpoint not of philosophy but of psychology and anthropology. For parallels in psychology see, for instance, Silvano Arieti, *Creativity: The Magic Synthesis* (New York: Basic Books, 1976); C. J. Jung, *Psyche and Symbol,* ed. Violet S. de Laszlo (Garden City, NY: Doubleday-Anchor, 1958); Ernst Kris, *Psychoanalytic Explorations in Art* (New York: Shocken, 1964); and Erich Neumann, *Art and the Creative Unconscious* (New York: Harper-Torchbooks, 1959). For parallel studies in anthropology, see Clifford Geertz, 'Art as a Cultural System', in *Local Knowledge* (New York: Basic Books, 1983); Carol F. Jopling, ed., *Art and Aesthetics in Primitive Societies* (New York: Dutton, 1971); Robert Layton, *The Anthropology of Art* (New York: Columbia University Press, 1981); and Jacques Maquet, *The Aesthetic Experience: An Anthropologist Looks at the Visual Arts* (New Haven, Conn.: Yale University Press, 1986).

6.   Nasr, *Islamic Art,* p. ix.

Suggested Readings

This bibliography is of necessity highly selective. Being restricted to writings that deal with issues of religion and aesthetics together, it omits studies in strictly philosophical aesthetics as well as many in theology and religion whose implications for the present kind of project are only tacit. For this reason, among others, the works mentioned in the notes to the present book form an essential supplement to the suggested readings. And even in the notes it is not possible to refer the reader to everything of interest – to relatively technical studies in artistic expression and representation, for instance. Thus the reader also will need to be attentive to bibliographies that are part of the works cited below and in the notes.

The following list includes a mixture of introductory and specialized writings representing a very wide range of views and several different disciplines. Most of these writings are of course theoretical; but a sampling of theoretically suggestive historical and critical studies has also been included, since these provide an essential basis for theorizing in religious and theological aesthetics.

Adams, Doug, and Apostolos-Cappadona, Diane, eds, *Art as Religious Studies* (New York: Crossroad, 1987).

Apostolos-Cappadona, Diane, ed., *Art, Creativity, and the Sacred* (New York: Crossroad, 1984).

Balthasar, Hans Urs von, *The Glory of the Lord: A Theological Aesthetics*. Various translators. 7 vols.; vol. 1 (San Francisco and New York: Ignatius-Crossroad, 1982); vols. 2–3 (San Francisco: Ignatius, 1984–6); vols. 4–7, trans. in progress.

Barth, Karl, *Wolfgang Amadeus Mozart*. Translated by Clarence K. Pott (Grand Rapids, Mich.: Eerdmans, 1986).

Brandon, S. G. F., *Man and God in Art and Ritual: A Study of Iconography, Architecture and Ritual Action as Primary Evidence of Religious Belief and Practice* (New York: Scribner's, 1975).

Brown, Frank Burch, *Transfiguration: Poetic Metaphor and the Languages of Religious Belief* (Chapel Hill, NC: University of North Carolina Press, 1983).

Burkhart, Titus, *Sacred Art in East and West* (London: Perennial, 1967).

Christensen, Carl C., *Art and the Reformation in Germany* (Athens, Ohio: Ohio University Press, 1979).

Coomaraswamy, Ananda K., *Christian and Oriental Philosophy of Art* (New York: Dover, 1956).

Coulson, John, *Religion and Imagination: 'In Aid of a Grammar of Assent'* (London: Oxford-Clarendon, 1981).

Davies, J. G., *Liturgical Dance: An Historical, Theological and Practical Handbook* (London: SCM, 1984).

Dean, William D., *Coming To: A Theology of Beauty* (Philadelphia: Westminster, 1972).

Delattre, Roland, *Beauty and Sensibility in the Thought of Jonathan Edwards* (New Haven, Conn.: Yale University Press, 1968).

Detweiler, Robert, ed., *Art/Literature/Religion: Life on the Borders* (Chico, Calif.: Scholars Press, 1983).

Dillenberger, John, *A Theology of Artistic Sensibilities: The Visual Arts and the Church* (New York: Crossroad, 1986).

Dixon, John W., Jr, *Nature and Grace in Art* (Chapel Hill: University of North Carolina Press, 1964).

—, *Art and the Theological Imagination* (New York: Crossroad-Seabury, 1978).

Eck, Diana L., *Darsan: Seeing the Divine Image in India* (Chambersburg, Penn.: Anima, 1981).

Eco, Umberto, *Art and Beauty in the Middle Ages.* Translated by Hugh Bredin. (New Haven, Conn.: Yale University Press, 1986).

Edwards, Michael, *Towards a Christian Poetics* (London: Macmillan, 1984).

Eliade, Mircea, *Symbolism, the Sacred, and the Arts.* Edited by Diane Apostolos-Cappadona. (New York: Crossroad, 1985).

Fraser, Hilary, *Beauty and Belief: Aesthetics and Religion in Victorian Literature* (Cambridge: Cambridge University Press, 1986).

Garside, Charles, Jr, *Zwingli and the Arts* (New Haven, Conn.: Yale University Press, 1966).

Geertz, Clifford, 'Art as a Cultural System'. In *Local Knowledge: Further Essays in Interpretive Anthropology* (New York: Basic Books, 1983).

Goethals, Gregor T., *The TV Ritual: Worship at the Video Altar* (Boston: Beacon, 1981).

Green, Garrett, ed., *Scriptural Authority and Narrative Interpretation* (Philadelphia: Fortress, 1987).

Gunn, Giles, *The Interpretation of Otherness: Literature, Religion, and the American Imagination* (New York: Oxford University Press, 1979).

—, *The Culture of Criticism and the Criticism of Culture* (New York: Oxford University Press, 1987).

Gutmann, Joseph, *Beauty in Holiness: Studies in Jewish Customs and Ceremonial Art* (New York: KTAV, 1970).

—, *No Graven Images: Studies in Art and the Hebrew Bible* (New York: KTAV, 1971).

Halewood, William H., *Six Subjects of Reformation Art: A Preface to Rembrandt* (Toronto: University of Toronto Press, 1986).

Hardison, O. B., Jr, *Christian Rite and Christian Drama in the Middle Ages* (Baltimore: Johns Hopkins, 1965).

Harned, David Baily, *Theology and the Arts* (Philadelphia: Westminster, 1966).

Harries, Karsten, *The Bavarian Rococo Church: Between Faith and Aestheticism* (New Haven, Conn.: Yale University Press, 1983).

Hart, Ray L., *Unfinished Man and the Imagination: Toward an Ontology and a Rhetoric of Revelation* (New York: Herder & Herder, 1968).

Hartt, Julian N., *Theological Method and Imagination* (New York: Seabury-Crossroad, 1977).

Hazelton, Roger, *A Theological Approach to Art* (Nashville: Abingdon, 1967).

Hirn, Yrjö, *The Sacred Shrine: A Study of the Poetry and Art of the Catholic Church*, 1909. Reprint edn (Boston: Beacon, 1957).

Hunter, Howard, ed., *Humanities, Religion, and the Arts Tomorrow* (New York: Holt, Rinehart & Winston, 1972).

Irwin, Joyce, ed., *Sacred Sound: Music in Religious Thought and Practice* (Chico, Calif.: Scholars Press, 1983).

Kramrisch, Stella, *Exploring India's Sacred Art*. Edited by Barbara Stoler Miller. (Philadelphia: University of Pennsylvania Press, 1983).

Küng, Hans, *Art and the Question of Meaning*. Translated by Edward Quinn. (New York: Crossroad, 1981).

Laeuchli, Samuel, *Religion and Art in Conflict* (Philadelphia: Fortress, 1980).

Leeuw, Gerardus van der, *Sacred and Profane Beauty: The Holy in Art*. Translated by David E. Green. (New York: Holt, Rinehart & Winston, 1963).

Lewalski, Barbara Kiefer, *Protestant Poetics and the Seventeenth-Century Religious Lyric* (Princeton, NJ: Princeton University Press, 1979).

Lynch, William F., *Christ and Apollo: The Dimensions of the Literary Imagination* (New York: Sheed & Ward, 1960).

—, 'The Life of Faith and Imagination: Theological Reflection in Art and Literature'. In *Fordham University Quarterly*, Special Issue on Faith and Imagination, 57 (March 1982): 7–16.

MacGregor, Geddes, *Aesthetic Experience in Religion* (London: Macmillan, 1947).

Mackey, James P., ed., *Religious Imagination* (Edinburgh: Edinburgh University Press, 1986).

Maritain, Jacques, *Creative Intuition in Art and Poetry* (Princeton, NJ: Princeton University Press, Bollingen Series no. 35, 1978).

Martin, F. David, *Art and the Religious Experience: The 'Language' of the Sacred* (Lewisburg, Penn.: Bucknell University Press, 1972).

Martland, Thomas R., *Religion as Art* (Albany: State University of New York Press, 1981).

Mathew, Gervase, *Byzantine Aesthetics*, 1963; reprint edn (New York: Harper & Row-Icon, 1971).

Miles, Margaret R., *Image as Insight: Visual Understanding in Western Christianity and Secular Culture* (Boston: Beacon, 1985).

Moore, Albert C., *Iconography of Religions* (Philadelphia: Fortress, 1977).

Nasr, Seyyed Hossein, *Islamic Art and Spirituality* (State University of New York Press, 1987).

Nichols, Aiden, *The Art of God Incarnate: Theology and Image in Christian Tradition* (London: Darton, Longman & Todd, 1980).

O'Connell, Robert J., *Art and the Christian Intelligence in St. Augustine* (Cambridge, Mass.: Harvard University Press, 1978).

Ong, Walter J., *The Presence of the Word: Some Prolegomena for Cultural and Religious History* (New Haven, Conn.: Yale University Press, 1967).

Pelikan, Jaroslav, *Bach Among the Theologians* (Philadelphia: Fortress, 1986).

Petersson, Robert T., *The Art of Ecstasy: Teresa, Bernini, and Crashaw* (New York: Atheneum, 1974).

Pilgrim, Richard B., *Buddhism and the Arts of Japan* (Chambersburg, Penn.: Anima, 1981).

Rahner, Karl, 'Priest and Poet'. In *Theological Investigations*, vol. 3. Translated by Karl H. Kruger and Boniface Kruger. (London: Darton, Longman & Todd, 1967).

—, 'Theology and the Arts'. In *Fordham University Quarterly*, Special Issue on Faith and Imagination, 57 (March 1982): 17–29.

Ryken, Leland, *The Christian Imagination: Essays on Literature and the Arts* (Grand Rapids, Mich.: Baker, 1981).

Scott, Nathan A., Jr, *Negative Capability: Studies in the New Literature and the Religious Situation* (New Haven, Conn.: Yale University Press, 1969).

—, *The Poetics of Belief* (Chapel Hill, NC: University of North Carolina Press, 1985).

—, ed., *The New Orpheus: Essays Toward a Christian Poetic* (New York: Sheed & Ward, 1964).

Terrien, Samuel, *The Elusive Presence: The Heart of Biblical Theology* (San Francisco: Harper & Row, 1978).

Thompson, Robert Farris, *African Art in Motion* (Los Angeles: University of California Press, 1974).

Tillich, Paul, *On Art and Architecture*. Edited by John Dillenberger and Jane Dillenberger. (New York: Crossroad, 1987).

Tracy, David, *The Analogical Imagination: Christian Theology and the Culture of Pluralism* (New York: Crossroad, 1981).

Turner, Victor, *The Ritual Process: Structure and Anti-Structure* (Chicago: Aldine, 1969).

Vogt, Von Ogden, *Art and Religion*, 1921; reprint edn (Boston: Beacon, 1960).

Von Simson, Otto, *Sacred Fortress: Byzantine Art and Statecraft in Ravenna*, 1948; rev. edn (Princeton, NJ: Princeton University Press, 1987).

—, *The Gothic Cathedral*. Rev. edn (Princeton, NJ: Princeton University Press, Bollingen Series no. 48, 1988).

Wolterstorff, Nicholas, *Art in Action: Toward a Christian Aesthetic* (Grand Rapids, Mich.: Eerdmans, 1980).

Yates, Wilson, *The Arts in Theological Education* (Atlanta: Scholars Press, 1987).

Zimmer, Heinrich, *Artistic Form and Yoga in the Sacred Images of India*. Translated by Gerald Chapple and James B. Lawson. (Princeton, NJ: Princeton University Press, 1984).

Index

Abrams, M. H., 209 n.27
Adams, Hazard, 211 n.17
Adams, John, 83
Adorno, Theodor, 93
aesthetic, the: as an abstraction, 11–12
aesthetica (sing.: aestheticon): defined, 6, 22, 50; etymology of, 21; features and identity of, 12–13, 21, 22, 49–76, 77–8; as focus of aesthetics, 22–3. *See also* art; beauty; sublimity
aesthetic attitude, 7, 25, 26, 54, 200 n.12
aesthetic experience (aesthesis), 6, 14, 24, 26–36, 47–9, 51–76 *passim*; complexity of, 12–13, 32–6, 62, 64–76, 78; and religious experience, 74–6, 91–2; 101–11, 114–38 *passim*, 146–7, 152–7
aesthetic ideas, 67, 71–2, 96, 97, 193, 199 n.38
aestheticism, 7, 9, 11, 19, 25; and the aesthete, 135, 152–3
aesthetic milieux, 49, 51, 54–8, 74–6, 81
aesthetics: Christian, xi–xii, 2–3, 5, 7, 14–15, 16–46 *passim*, 47–50, 58–63, 115–35, 185–7, 191–4; 101–11, 185, 186, 187, 191–4; critiques of, 5–13, 20, 21–2, 19–30, 47–50, 58–63; ethics compared with, 16–19, 29; formalist and purist, 4, 5–9, 25–30, 47–50, 62, 63, 72–3, 142, 145; and hermeneutics, 11, 14, 23, 24, 29, 41, 42, 45, 196 n.5 (to chap. 1); of Kant, 63–72; of nature, 44, 68–9, 70, 118, 122, 126, 129, 192, 201 n.40; and psychology, 10, 12, 47, 55, 94, 213 n.5; and religion, xi–xiii, 1–9, 14–15, 16–45, 47–50, 51, 55, 56, 57, 59–60, 62–3, 64–5, 67, 74–6, 78, 81, 82–3, 84–5, 91–2, 185–94; Romantic, 24–5; scope of,

22–4; and semiotics, 10, 23, 29, 47; and sociology, 10, 47; standpoints for, 185–94
African American worship: Free Church, 123, 126–8
African art, 9, 150
Albers, Joseph, 83
Aldrich, Virgil, 26–7, 32, 33
'Alleluias', 125
Alter, Robert, 204 n.19
Angelico, Fra, 163–4
Anglicans, 120, 121, 123, 180, 184
anthropology, 81, 213 n.5
anti-aesthetics, 9–10, 11, 47, 48, 49
apperception (aesthetic), 140–2, 145–57 *passim*
appraisal (aesthetic), 53–4, 140–2, 145–57 *passim*
appreciation (aesthetic), 140–2, 145–57 *passim*
architecture: aesthetics of, 58–63, 67, 79
Arieti, Silvano, 213 n.5
Aristotle, 80, 81, 95, 98
Arnheim, Rudolf, 204–5 n.30
Arnold, Matthew, 41, 42
Arsat, 60, 64, 73, 74, 75
art: bodily/sensory aspects of, 3, 50–1, 52, 92–4, 96–7, 99, 100, 103, 106, 109, 110, 116, 160–1; classics and non-classics of, 158–84; communal/public nature of, 56, 57, 87, 203 n.16; concepts and definitions of, 78–91; diversity of, 80–91; and expression, 28, 34, 82, 84, 86, 88, 93, 101–11 *passim*, 109–10, 203 n.16; and feeling, 1, 6, 25, 28, 39, 48–9, 93–4, 97–9, 104, 106, 110; and gender, 8, 13, 154, 174; and making, 11, 14, 20, 27–8, 31, 43, 58, 71, 74, 81–3, 86–90, 99, 102–3, 105–11; and meaning, 11, 12, 13, 14, 23, 26, 28, 31, 32, 33–5, 39–43, 54, 58, 77–8, 91–111 *passim*, 146–7,

218

222 *Index*